# THE
# HEART
## OF
# ADDICTION

# THE
# HEART
## OF
# ADDICTION

# LANCE M. DODES, M.D.

HarperCollins*Publishers*

HarperCollins books may be purchased for educational, business, or sales promotional use. For information, please write: Special Markets Department, HarperCollins Publishers Inc., 10 East 53rd Street, New York, NY 10022.

FIRST EDITION

*Designed by Joseph Rutt*

Printed on acid-free paper

Library of Congress Cataloging-in-Publication Data

Dodes, Lance M.
    The heart of addiction/ Lance M. Dodes.
    —1st ed.
        p.     cm.
    Includes bibliographical references and index.
    ISBN 0-06-019811-7
    1. Alcoholism—Treatment.   2. Substance abuse—Treatment.   I. Title.

RC565 .D597   2002
616.86'06—dc21

                                                        2001026477

02 03 04 05 06 ❖/RRD 10 9 8 7 6 5 4 3 2 1

To Connie, Joshua, and Zachary

# CONTENTS

# ACKNOWLEDGMENTS

In order to write this book, I first had to have the help of brilliant teachers, from the beginning of my training in psychiatry through my later training in psychoanalysis. I especially want to thank Dr. Edward Khantzian as not only a giant in this field, but a man who has been over many years a teacher, a mentor, and a friend.

I am grateful also to Judy Phillips, Pam Douglas, Sarah Lamstein, and Dr. Isabel Murphy, who read portions of the manuscript and offered valuable suggestions. I am indebted to my agent, John Ware, for his fine work as well.

It is a pleasure, too, to thank my editor at HarperCollins, Megan Newman, who had the confidence to champion a book so different from others in this field.

I am also immensely fortunate that I could call and call upon my wife and two sons for help, since they are all gifted writers. Zach first showed me how to move beyond a style of writing more appropriate for academic works, and integrate dialogue with description. Josh's dedicated reading pointed to countless ways the text could be made more understandable and flow more easily. Connie's skill as a writer and as a teacher of writing gave me the confidence that what I had put on paper was, in the end, all right. And, needless to say, beyond their practical help I could never have written this book at all without my family's love and support, which sustain me.

Finally I deeply thank the many patients who have allowed me to know about their lives, both inner and outer, and to share with them their journey toward understanding themselves.

# THE
# HEART
## OF
# ADDICTION

# Time for a Change

Len, a forty-three-year-old man with long-standing alcoholism, had managed to stay sober for six months. He couldn't remember when he had been able to go this long without a drink. As he stood in his home looking up at the botched handiwork of the man he had hired to fix his ceiling, he abruptly made a decision. Striding purposefully over to the refrigerator, he pulled out a beer and began to drink.

It was late afternoon when Susan drove by the convenience store on the way home from work. Still ahead of her were food shopping, a trip to the vet to pick up the dog's medicine, and straightening up for the impending weekend visit of her parents-in-law. Thinking about these chores, she began to slowly shake her head back and forth. Although she had sworn to her husband that she would not waste any more of their money on lottery tickets, she parked the car and with grim determination entered the store that she knew contained the Lotto machine.

A hard rain made it difficult for Steven to see out the windows of his car. His search was already hindered by the fact that in this weather the prostitutes would be huddling in doorways, instead of strutting openly as on most nights. But he had to find one. Almost every night, he had to find one.

————

Alcoholism and other addictions are among the most important problems we face in our society. Yet, if you look beyond pat ideas about their cause, such as "alcoholism is a disease," nobody has really had an answer for why people with addictive behaviors continue to repeat them in the face of their awful consequences. This book will offer an answer to the core "Why?" question of alcoholism and other addictions, and will provide the chance for you to do what so many of my patients have done: use this new understanding and the practical tools that flow from it to take back control of your life.

You may be concerned about this subject because you are suffering with an addiction, and perhaps have wrestled with it on your own or have tried one or another treatment approach, without much success. Or, you may worry that a behavior of yours is addictive and want to know the difference, beyond simple formulas and labels, between just doing something too much and having a real addiction. You might also be concerned about a loved one who suffers with an addiction and has not been able to get well—or hasn't found a way to look at his or her problem in a way that feels safe enough to begin to deal with it. Finally, you may be interested in a new way to think about addictions because you provide professional help to people suffering with these problems, and have been dissatisfied with the help you are offering using the usual traditional approach.

In this book, I am going to tell you things that are very different. In fact, in some ways this new approach stands traditional views on their head.

For over twenty years, as a psychiatrist in both substance abuse units of hospitals and in my private office, instead of trying to sell people on a set, preexisting program, I have spent my time *listen-*

*ing* to the experiences of people suffering with addictive behaviors. Often I have been moved by their stories of struggling with an urge that seemed so much more powerful than they were. It was after listening to a great many people that I realized I was being told something new about the very nature of addiction. And with the limited success I saw with the standard approaches, it seemed to me that it was time for something new.

This new approach is not a simplistic, one-size-fits-all recipe of quick fixes that cannot possibly work for everyone. This book is self-help of a different sort. I will give you the tools to help you understand and master your addiction, illustrated with many examples of how people have individualized these new ideas for themselves. I believe that you will find in the stories of these people and situations elements that resonate with who *you* are as an individual—and that these stories and my discussion of them will enable you to thoughtfully and usefully apply this new understanding of the nature of addiction to yourself. This is, in fact, just what they did.

## A NEW WAY OF THINKING

I first noticed the pattern that I discovered underlies addictive behavior when I treated people such as Michael Franklin,* a man who suffered with alcoholism. Michael had been sober for three months until the day he waited, futilely, two hours for his wife at a downtown street corner. Earlier in the day they had arranged to meet there, but she hadn't shown up. He wasn't worried, because she tended to be forgetful and this had happened before. But he couldn't leave, because she wouldn't know where he was and she didn't have a car. In addition, he had no way to reach her. There was nothing he could do. He paced back and forth. The rush hour crowds around him began to thin. He was trapped, and he hated

---

*To preserve the confidentiality of the people described in this book, all of the examples are composites. In each case all names and identifying characteristics are fictitious.

being trapped. Then, on the far corner, he spotted a cocktail lounge. At that moment, his months of effort to stay sober disappeared from his mind. He walked across the street, went into the bar, and ordered a vodka martini, immediately followed by two more.

The next day when I met with him and he recounted his experience, something surprising emerged. We learned that he began to feel better not when he started to feel the physical effects of the alcohol or when the first sip of martini passed his lips. He had begun to feel better *the moment he decided to walk into the bar*. The drink itself was almost irrelevant!

We soon discovered that the moment Michael *decided* to drink, he had already accomplished something. In making the decision, he had the sense that he had reversed the helplessness he felt while standing outside waiting. He no longer felt helpless, because he knew at that moment that he could, and would, take an action that would make him feel better.

Once Michael realized this, the emotional purpose of his drinking began to make sense. He had felt driven to drink because he had to get out of his trap. Drinking reversed his helplessness by placing *him* in control of how he felt (alcohol and drugs in general are particularly apt for this purpose—altering how one feels is just what they do). But he had actually begun to achieve this goal before he had swallowed a drop. So, although alcohol could change his mood, it was clear that it was the meaning of feeling empowered that was critical here.

I have heard of experiences just like Michael's from an enormous number of people with all kinds of addictive behaviors, and I will offer many detailed examples of this in this book. But for now, I will simply state my conclusion. *Virtually every addictive act is preceded by a feeling of helplessness or powerlessness. Addictive behavior functions to repair this underlying feeling of helplessness. It is able to do this because taking the addictive action (or even deciding to take this action) creates a sense of being empowered, of regaining control—over one's emotional experience and one's life.*

Of course, addictive behavior is actually out of control at the same time that it serves a deeper purpose of regaining control. This paradox is not unusual in emotional life. It arises because your other goals are temporarily ignored while you are under the sway of a powerful need to act in the moment. So, if you have an addiction, while you are trying to create a *sense* of control, the net effect of this behavior is all too often contrary to what you want in general for yourself. The net effect is to be out of control.

Naturally, we all have to live with a certain degree of helplessness in our lives, and everyone, including you if you suffer with an addiction, puts up with this annoyance much of the time without having to take a drink or perform another addictive act. But what I have found is that for people suffering with addictions, there are quite specific kinds of helplessness, *specific to them as individuals*, that set off critical issues inside them that they find intolerable. Once that happens, the intense need to take an action that reverses the feeling of helplessness takes over. As I will discuss later, a response to act against helplessness is at heart actually quite normal. It is just that when the response is an addiction, the results are typically disastrous.

———

The action of addictive behavior to reverse helplessness explains its *purpose*, but it is only one factor in the new way to understand addiction. The second factor is an explanation of the *drive* behind addiction. When anyone is trapped, physically or emotionally, he or she will sooner or later feel a great anger—a rage, really, at being helpless. *It is this rage at helplessness that is the nearly irresistible force that drives addiction.* Michael's case is typical. When he described to me a day later how he was filled with feeling walking into the bar, the intensity of his emotion was palpable. Nobody was going to stand in his way. He had waited helplessly for a long time—and now he was going to act. The rage driving his addiction was evident when he talked about it, and it was certainly present the day before in the fury of his determination as he walked over to that bar.

When Michael understood the purpose behind his seemingly irrational decision to drink, and understood the drive that made drinking so irresistible at that point, he found this to be deeply meaningful. He had never known any sensible explanation for his drinking. Actually, he didn't think there could be any sensible explanation. As a consequence he had always thought of himself as weak, or selfish, or stupid. But now he had a way to think about not only *why* he felt a compulsion to drink, but why he felt it *when*. He began to be able to predict the occasions that he would be flooded with the urge to drink, because *they were always occasions in which he felt the particular kind of helplessness that was critical to him.* Once he had identified what sorts of things made him feel intolerably helpless, he could predict when he was at risk of drinking.

As I mentioned before, the sorts of problems and concerns that make a person feel helpless in a way that leads to addictive behavior vary from individual to individual. You will find many quite different examples of this throughout the book. I expect these will help you to genuinely understand what leads *you* to feel compelled to repeat addictive behaviors, and to figure out alternate ways to manage this drive—ways that are based on the specific factors that lead to the addiction in your own life.

———

There is also a third, critical, aspect of the new way to understand alcoholism and other addictions. It arises from this fact: if the purpose and drive behind addictive behavior—an effort to preserve one's power and control against helplessness—make sense, and if an addictive act is merely a very unfortunate way to express this sensible function, then it follows that there must be a better way to achieve this sensible aim. That is, addictions must be *substitutes* for some other, more useful actions to respond to the helplessness. Indeed, I have found that *every addiction results from a redirection of energy to a substitute or displaced action (usually because another, more direct, action is not considered permissible)*. In Michael's case, for instance, it was understandably not permissible to him to perform the direct action of leaving his wife stranded. So, he displaced his need to reverse his sense of helplessness to the one option— drinking—that had leapt automatically and forcefully to mind. But if he had been fully aware of what was driving this action at that moment, then instead of having a drink he might have been able to consider other options to reverse his feelings of helplessness and the rage that accompanied them. Indeed, it would have been easy for him to find other solutions, ranging from simply thinking the issue through, to composing an angry harangue to give his wife when she appeared, to buying a newspaper or a book that he wanted to read, to making a phone call to a friend, and so forth. Throughout this book, you will read about a great many examples of the kinds of alternate solutions that people have been able to find, once they know what is driving their addiction.

Put another way, knowing that every addiction is a displacement means that there is always another, specific behavior that is being ignored or denied by the substitute behavior of the addictive act, and that this alternative can be found. This idea of looking for the specific alternative is very different from finding general "triggers" to addiction, such as walking into a bar or being with drinking friends. It also differs from the usual advice to distract yourself or keep busy when the urge is upon you. Those efforts often fail because they do not address the individualized issues that are driving the addiction.

A final word about displacement. The fact that all addictions are displacements, or substitutions, is of great importance because without this displacement, addictions would not exist! It is precisely the shifting of the effort to reverse helplessness to another activity, such as drinking, that creates the phenomenon that we call addiction. When actions are taken directly to deal with helplessness, there is no addiction.

## THE WAY IT HAS BEEN

I recognize that the view of addictions I have outlined may seem very strange if you have been exposed to only the usual way of thinking about this problem. Indeed, it is an extraordinary fact about alcoholism and all other addictions that not only has there not been a satisfactory answer for *why* people repeat addictive behaviors, but—perhaps because it seems to be so hard to answer this question—it has even become fashionable to say that the "Why?" question should not be asked at all. It has become the tradition to suggest that people accept the vague idea of addiction as a disease—and not inquire what sort of disease this is, or what causes it, or how it makes a person walk into a bar against his best judgment. More recently, it has become common practice to suggest that alcoholism, or any addiction, is a genetic disorder—and overlook the fact that nobody has ever found a gene for alcoholism (contrary to what you might have heard), or that if one person has alcoholism, his or her identical twin, with exactly the same set of genes, is more likely *not* to have alcoholism than to have it.

It was in the context of this lack of any clear understanding of the problem that I began working many years ago as the psychiatrist at an inpatient alcoholism treatment center. Like most traditional centers, treatment there consisted of physical detoxification (physical withdrawal from alcohol), coupled with individual and group counseling centered on the disease concept of addiction and on the twelve steps of Alcoholics Anonymous. While there were some people who seemed to be doing well, many others had to be rehospitalized again and again, sometimes for their one hundred fiftieth or even two hundredth admission. When I asked the counselors on the treatment floor about these returning people, I was surprised to find that, even after knowing these patients for many years, the counselors knew next to nothing about their personal or emotional lives. It wasn't that the counselors were cruel or uncaring people. It was just that in their view, the personal lives of their patients were not important. When people repeatedly did not improve, they would say, "When he's ready to get sober, he will." Hence they could see no point in learning more about, or from, their patients.

This idea of essentially blaming the patients for not benefiting from the single treatment approach they were offered was very different from customary medical practice. In the rest of medicine, treatments are changed if they are not effective. It seemed that for alcoholism, and I later learned for addictions generally, somehow the treatment had become stuck. Because of a widely held belief, even a faith, in the correctness of their standard approach, people—both those suffering with alcoholism and those trying to help them—stayed with it whether it worked or not.* This left nobody but the patient to blame.

Clearly it made sense for those people who did well in the traditional AA-oriented treatments to continue with them. But for the majority of people who have not benefited, or not benefited enough, I have found that it is essential to pay attention to exactly those aspects of their emotional lives that are routinely ignored in standard treatments.

———

I invite you to sit in with me to hear the stories of people with alcoholism and other addictions who have been able to take control of their lives by making use of the new way to understand the nature of addiction that I have outlined. As I discuss their experiences, you will have the opportunity to do for yourself what they have done. For once they understood for themselves how the critical kinds of emotional factors worked in *them*, they were just like anyone else who has discovered the basis for what he or she is doing. Armed with this deeper understanding of their compulsion to repeat their addictive behavior, *they were no longer helpless in the face of it.*

———

*Considering Alcoholics Anonymous, for instance, two studies cited by Fingarette that looked at eighteen-month followups of people in AA found that at the most, 25 percent of people were still attending meetings, and that among regular AA members, only 22 percent consistently maintained sobriety. Taken together, these numbers indicate that fewer than 6 percent of people both attended and stayed sober (Fingarette, H. *Heavy drinking.* Berkeley, Calif.:University of California Press, 1988).

TWO

# *The Man Who Had No Time*

Ted Baldwin left work at 5:15 P.M. and, as he usually did, walked directly to his bar two blocks away. "Tony!" he said as he caught the bartender's eye. Tony smiled and put a glass under the long-handled spigot that dispensed Ted's favorite beer. He put the glass in front of his regular late-afternoon customer.

"How's it going?" he asked.

"Can't complain," Ted answered. It was their usual exchange. Ted began to drink the first of the four beers that he would have before going home.

This was "his" bar. It was his because he went there most days, and because, in a way, it was like a friend. But today, even as he began drinking the first beer, his mind drifted back to the unpleasant visit he had made to his family doctor several days before for his annual appointment. It had shaken him up, and though he managed to put the experience out of his mind for a couple of days, now he couldn't help having the thought that maybe the doctor was right. Maybe this bar, his place, was not the best place for him to be.

Dr. Moss had read him the riot act. He was one of those doctors who became genuinely angry with patients when they didn't take care of themselves. And he had been wound up this time.

"Look at these tests!" he had said, holding out a piece of paper that meant nothing at all to Ted. "You're drinking every day again, aren't you?" Dr. Moss had bushy eyebrows, and when he was angry they came together in a long bristly line. Ted focused on that line. From previous experience, he knew that there was nothing he could say in this situation, and that the best course of action was to stay quiet. Dr. Moss went on for almost ten minutes. When Ted finally left the office he was holding a piece of Dr. Moss's notepaper with my phone number on it.

————

Ted didn't drink for the next two days, and the paper from Dr. Moss with my phone number was left folded in his wallet. But on the third day he was back in the bar, and when he woke up with a hangover on the fourth day he knew he couldn't put it off any-more. Reluctantly, he dialed my number and we agreed to meet the next week.

Ted arrived on time. "Come in," I said as we shook hands in the waiting room. He was a handsome thirty-five-year-old man, slightly above average height and a little on the thin side. He clearly seemed fit, even athletic, in his easy walk. But his face was drawn and tense, and he seemed to find it difficult to return my smile. I showed him to a chair in the office and sat down myself.

"How can I be of help?" I said.

"You were recommended to me by my doctor," he began. "He said that you specialize in alcoholism." He paused awkwardly.

"Please go on," I said. I knew that people often have trouble talking to a complete stranger, psychiatrist or not.

"Well," he resumed, taking a breath, "if you want to know the truth, and don't take this the wrong way, I'm not sure this is going to do me much good." His eyes met mine and he seemed to half expect me to ask him to leave, and half wish that I would.

"Why is that?"

"Well, I've already been to a lot of treatment. I pretty much know the standard line. I know that I'm an alcoholic." He looked carefully at me again, gauging my reaction. "Let's face it," he continued after a moment, "what it all boils down to is that I have to stop drinking." He shrugged resignedly. "It's a matter of willpower. When I'm ready to stop, I'll stop, and, no offense, but it's not going to depend on what anyone else says. When I decide to stop screwing up, then I'll stay sober."

I frowned. "That's awfully hard on yourself."

"Well, stick with the program, don't drink. That's basically what they told me at all the treatment centers."

"You were in more than one?"

"Oh yeah. I've been to three of them. I've seen maybe four or five counselors."

I asked him about those treatments. He said that all of his therapists had been alcoholism counselors, and he had seen them for varying lengths of time, from two months to a year. Each had emphasized the self-destructiveness of his drinking and how important it was to stop. Each had reminded him again and again of everything he had lost because of his drinking, hoping to strengthen his determination to remain sober.

"They kept telling me I was going to lose my job, then my marriage, and my health. And hey, guess what?" He shook his head self-mockingly. "They were right."

Ted's tone was sadly familiar. Many people with alcoholism (as well as with other addictions) are incredibly cruel to themselves, telling themselves they are fools or worse, because they can't stop. Since no one has ever helped them find a reasonable explanation for why they drink, it has been easy for weakness or stupidity to seem the only logical explanations.

Ted went on to describe how painful it was to end his marriage after twelve years. He lost his career as a financial adviser. He embarrassed himself many times by being drunk at parties. He was arrested for driving under the influence after a few of the parties. "Those were bad times," he said. "You ever been in jail?"

"No," I admitted.

Ted just shook his head. Then he lowered it into his hands. "When my wife left me, that was the worst." He paused. "I don't know what I've done with my life," he said softly.

As he spoke more about how unhappy he was and how ashamed he felt, I thought of what he had said about his previous treatments. Like so many other people I have seen, he had not needed all the reminders he received. Ted was all too aware of his many losses. In fact, he seemed tortured by them. In a sad irony, it appeared that the reminders and the reproaches about his drinking that had been intended to be helpful had mostly resulted in Ted's feeling more ashamed—without helping him to stop. How awful he had felt was even more clear when he told me that on several occasions he had considered suicide.

I asked him whether in his previous treatments he ever talked about anything besides the importance of not drinking. He said he hadn't. Although I could not say I was very surprised, I was still troubled by his response. So, I asked another way. "Well, didn't they ask about you as a person, your life and so on?"

"Not really. When I got started at each treatment center, they asked some questions about where I grew up, who was in my family, that sort of thing. They wrote it down, but they didn't really get into it. While we were meeting, the counselors sometimes wanted to know what was stressful in my life now. But that's about it." He shrugged. "Anyway, stuff like what happened in your past life isn't important."

I must have looked surprised, because he went on to explain.

"See, talking about your life is just looking for excuses." His tone shifted, and he spoke in a sort of monotone. "Alcoholics drink because the sun comes up, and if it's cloudy, they drink because there is no sun. There's always a reason to drink if you're an alcoholic." It was clear that Ted had both said and heard this sentiment countless times.

A lot of people think about alcoholism, or any addiction, this way—that it has a life of its own, separate from the life of the person. And it is true that people with alcoholism sometimes make up unrelated reasons to explain, or explain away, their drinking—proposing explanations to fill the vacuum left by an absence of real answers. But, of course, there are real motivations for drinking just as there are for any other action. As I said in the last chapter, I have seen a lot of people struggle with addictions, and without exception they all have something *within* them that drives their behavior. It is definitely not the sun coming up.

"We're going to want to try to understand your drinking as best we can," I said. "As we look at your life, maybe we can make more sense out of the drinking than you've been able to so far."

"I hope so," he said without much enthusiasm. But for the first time he gave me a little smile. "Nothing else has worked."

———

Ted was still drinking when we began meeting, but not in a way that was causing a crisis in his life, so I mainly listened as he began to talk about himself.

I learned that Ted was an only child. His father was a computer programmer and his mother worked as a research assistant at a medical lab. Ted had always done well both in school and at sports. He said that he pushed himself to achieve, although he quickly added that he didn't really mind.

"It's just that I had to accomplish things, you know what I mean? It's like I had to uphold something for the family, the family pride or something." He paused and added, with what seemed to be a touch of that family pride, "I did a pretty good job of it."

In fact, he did a very good job. Ted worked hard in school, making almost straight A grades from elementary through high school. His father was interested in sports, so Ted went out for the football team in both junior and senior high school. Although he wasn't especially big, he threw himself into football as he had into schoolwork, knowing that his father would be in the stands with praise or criticism for him afterward.

When it came time to go to college, his impressive achievements gave him a wide selection of schools. His first choice was a fine small rural college. However, he felt his father would be disappointed if he didn't attend his own alma mater, a large research university in a nearby city. He enrolled at the university. "I was just doing what seemed the right thing," he said. When he got there, he began to drink heavily for the first time.

"College was when alcohol really started to interfere with my life. I was very concerned with doing well, and I got good grades and all, but it was a thousand times harder than it should have been." He spread his hands in exasperation. "In a way, the problem was really time. I ended up spending so much time drinking that I was always in a crisis before exams, or when papers were due. Then I'd cram for twenty-four or forty-eight hours, and get no sleep or close to it. It was ridiculous. I'm a smart guy, and if I'd taken even a quarter of the time I spent drinking to do the studying I should have done . . ." He shook his head in disgust. "And after college, I just drank more."

He talked about his marriage, the spoiled special occasions, the arguments, the evenings lost to drinking. He spoke at length of his failed career as a financial adviser, the accounts he'd let slide, the appointments he'd missed. He kept returning to the time he had lost. "If only I could have that time back," he said.

But in our next meeting as Ted continued to speak about time, his focus shifted. Instead of time he had lost to drinking, he surprisingly began speaking of almost the opposite—the time he had lost by working so much and so hard. And as he talked about this, he became more upset. As much as he regretted the loss of time because of his drinking, it was as if this other kind of time loss, caused by pushing himself, was even more important.

"There's *never* time to do things—the things I really want to do," he said. "I don't know how it happens, but no matter how much I cross things off my 'To Do' list, there's always more." He chewed methodically on his lip. "There's never time for myself. I don't mean just time to relax, although *that* would be nice. But I mean time to do stuff that's really mine."

Ted paused and looked off. Then he continued as if he were exploring the idea as he was saying it. "You know, there's never time for stuff that I would do with my life, if my life were up to me." As soon as he finished speaking he seemed genuinely surprised at what he had said.

I was also surprised. "You seem to feel that your life isn't really in your hands," I said. "It would be good if we could learn more about that."

In our next few meetings, Ted spoke further about his sense that he was not in control of his own time. He wanted to go fishing with his friends on the weekend but he had to pay his bills, balance his checkbook, paint his basement, and on and on. He brought home work (from his new position in the comptroller's office of a large company) during the week because he felt he should be more productive at his job, then struggled between doing it and taking the breather—watching TV or going for a walk—that he felt he needed and deserved.

"This weekend is going to be a cruncher," he said a couple of weeks later. "I've got to start working on my taxes, and now's the time to start cleaning up the yard for spring. Plus, I really should write back to that guy about the school reunion, which I'm dreading."

"A lot of work for a weekend," I said.

"Yeah, well, you know there's always something that has to get done." We had already established that this was his outlook.

"I can see there are things that you have to get to," I said, "but the great pressure you feel about it seems to come from you."

"I guess so, yes. I've always told myself I should be doing more. So yeah, I guess in a way it's me that keeps me from having enough time for other things." He looked off at the wall. "But you know," he continued, "it's more than just having enough time. It's like there's never enough time to *be* myself." Ted paused a moment, then he went on, seemingly following rather than guiding the thoughts that were flowing inside him. He began to talk of how proud his mother had been because he was always so good. Then he began to speak about his father. He recalled their sitting at the kitchen table, going over his report card together, looking at each category from Arithmetic to Socializing with Others. He spoke of the mix of feelings he had at that table, a sense of pride at his superior work that was mingled with a tightness in his stomach as his father emphasized the importance of keeping up his good grades. As he talked about this and other memories from his early life, it seemed to be clear that in pushing himself to work so hard as an adult, he was continuing a pattern of being good that he had lived out as a child.

———

During our meetings, Ted often told me he thought about drinking, and we regularly discussed it. He had not had a drink for about a week when one rainy Tuesday morning, not long after he had told me about his father and the report card, he walked in dripping wet and shaking his head disgustedly. "I blew it last night," he said. "I drank. What an idiot I am!"

He took off his coat and sat down, running his hand through his hair. "It really makes no sense at all."

"What happened?" I asked, as he caught his breath.

"Yesterday was actually a very good day! That's why it makes no sense. Why would I ruin it by drinking? My new boss, Paul, came into my office to tell me what a great job I did on the last project. Man, I was flying high all day. Then about four o'clock he came back to give me a new project. There was a ton of paperwork in it, and it was really Mickey Mouse stuff. But it had to get done before the department meeting next week. I ended up staying at the office until about nine o'clock, and I got nearly all of it done. Then, on the way home, I went into my old bar and got a couple of beers. Just the way I always used to! No reason for it, I just felt like having a beer." He shook his head back and forth several times. "I've been trying so hard to stay sober. I really am a loser."

It was hard to hear him say this, but we had talked about his self-criticism a number of times, and he already knew I did not share his view of himself. So, instead I said, "There's something I don't understand. Did you say that the project wasn't due until next week?"

"Yes."

"Then why did you work so late last night?"

"Well, I was feeling good. Paul told me what a great job I did on the last project and I guess I wanted to keep up the good work." He shrugged. "That's nothing new for me."

Here it was again, the pressure to perform that was such a constant in Ted's life. And this time it was linked with his drinking. This seemed to be an opportunity to learn something more.

"When did you start to think about having a beer?" I asked him.

"When I went into the bar," he answered quickly. Then he thought about it a minute. "Well, I guess I started to think about getting a beer while I was still at the office. It was around five-thirty. Yeah. I know it was around then because I remember I was thinking that I was going to buy some new CDs and listen to them last night. You know, to sort of celebrate finishing the old project. Then, when it started getting to be about five-thirty and I could see that there was no way I was going to get home early . . ." He nibbled on his lip, then he nodded. "Yeah, that's when I started to think it would be good to stop and have a beer when I got out of work."

"Say some more about that."

Ted paused. Then he began to focus more intently on his feelings of the day before. "The thing is," he said, "I guess it bothered me to be working so late. I mean, I just finished working on the last project, and now here I was working late again on a new project." He shook his head. "I started to think about how the whole evening was going to be lost. It was one of those time things again." Some color came into his face. "You know, I thought, when am I going to have *my* time? I even started slapping the papers around on my desk." He shook his head more vigorously. "I guess I finally thought to myself, 'Fuck it! I'm going to have a drink!'"

"Because you were having to work late and losing your time?"

"Yeah. I guess by the time I got to the bar, I had already made up my mind. I figured that if I'd blown the evening, then fuck it, I was going to have a drink." He paused, thinking again about how he felt. "That was going to be *my* time to relax." There was another moment before he added, "It was pretty stupid, huh?"

I shook my head. "I don't think it was stupid. The way you're describing it, it's as though your drinking was supposed to somehow make up for what you'd lost."

"That's right!" he said instantly. "I lost my evening! But I was going to have my beer."

"Go on," I said.

Ted was energized. His thoughts began to tumble out of him. "Damn it, I've *always* done what I was supposed to do. I can't tell you how many times as a kid I didn't go out to play ball because there was something to get done in the house, something I knew my folks would like me to do. Or there was some homework that I didn't really have to do, but if you did it you'd get extra credit." He looked off toward the window and it seemed to jog another memory. "There were even times I *did* go out to play ball because I knew that it would make my father happy. You know, if I worked on my catching or something." He stopped a moment. "There was always something that I had to do."

"Yesterday was like that?"

"Yes. It felt just like that." His face colored again. "I was giving up my whole goddamn evening just the same way. . . ." He paused. Then his face hardened and he looked straight at me. In an even, intense way, he said, "Except that I could get a drink. That's for me. And nobody was going to take that away."

His words hung in the air between us.

"Yes," I said after a moment. "It sounds as though you felt that you were not free to make your own choice. But drinking was a way to have your choice. You said 'Fuck it,' nobody was going to stop you. You used strong words because of how strongly you felt. There is a lot at stake for you when it comes to having the power to decide for yourself."

It seemed to me now that the reasons that Ted drank the night before, why he had felt compelled to drink, were becoming clear.

He had felt that he was in an old trap, having to give up his time out of his old sense that he should work harder, be "good." But in making the decision to drink, he made a choice that was his own and that was entirely in his control. Making this decision meant that, for a little while at least, he was no longer helpless over his time and his life. This was why he felt an overwhelming compulsion to drink.

————

The reason behind Ted's compulsion to drink is quite typical. As I mentioned in the first chapter, I found out years ago that when I asked people at what point they began to feel better from their drinking, they often said something surprising. At first they would say they felt better when they began to drink. But then, when they thought about it, people said they felt better even before they drank. Finally, on further reflection, many people said they really started to feel better as soon as they *decided* to drink.

I began to hear story after story of how relieved people felt as soon as they made this decision. One man with alcoholism described how he had spent most of a day trying to fix a problem with his computer before he put on his coat and walked out to a liquor store to buy a bottle of vodka. He spoke with feeling about how helpless he had felt trying to follow the advice he had received over the phone from the computer assistance line he had called. No matter what he had done, it hadn't worked. As the hours went by, his frustration increased. But when he decided to go out to the liquor store, his frustration lifted. As with Ted and with Michael Franklin (chapter 1), this man could feel better just by deciding to act, because making the decision in itself fulfilled the purpose of addiction to undo a sense of helplessness. (Some people are so overwhelmed by the awful effects of their addictive actions that they overlook this sense of control they gained *immediately* upon deciding to act. But they usually can recognize this later, when they look back at what happened.)

Ted's experience also illustrates the role of rage at helplessness as the drive behind addictive behavior. When he finally decided to leave work and go to the bar, Ted's exclamation, "Fuck it!" reflected this rage. In fact, Ted's words are probably the most common expression used by people when describing how they feel at the point they decide to go ahead with an addictive act.

A fascinating aspect of the role in addiction of rage at helplessness is that it explains a lot of the most important qualities of addiction. When people in general are enraged at feeling trapped or helpless, they become powerfully focused on doing what they feel they have to do to deal with the immediate threat. Along with their narrowed focus, they often disregard any long-term consequences of their actions. At the same time, in the fury of the moment, they frequently lose some of their ordinary capacities to think clearly and weigh other options. But these qualities of rage at helplessness—an intense, narrowed focus, a loss of usual judgment, and a temporary blindness to consequences—are precisely the characteristics that describe addiction. So, it turns out that rage at helplessness not only is the drive behind addiction, but it also gives addiction its most distinctive qualities.

———

I mentioned in chapter 1 that, despite all its terrible consequences, addictive behavior at its core has an element of emotional health. How can this be?

The answer is that acting against helplessness is, after all, a normal, and valuable, feature of life. A good example of the healthy nature of this kind of action can be seen in survivors of hostage situations or political prisons. When these imprisoned people found secret ways to express an aspect of their identity that was not controlled by their captors, they found they were able to preserve a sense of themselves. Sometimes they accomplished this by recalling events from their past, or just by keeping track in their own way of their history of imprisonment. But those who entirely gave up all sense of personal power tended to sink into a deep depression, or even died. The experience of these people underlines the fact that *acting* in some form when one is trapped and helpless is not only normal, it is psychologically essential. And attempting to act against powerful feelings of helplessness is just what lies at the heart of addiction.

Seeing things this way also points to another truth. Contrary to what you have heard, suffering with an addiction in itself does not make you fundamentally psychologically "sicker" or less mature than people with a wide variety of other difficulties, who generally are not so harshly judged. The feelings and conflicts that underlie addiction are easily understandable in human terms and do not set you apart from anyone else.

——

Our discovery of what drove Ted to drink the night before, of the relationship between his drinking and his need to feel in control of his time and his life, was a critical point in his treatment. Still, for a while, he had a few more drinking "slips." Although we had learned what appeared to be the key meaning of his drinking, it took some more experience, for both of us, to be able to recognize the various forms that this issue could take in his life. We began to learn of other circumstances besides time and work that could carry the meaning for him of being controlled.

On one occasion, Ted drank when a friend set him up with a blind date. Talking about this, we discovered how deeply he resented his friend's pushing him to go out. But he had not seen a way to refuse his friend's good intentions, so he went anyway. He was doing what he thought was the right thing, again. Just as with his new project at work, Ted took back his sense of control of his life when, immediately after dropping off his date, he drove directly to a bar.

But, over time, Ted increasingly used his newfound understanding of himself to manage his addictive impulse. "I used to work to avoid thinking about having a drink," Ted said one day. "I'd really bear down. But these days when I start to think about drinking, instead I try to figure out what's getting to me. It isn't always easy, because when I want a drink, I want a drink. But now that I know the sort of things that set me off, I'm getting better at figuring it out." He paused briefly. "And you know, when I do figure out why I want a drink at that moment, when I know what's bothering me, I start to focus on that. It's like last Saturday, when I started to clear out my attic. I got up there and started to sort through some of the junk that's piled up. Then, while I was going through a box I began to think of going to the liquor store. Right then, I just stood up and said, 'Wow.' I knew right away that I thought about drinking because I was working on a Saturday. It was the old time thing again—I wasn't letting myself do what I wanted to do. I really felt the anger rising up in me." He paused reflectively, remembering how he had felt. Then he said, "You know what I did? I just left all that stuff sitting there and I went out for a run. It was a beautiful day." He smiled at me. "I'll get to the attic someday. But let me tell you, it won't be a Saturday."

––––––

Ted's decision to go for a run is an example of finding an act that deals more directly with the underlying helplessness that precipitates an addictive impulse. Once he knew what set off these feelings *for him* he was in a position to find a solution that addressed them directly. Put another way, he *turned the tables on his addiction and used his addictive drive as a* signal. In a real sense, he replaced being controlled by his drive to drink with using this drive to help him be in control of his life in a better way for him.

––––––

As you read the examples in this book, they will provide a clue to the kinds of issues that are likely to set off your own addictive urge. You can also identify these core issues directly from your experience. Try to catch those moments when the addictive drive *first* comes to mind. This is the key moment in the process, and it always occurs before the actual addictive act. Ted, for instance, made the choice to drink at just the moment he felt that his choices were taken away from him, at five-thirty. When we later understood this, it made sense why this was the moment that drinking came to his mind.

For yourself, when you catch this key moment, think back to what has just occurred. If you look consistently for these moments when the addictive drive is awakened, you will eventually discover a pattern of the things that you find intolerable—events or situations that set off the impulse to take back a sense of power and control. You will find that while the details of what has just occurred before each of these moments vary, there will nearly always be something about them that is the same. This is what you are looking for. When you get to know this underlying issue, you will be more and more able to recognize the different forms it takes that can set off your impulse to repeat the addiction. And then you will be in a position to figure out what you are *not* doing to deal with this issue, to figure out what alternative choices you have that will directly address this underlying problem.

There are many examples in this book of people finding actions that can replace their addictions that work because they are specific to the issues that concern them. In addition, even in situations where there is not much choice of other things to do, you may find that just having thought through the purpose behind your addictive impulse is an empowering experience. One woman described it this way: while she was reaching into the hiding place where she stored her supply of liquor in her house, she suddenly realized what had triggered the urge. She told me she thought, "I can't believe I almost got caught by *that* again! I just sat there on my stairs for about two minutes. Finally, I actually had to laugh. Boy, was that strange—I'm usually pretty grim when it comes to reaching for a drink." She never did remove a bottle from the secret stash. Once she knew what was happening to her, she felt back in control and the impulse passed.

Since every person has his or her own personal history, the specific areas that make any individual feel helpless vary enormously. This is part of the reason that programs that expect everyone to get better with the same superficial approach don't work well. As you experiment with identifying and trying to understand the moments when your addictive drive emerges, don't become discouraged.

Anyone can become good at this with practice. When you get the hang of it, you will have turned the tables on your addiction and made it your tool instead of your master.

———

Ted succeeded with his alcoholism even though his earlier efforts had failed because he thought about it in a radically new way. Rather than focusing on its destructiveness and his powerlessness over it, he learned the opposite: how his drinking empowered him. In place of assuming that he had a failure of willpower, he discovered how his drinking was an expression of his will. Instead of thinking that his emotional life was separate from his alcoholism, he learned how much his alcoholism was connected with the rest of what was emotionally important to him.

In the end, Ted was able to prevent his drinking in a way that was unprecedented for him: not by feeling guilty, or ashamed, or by trying harder, or by remembering all the bad things that his drinking had done to him. Instead, he could master his addiction by finally understanding it and by using his understanding to find other solutions. Having an addiction does not mean, after all, that there is anything wrong with your ability to think about yourself— or to use your good mind to take back control of your life.

# THREE

# *A Good Woman*

Marion turned on the washer she had just loaded, and began look-ing for her car keys to pick up her eleven-year-old from baseball practice. Her mind drifted to the dinner she would be preparing this evening. Gerry had invited some business friends for dinner again, so it would take some more work than usual. Well, he told her about the dinner yesterday, which was better than the shorter notice he'd given her some other times, so she didn't know why she felt so pressured. If only she liked these business-entertainment evenings more.

The telephone rang. Marion knew it was her mother. They had talked just last evening, but they talked often.

"Hello?"

"Hello dear, it's me."

"Oh, hi Mom. Listen, I've got to run out to get Sam. Can I call you back later?"

"Well, I just wanted to see how you're doing."

"I'm fine, Mom."

"I was just thinking about going to the canasta game tonight with the girls. Then tomorrow, we're going to the movies. It's pretty much the same every week. Of course the town sort of empties out in the summer, and with the heat and all, I really can't do anything outdoors."

"I know, Mom. Look, can I . . ."

"Things have changed so much here. You remember Barney Fields? I just heard that he sold his store and moved to Florida. There really are no good places to shop anymore, I mean right here in town."

"I know, Mom. I just . . ."

"I think about how it is where you are, in a big city with lots of stores and things going on." Marion's mother paused a moment. "So, how is Gerry?"

"Gerry's fine. He's at work now, but he's bringing home some business associates for dinner, so I really have to get going."

"With the town emptying out the way it is, I was thinking of coming up to stay with you for a while."

"Mom, we'd love to have you but remember we talked about how we couldn't afford to put you up in a place here during the summer?"

"Well, it doesn't cost anything for me to stay with you."

"We just don't have the room. Our house isn't big enough. Please, Mom, we talked about this."

"Lilly and Sam could stay together for this little while. You know, when you were growing up we didn't have a separate room for each child until you were older."

"Sam is already eleven, and Lilly is eight. They would both hate it if they had to share a room together for such a long time."

Marion's mother made a tisking sound. "I just don't think it's right."

"Mother, please, I have to go pick up Sam."

Several more minutes went by before Marion could escape from the phone. She stood next to the piles of laundry still to be folded and took a deep breath. Then she went into the bathroom and opened the medicine cabinet. There was her prescription bottle of Percodan on the top shelf.

She had promised Gerry a number of times that she would stop taking it unless her headaches were really bad. On several occasions after he found her unsteady or asleep on the couch when he came home he had flushed a whole bottle of the pills down the toilet. She looked at the bottle in the cabinet, and thought about how this morning especially Gerry had asked her to be at her best for the guests.

Marion took down the bottle and poured two pills into her hand. "I'll just take these," she thought. "Then I'll pick up Sam."

———

Two hours later, Gerry came in the back door to the kitchen. Marion was standing at the stove, stirring a pot. She had picked up Sam, then had another Percodan. She didn't turn around when she heard Gerry come in.

"Hello," he said.

"Hello," she answered. Although she tried hard to sound bright and alert, she couldn't quite pull it off and he knew immediately.

"Jesus, have you been taking those pills again? I told you this was an important dinner tonight!" He threw his briefcase on the floor.

Marion turned around. "I had a headache."

"Oh, sure, a headache. You always have a headache." He glowered at her. "I'm sick of this! You should be ashamed of yourself."

"I know. You're right. I'll stop."

"Give me a break. You'll never stop," he said.

"I will, Gerry. I'm sorry."

He looked helplessly around the room, then back at her. "I don't know what I'm going to do," he said. In a lower voice, he added, "I don't know why I married you."

"Please, Gerry, I'll stop. I know I should stop."

He raised his voice again. "You know you should stop! I have important people coming over tonight. Do you know that?" He glared at her again. He took some deep breaths, trying to control his rage. In a barely controlled voice, he said, "Do you know what a useless wife you are?"

Marion began to cry. "I know. Please, Gerry. I know."

He stared at her another few seconds, then with a shaking voice he said, "I'm not putting up with this anymore. Do you hear me? This is it. You stop, or I'm getting a divorce." Gerry started to walk away, then turned back. "And I'm taking the kids. I don't care where you go."

Marion sat down heavily at the kitchen table. She was still crying. After a few minutes she stopped and sat clutching her wrinkled handkerchief in front of her on the table. She had seen Gerry mad many times before. He had even talked about getting a separation before. But tonight it seemed to be more serious. He had never said he would leave her and get a divorce, and he had never talked about taking the kids. She began to feel a deep fright at the thought of being left alone.

"I have to get help," she thought. "Now I really have to get help."

————

When Marion came for her first appointment, it was one of the hottest days of the summer. "This is my kind of weather," she said when she walked in.

"This hot?" I said with a smile.

"You bet. We lived in Texas until we moved up here three years ago."

"What brought you up North?"

"My husband, Gerry, changed jobs. He's a personnel executive and this was a terrific opportunity for him." She began to tell me at length about Gerry's career. She spoke earnestly, as though she wanted me to understand the importance of Gerry and his work. After a few minutes she fell silent.

"What are you thinking?" I said.

"Oh, it's nothing, really. Things are really great up here." There was another pause. "Of course, we had lots of friends in Texas," she said, "and I do miss them." She sat a minute, then said, "Well, I suppose I should tell you why I'm here. I've been taking some pills prescribed for my headaches, too many pills."

"Tell me about it."

"I have Percodans for my headaches, but I also take them at other times. They calm me down. But, well, it's become a problem. Gerry gets very upset about it and it's to the point that I've got to stop. It isn't fair to Gerry."

"And to you?"

"Well, the pills interfere with my getting the things done that I should, and I haven't been able to stop. I wish I could stop, but I guess I can't." She paused and looked at the floor. "I feel so bad for Gerry," she said. Marion raised her hand and nervously brushed it through her hair, then put it back in her lap. "He told me he's going to leave me if I don't stop. I can't fault him. I know he's right." A thought seemed to come to her and she abruptly looked at me and said, "I take good care of the children, Sam and Lilly. I would never not take care of them. The pills don't interfere with my being their mother." Then she dropped her eyes again. "But I'm a bad wife."

"Because you take the pills?"

"Yes. I let Gerry down all the time. Just the weekend before last, I took some Percodans before a dinner meeting at our house. Gerry sometimes invites people over to talk about business things, and it's important for me to be a good hostess. It was awful. I had to stay in the bedroom."

"You didn't go to the dinner?"

"No. Gerry told me to stay out of the way."

"You mean that after you took the pills you didn't think you could deal with the dinner?" I asked.

"No, I thought I would have been okay."

I looked at Marion in puzzlement.

"Gerry told me to stay out of the way. He told the guests that I was sick." She looked at me and spoke with the same earnestness as when she was describing Gerry's career. "He didn't want me to spoil the occasion. These were important business contacts for him."

"You didn't tell him you thought you were okay?"

"Yes, I told him, but I shouldn't have had the pills. Gerry was right." She paused a moment. "You have to understand," she said, "this is all my fault. I've put him through a lot."

Whether or not Marion had put him through a lot, it sounded as though her view of whether she could have attended the dinner hadn't counted in the final decision, to either Gerry or her. I thought this was important, but since she was so certain about the rightness of what she was saying, I thought I should know her better before pursuing it with her.

"When do you usually use the Percodans?" I asked her.

"Mostly, I take them in the afternoon, after I pick up the kids from school and I'm starting to get dinner ready. And weekends. I've been using them on weekends."

"Are you at home all during the week?"

"Oh no, I work part time. I'm a registered nurse, and I work a few shifts a week, while the kids are in school."

Her answer surprised me. Marion's having described Gerry's career in such detail without mentioning her own field had led me to assume that she did not work outside the home.

"It sounds like you're busy," I said. Marion shrugged. "Since you have work of your own out of the house," I asked, "are you the primary caretaker for the kids?"

She laughed. "Primary? I do the laundry, I go to the school conferences, I shop for them, I take off time from work when they're sick, I do the bake sales for the PTA." She seemed to catch herself then, and added, "But Gerry is a wonderful father to them too. He just doesn't have a lot of time, with his job."

"It's hard to see how you have time to do so much, either."

"Somebody has to do it," she said.

It wasn't clear to me why Gerry didn't share more of the burdens of housework, but again I thought I should know more about the situation before coming to any conclusions. "You were saying that you take the Percodans mainly in the afternoon and on the weekends," I said.

"Yes. I don't know why I do it. There's no good reason, really.

There are people who use drugs who have an awful life—I see them when I'm working at the hospital. They're homeless, or they come from terrible situations. I can see why they would need to get away from it all. But for me, I couldn't ask for a better life. I have a wonderful husband, two wonderful children, a nice place to live. I shouldn't complain." She shook her head. "There's no excuse for what I do."

I said, "Well, I think we'll have to see what the reasons are for what you do. It will be helpful if you can notice anything special about those times when you take the Percodans, or even times when you just feel like taking them." Marion nodded. "In the meantime, it would be good to know something about your life— how you got to be you."

––––––

"Well," Marion began, "I grew up in a small town in Kansas. I have one brother—he's four years older than me. He's an accountant now, like my dad. My dad was sweet, but he was pretty busy when we were growing up, and I don't remember doing too much with him. I guess I would have to say that my mother was at the center of my life. We did everything together. I think it's because I was so close to my mother that I stayed home as long as I did. I went to college near enough to where we lived so I could still live at home. Then, when I got my B.S. in nursing I worked at our local hospital until I met Gerry." Marion smiled. "It's sort of a strange story how we met. He was working in an ad agency in Kansas City, and he was admitted to my unit at the hospital. He had been driving home in a blizzard and ran off the road. He broke his leg and a couple of ribs. I was his nurse. Well, we hit it off, and after he was discharged we kept seeing each other, and eventually we got married. Then, when he took a job at a new agency in Dallas we moved there, and that's where we were until three years ago. Sam came along while we were in Dallas, he's eleven now, then Lilly, she's eight. So," she said, "that brings you up to the present."

"Okay," I nodded. "What about the Percodans, when did you start using them?"

"It was pretty soon after we moved to Dallas. I started getting bad headaches, and I went to see my doctor. He sent me to a neurologist, and I ended up getting the full workup—CAT scan, the whole works. They didn't find anything that was causing them, which was basically good news. They finally diagnosed them as tension headaches."

"I see," I said. "I wonder what was making you tense."

"Oh, I don't know. Probably it was leaving home. It was really hard leaving my mother."

"You said you were very close."

"Yes, well, I still talk with her every day. Sometimes more than once a day. It's good we keep in such touch." Marion smoothed her skirt and looked out the window, then looked back. "Sometimes she calls when I'm busy. Then, it can be hard to get other things done."

"You don't tell her you're busy?"

"Yes, I do, but I know it's important for her to talk about things."

"So, what happens?"

"Oh, we just talk. Sometimes it goes on for quite a while." Marion gave a small laugh, as if to say, "It's nothing."

I thought a moment. "You know, this reminds me of what you said about the dinner party."

"What do you mean?"

"You have your own point of view—that you're too busy to talk, or that you're okay to go to the dinner—but the way you describe it, your view doesn't affect what happens."

"Well, I suppose. But Gerry's business contacts are very important for him. And it's important for my mother to be able to talk about the things on her mind. After all, what sort of person would I be if I didn't listen to my mother, at her age?"

I nodded. "Sure," I said. "Still, while you're looking after the needs of your husband and your mother, I do wonder about what happens to things that are important to you." Marion shrugged, then brushed her hand through her hair.

In the next couple of sessions, Marion began to tell me more about her life. As she had said, she did not recall much about times spent together with her father. But her mother was apparently everywhere in her childhood. By and large, these were good memories: her mother combing her hair, taking her shopping, even their talking together about boys when she was a young teenager. But there was a hint of something more. For instance, Marion told me a story about a time she wanted to sleep over at a friend's house.

"I was ten years old and Susan, who was my best friend, invited me over for a pajama party. Mom wouldn't let me go, because she wanted me to go with her somewhere the next day—to meet some friends of hers, I think—and she thought I wouldn't be able to get up and come home in time. I argued and argued, but she wouldn't change her mind." Marion paused, and I thought she was about to say how much she resented this. But instead she continued, "I was really a brat. I shouldn't have given her so much trouble."

"You felt you were being a brat?"

"Oh yes. I probably would've stayed up late talking to Susan and been cranky the next day with my mother's friends."

"I can see that might have been your mother's perspective, or maybe even yours now," I said. "But I can't imagine your feeling that way then."

Marion shrugged. "I'm sure I got over it quickly."

It seemed to me that I was having more feeling about this story than Marion was. I said, "It's as though you're thinking of this from the point of view of what your mother needed, not how you felt."

She frowned. "Well," she said, "you grow up and you see things differently."

"Sure," I agreed. "But this sounds like you can't remember what it was like for you then." I paused a moment, then continued gently, "Maybe you don't want to."

Marion started to say something, then stopped. In a quiet voice, she said, "My mother is very important to me. I try to do what's right for her. I don't like to think about disagreeing with her."

"Yes, it sounds like you don't like to even remember disagreeing with her."

"No, I guess not."

———

Marion and I talked quite a bit about her use of Percodans over the course of the time we met. At first, when she had described the big fight with Gerry that had led her to come see me, she focused on how she had let him down by taking the pills. Later, when I asked her more about what happened that day, she told me about the phone call she had received from her mother that had upset her and made her late to pick up Sam. Then, when I pressed her about the rest of the story around the dinner party, she began to talk about how much she hated Gerry's bringing business associates home for dinner. Eventually, she revealed that Gerry had not told her about the dinner party until the night before.

"You didn't want to talk about that," I said.

"No. I don't like to complain about Gerry. He works hard for us, and I can't expect him to always know way in advance when he'll have people over."

"I know you don't like to complain." I thought a moment. "Let me go back to when you decided to take the Percodans. What were you feeling then?"

Marion looked out the window. "I was upset, so I took the pills," she said softly. "I was upset with Gerry. It is hard when he gives me such little notice before we have guests." She smoothed her skirt. "And I guess I was upset with my mother."

"You took the Percodans after the phone call with her?"

"Well, that day, I took them before I picked up Sam. Yes, it was right after I hung up with my mother." Marion looked around the room. "I don't really want to talk about this."

We were both silent. After a minute, I said, "You felt something just now."

Marion's face began to color and there were tears in her eyes. "It's not right," she said. She began to cry softly. A few minutes went by before she stopped and sat up straighter in the chair. She blew her nose. "I know what I felt," Marion said. She looked at me. "Did I tell you what he said to me that night?"

"No, you didn't."

"He told me I was a useless wife. I was making him his damn dinner, and he told me I was a useless wife. It's how he always feels when I don't do what he wants."

"And that's connected to when you took the pills?"

Her voice rose. "Don't you see? I have to do what they need for me to do."

"They?"

"Gerry, my mother, God only knows who else." Abruptly, Marion seemed to collapse again. "I know I shouldn't complain," she said more quietly.

"You were talking about how you felt when you took the pills," I persisted. "Go on."

Marion seemed to struggle with herself, then she sat up taller again. "It was just too much right then. I was already starting to think about preparing for the stupid dinner that I didn't want to have anyway. Then I couldn't get off the phone with my mother, and I had to rush to pick up Sam. It's all for them. I couldn't put up with it just then. I know it's wrong," she said, and took a breath, "but sometimes I feel I have to do something that isn't to take care of someone else."

We both were quiet for a minute. Then I said, "Mostly, you do feel that you should be doing something for somebody else. And most of the time, that's what you do. But you're right: when you made the decision to take the pills, you did something for yourself."

"But it was something wrong!"

"Well, it certainly wasn't good for you. And it would be very good for you to stop using the Percodans. But it's important to remember that you used them to solve another problem—the problem of ignoring yourself—your feelings—while taking care of the people around you."

"I've always thought that taking care of people is the right thing to do."

"Of course, taking care of people is wonderful. But for you, for some reasons within you that we don't yet understand, it's been a trap. In focusing so much on others' needs, it seems you've trampled on your own feelings and your own views—on your own needs to be heard and to be counted."

Marion was listening quietly. "I guess," she said.

"It looks like that's why you had to take the pills," I went on. "At that moment, you couldn't put up with being ignored, or with ignoring yourself. And you shouldn't have had to put up with it."

"I don't know. You make it sound like it was a good thing to take the pills."

"No, not to take the pills exactly. But it sounds like the reason you took them was a good thing. It would be awful if you were controlled forever by your need to take care of others at your own expense, without having something that you could do about it."

Marion nodded slowly. "Maybe you're right. I have felt like I have no say in things. When I took the pills I did feel like I had at least that little bit of say in my life." She sat still a minute. "I had some say, but it doesn't seem right to have it." She paused and stared out the window. "It never seemed right."

———

Marion had made it clear that she felt that serving others was morally correct. But as we continued to meet and she talked about her terror of Gerry leaving her, another, deeper reason for her self-ignoring devotion to the people in her life became clearer. She was desperately afraid of being left alone. She felt that if she placed her own needs secondary to Gerry's, then he would stay with her. This sense of what she must do for others in order for them to stay with her had a long history in her life. Indeed, this is what she had felt with her mother, who had subtly required the little girl to put her mother's needs first. It was what had happened, for example, when Marion couldn't stay overnight with her own friend so her mother could bring Marion to meet her mother's friends. Even in her adult life, Marion was still afraid to keep her mother from imposing on her, in the same way she felt afraid to stand up to Gerry's demands upon her.

The combination of Marion's fear of being left alone and her sense that she was doing the morally right thing when she took care of others' needs at the expense of her own created an airtight trap in which she could rarely act on her own feelings in any relationship. But when she used the Percodans, she finally, privately, fought back. Fueled by her intense frustration at constantly ignoring her will, she managed to achieve some sense of control in her life by making the decision to perform this act. With this drive behind it, her taking Percodans became an addiction.

————

Some people take longer than others to get better, and Marion turned out to be one of those who struggled. At first, she made some quick strides. It was very helpful for her to see that her addictive use of Percodans was her way to restore a sense of control against her subservience. Knowing this, she was able to interpret her urge to use Percodans as meaning that she had just failed to protect herself against bending to the needs of others. Or, even better, she could use the addictive urge to catch herself as she was about to overlook herself and her own feelings. With this new awareness, there were an increasing number of times that she was able to stop herself before she used a drug. Instead, she tried to think through her other choices to deal with this underlying issue.

This was the hard part for Marion. If she wasn't going to use drugs to reassert a sense of power against her usual helplessness, she would have to begin to stand up for herself. But this ran directly into her old ideas of the virtues of self-sacrifice, and into her fears of alienating Gerry or her mother. As a result, most of her early triumphs were in less critical areas. When the PTA called for a third time asking for her to do more work for them, she at first automatically agreed. After she hung up she kept busy cleaning for an hour, then found herself wandering over to the medicine cabinet. She stood there for a full minute before she remembered the call from the PTA. She looked up at the ceiling and closed her eyes. "Oh, my God," she said out loud to herself. Then she walked out into the bedroom and phoned the PTA to let them know that she simply did not have the time to be the cashier at the book sale. The urge to take Percodans passed, and she did not think of them for the rest of the day.

After a short while, Marion's "slips" using Percodans occurred almost exclusively when she complied with pressure from Gerry or her mother to do something to which she objected. She felt that standing her ground with either of them was a minefield. But, gradually, she tiptoed into it. On one occasion, Gerry again called to say he was bringing home guests for dinner that night. She could not bring herself to object, and felt a nearly overwhelming compulsion to take some of her pills. And this was not the PTA—she could not bring herself to call him back and tell him she was not going to entertain anyone that evening. Finally, she came up with a solution that I heard about at our next appointment.

"I didn't use any Percodans!" Marion said with some pride, after she had told me about the conversation with Gerry.

"How did you do it?"

"Well, I knew I had no chance to stay out of the medicine cabinet if I didn't do something about the damned dinner. Then I thought of it: Why should I make the dinner? I called up a Chinese restaurant and ordered takeout." She laughed. "Gerry wasn't thrilled, but I have to say, he wasn't as upset as I thought he would be." Marion smiled a little, then looked serious. "I know I have to do better for myself," she said. "But it's a start. And I didn't use any drugs."

I nodded. "You're getting better," I said, and smiled.

Marion continued to look at the fears she had felt her entire life, about being left alone and about the risks of being too aggressive.

Gradually, she found new and better ways to manage her conflicting wishes and fears. She became more assertive in her marriage and in the rest of her life. In the end, knowing what the issues were behind her compulsion to use Percodans enabled her not only to give them up entirely but slowly to work out a new way to live her life.

# FOUR

# The Secret General

Mark Wheeler was thirty-one years old when he came to see me for treatment of his compulsive gambling. He walked in with a big smile and a firm handshake. He was about five feet seven inches tall and about twenty pounds overweight. He created the instant impression of being gregarious and outgoing.

"I've got a problem," he began as soon as he sat down. "I gamble and I've gotten into a big financial mess."

"What do you gamble at?" I asked him.

"Oh, I go down to the track—horses that is, not dogs—and I buy lottery tickets."

"And you have a financial mess?"

"Yeah, I owe about twenty-five thousand dollars. Mostly it's on credit cards. And I owe money to some friends."

"Oh?"

"Yeah. They helped me out a few times when I was in a bind." He shook his head with a wry laugh. "That's over, though."

"How come?"

"You can't expect people to lend you more if you still owe them for the last couple times." There was a short pause, then Mark said,

"See, I've got four credit cards and they're all maxed out. I figure if I can just win a couple hundred at the track, I can pay off the minimum balance on a couple of them and I can throw a little bit to my friends, too." He went on to talk about the details of his financial troubles. He had ideas about making money, winning money through the new Keno game that the lottery was promoting, and managing his debts by borrowing from one source to pay another.

After a while I asked, "So, do you have a family?"

"Yeah, wife, two kids, but we're separated. We've been separated for two months."

"What happened?"

"Oh, she didn't like me not telling her what was happening with the money, and taking some money from the savings account we were putting aside for the kids' college. I owe the IRS some dough too, and she didn't like that either. I'm getting a second job so I can give some money to the IRS and get them off my back. I can make maybe another two hundred fifty a week, and I could start putting money back into the college account and still have some money to make something at the track."

Mark had immediately returned to talking about the details of his finances. He did not say anything about his relationship with his wife. I did not know if he still saw his kids. I imagined that there had been a lot of emotional turmoil, not only with his wife but within himself, as he gambled away his marriage and his family. But none of this appeared in what he said.

"You seem to focus on money," I said with a smile.

"Sure," he answered with a quick grin. "That's what makes the world go round."

"Well, I can see it's awfully important for you."

Mark just shrugged.

There was a short pause. I asked, "Well, why do you think you gamble?"

"You can't win if you don't play!" he said with a laugh. I smiled.

"Hey, do you go to the track?" he went on. "I can help you. You want some good tips?" He gave me another big grin. I smiled again, then there was a silence. After a moment, Mark refocused on my question.

He spread his hands. "Why do I gamble? It's the thrill! There's nothing like the thrill of the action, watching the horses, or scratching the lottery tickets."

"It's a thrill to win," I said.

"Man, is it! But you got to understand, it's a thrill just to play."

I thought about this a moment. "And if you lose?" I asked.

He gave a bitter laugh. "It's horrible. You know, the best thing in the world is going to the track, and the worst thing is walking out when you've blown everything."

I nodded. "So, losing isn't where the thrill of gambling comes from. And I suppose it isn't thrilling to think you'll lose."

"No, of course not. That would be nuts."

"But you said it was thrilling just to play, just to be in the action." Mark nodded.

"Then maybe what's thrilling about the action is that you're thinking you're going to win," I said.

Mark furrowed his brow. "Well, I've always thought it was the thrill of being in action. You know, it's pretty exciting to watch those horses come around the last turn." But Mark fell silent for a moment. "I don't know," he added more slowly. "Maybe that's right. When I bet, I do think I'm going to win. I never figure I'm going to lose." He rubbed the side of his face thoughtfully. "Maybe betting and winning are like the same thing. For me, anyway." He paused. "At least until I lose."

Considering how much money Mark had lost in his life by gambling, it was remarkable for him to say that he always expected to win. I wondered if Mark was saying that winning was so important to him that it had invaded his ability to think rationally about his chances of winning. At a minimum, it seemed that winning, and money, had special meaning for Mark.

———

Mark was not the first person with compulsive gambling who told me that he gambled for the thrill of it. But this explanation was, I soon learned, as flawed for Mark as it had been for others. First of all, as he and I had just discovered, although the betting action was thrilling, it was really the chance of winning that made it so exciting. Then, soon afterward, Mark told me that he did not feel the same intense drive to perform exciting or thrilling activities in other areas of his life, especially if he felt they were hazardous. He had given up skiing on expert slopes because he didn't ski enough to permit himself to feel safe on them. He had also stopped riding the big roller coasters he had always loved as a child, because they now made him nervous. Mark, it turned out, was a fairly cautious man in the rest of his life outside of gambling. If there wasn't a chance to win, he had little interest in thrill-seeking itself.

————

Mark and I began to meet weekly. I soon learned he was the fourth of seven children. He told me early on that his childhood was happy. But there was something about his stories that made me wonder. He told me about his older brother Bill's all-star soccer game, his older sister Katie's appendicitis and how everybody was so worried, and his little brother Phil's excitement over receiving the train set he wanted.

At first, I couldn't put my finger on what troubled me. But then I began to see it: he was never the central character in any of these stories. This realization was crystallized for me one day when Mark brought in an old family photograph, taken when he was a child. On several earlier occasions he had referred to this picture, saying that it was one of his enduring images of his childhood.

"That's all of us, the whole crew," he said as he handed it to me.

I looked at the photograph. It was a scene around a Christmas tree. There were opened and unopened boxes scattered around the floor and everyone had, it seemed, just been told to look at the camera. In the center of the photo were Mark's parents, with his mother holding an infant, and two older boys standing to their right. An older girl was standing on their left in front of the tree, and two young children were lying on their stomachs on the floor.

That added up to six children. I couldn't be sure, but I thought none of them was Mark. I looked up from the photo.

"Where are you?" I asked.

"Over here," he said, pointing to the side of the picture. I looked where he pointed and saw a small boy half in and half out of the frame, facing sideways to the camera.

"I see," I said. Mark took back the photograph. I felt sad. This was a picture that he had said was an image of his childhood, but he was barely in it. I looked at him for a moment. Finally I said, "You're only partly in the picture."

He looked at it, then shrugged awkwardly. "Yeah, I guess."

I paused another moment, then asked gently, "What do you think about this?"

He looked at the photo again. "Well, there were a lot of us, and I guess I just thought of this as a picture of the family." But he had caught my meaning and he sat still, thinking. His face became more somber. "I don't know," he said after a while. "I guess it's the way I felt a lot of times. Kind of part of everything, but kind of not." He fell silent again. "You know, Bill and Frank and Katie were always doing things well, in sports or at school. Even Elizabeth and Phil and Mike were like something special, you know, they were sort of together a few years younger than me, the little ones. I wasn't in either group." He stopped again. "I don't know how to describe it, but it's like I was just . . . there." He shrugged. We both sat still for a while. Then he went on in a softer voice. "I don't think my folks ever really expected too much of me, anyway. If I made average grades in school, that was okay, no big deal. If I had problems with kids, it was like, 'Oh, it'll get better,' or 'It'll be fine.' I mean, my parents loved me and all, but I don't think I was . . . that important to them, you know what I mean?" He looked at me and seemed very sad for a moment. Then he rushed on in a stronger voice. "Sometimes I thought it was good, though,'cause I got left alone. I could spend hours in the basement fooling around with stuff and nobody even noticed I was missing. Sometimes I'd be down there all afternoon, making up battles with thousands of soldiers. I was the general, figuring out the strategies and everything." He stopped again, then sighed. "I was big on pretending that I could do great things. But no one else thought I could. Ah, what the hell. I can't blame them. There were a million times when I was a kid that I could've done things, like extra projects or joining clubs at school, or really pitching in on the big cleanups we did at home sometimes. But I never stepped forward." Mark shook his head but didn't say anything for a minute. "It's really my own fault that I was sort of a failure, a guy you couldn't expect much from. I didn't do too much." He sat quietly looking at his hands.

———

As Mark told me about his life over the next weeks, it was apparent that along with his feeling that his parents didn't expect much from him, he had come to expect little of himself. Indeed, he had lived much of his life on that basis. He had never followed a career path, instead just moving from job to job. He had never sought further schooling after high school, or any other training.

"I didn't think there was any point in doing those things," he explained. "I just wouldn't be anything special at it. Yeah, I could go through a school and finish, but there'd be half the class ahead of me, and they'd get the good jobs. I know I'm no world beater."

"You wouldn't be anything special, you said," I repeated. "That's what you said about yourself as a kid."

"Yeah. Nothing's changed. Once a failure always a failure."

"You talk about yourself as if you simply are a failure, as if this is somehow in your bones. But these decisions, not to go on in school and so forth, were yours, made later in life."

"So? That's the same as what I did as a kid. It was me that decided not to participate, not to do things. I've done the same things my whole life."

I nodded. "Yes. But I think you're saying that you keep *doing* the same things because you still have the same feelings about yourself—about being unimportant, and about being unable to do as well as others. The bad results of these feelings—the ways in which you say that you failed—are no more than that: just results of how you feel about yourself. That's different from *being* a failure."

Mark was listening carefully. When I finished he sat for a minute, then he nodded his head. "I think I get it. You're saying I keep screwing up because I still feel the same way about me as I did as a kid." He rubbed his cheek slowly. "Well, I guess that makes more sense than just that I'm a screwup." He continued to think in silence another couple of minutes, until our time was up.

Over our next few meetings Mark talked more about this new take on his life. To see the course of his life as having been determined by the way he had always felt about himself, rather than as a sign that he was inherently a failure, was new to him. His life story became increasingly more comprehensible to him. But I was aware that we did not yet know what all this had to do with his gambling.

––––

We talked a lot about his gambling. He especially loved to reminisce about his successes.

"You can't imagine what it's like to have the winning ticket in your hand," he said one day. "I know everyone at the track because the same crowd always shows up. When I'm a winner, there's nothing like standing there with that ticket. I feel like holding it up high and shouting! And I know it doesn't sound right to say it, but even though I like the guys at the track, I really get a charge out of beating them."

"Even though you're really betting against the track, not against them?"

"Sure. It's like when we start, we're all even with each other. But then I get ahead."

Mark's description of being in his group of friends at the track reminded me of the busy scenes he had described in his home as a child. "Getting ahead of the crowd sounds like what you would have wanted to do in your family," I said.

He laughed. "Yeah, I guess so. Except there was no way to get ahead in *that* crowd!"

Mark was being humorous again. I knew Mark well enough to recognize that this meant we were talking about something close to his heart. I said, "That must be one reason, then, that it's such a thrill to you to win. You stand out ahead of the others in a way that you couldn't do at home." Mark looked off to the side, then gave his awkward shrug.

We both sat still, but Mark didn't say anything more. Finally, I said, "I was struck by something else you mentioned. When you described holding the winning ticket, you didn't say that you won. You said that you were a winner. What did you mean?"

"Well, I always feel that way when I win. You know, I'm not the only one. You should see some of the other guys at the track when they win, strutting around like they own the place. Hey, everyone loves a winner, especially at the track. You win, you're special. Maybe you know something the rest of those losers don't know. Maybe you're luckier. Either way, you win, you're a big shot."

"Winning isn't just winning. It makes *you* a winner."

Mark nodded.

I thought a minute. "You're saying it changes how you feel about yourself," I wondered out loud. "So, winning isn't really about the money."

Mark looked surprised. "Well, money *is* important. I like playing the lottery games with the really big jackpots. I know the odds against winning big bucks are ridiculous, but I always figure I'm going to hit it on the next ticket. Then, boom, I'm going straight to the top." He smiled at the thought. He paused then and rubbed his cheek. "But I've got to say, there've been times I was happy winning some pretty short money. It was still great to win." He paused again. "I don't know. Maybe you're right. Maybe it's basically about winning."

"I think the way you said it before is right, that it's not just winning. It's what winning means—being a winner."

Mark sat quietly a moment, then he began to talk some more about the feelings that he had when he won—either at the track or with scratch tickets. After a few minutes, he returned to his idea about going straight to the top.

"That's what I want," he said with a nod. He made a motion with his hand swooping up.

"You said that before. So, winning at the track, or with a lottery ticket, is how to get there?"

"Yeah. How else?"

I thought about what Mark said earlier, about there being no hope for success through more schooling, or doing something else to advance himself. I said, "I think you feel that there's no choice about how to get to the top. With the way you've thought about yourself and what you can achieve, I can see why gambling must seem like the only way."

Mark looked at me. "You know, you may be right."

Over the next few weeks, it became clear to both of us that indeed whenever Mark had won, he had succeeded in creating a momentary experience of being at the top. But we already knew that he anticipated that he would win whenever he played. So each time he gambled, *just by playing* he was able to create a feeling that he was calling the shots—he was controlling his life, acting to make himself a winner. This was what was so thrilling about gambling, about "being in action."

At the same time, we also realized how sad it was that, while Mark was striving through his gambling to be empowered by becoming a winner, both he and his family had always viewed his gambling as just further evidence of his being a failure.

———

Once Mark was able to see that there were deeper emotional reasons—understandable reasons—why he gambled, he felt less degraded by his addiction. In turn, this helped him to feel better about himself. He also reported that he was gambling less. This was not really surprising, since his gambling had been at least partly driven by his need to feel more worthwhile. When he felt better, he had less need to create that brief feeling of being on top that he had tried to create through gambling.

But he was not all better. There were times when he abstained from gambling for weeks, then, seemingly heedless of what he had discovered about himself, returned to the track.

And when Mark gambled, it was like a fire, burning everything in its path. He could spend an entire day at the track, losing and losing. Or, he could scratch one lottery ticket after another, taking money that was earmarked for something important, and quickly burn it all up. Although Mark had been helped by learning that gambling was a way to feel more valued, there was clearly more that we needed to find out. What lit the fire of his gambling when it started to burn, and what made it burn so hot?

———

It was a bright fall day when Mark came in, after going a month without gambling, and told me he'd bought twenty lottery tickets.

"What happened?" I asked him after he gave me the news.

"I don't know. I just went to the store and bought them. And I lost my last twenty bucks," he said disgustedly.

"Something must have touched this off."

"I guess so," Mark said with irritation.

"So," I said softly, "what do you recall?"

Mark sat a moment then took a deep breath. "Well, I went to see a lawyer yesterday, about my debts. I was hoping maybe there was a way I could get some help with putting off payments or something. He told me that I should file for bankruptcy. I can't do that." Mark looked out the window, looked back, then put his head in his hands. "I'm not going to do that. I've got three brothers in business, and my father's run his business for thirty-five years, and no one has ever come close to going bankrupt." He shook his head. "Of course, I just lost more money! What a jerk I am, thinking I'm going to solve everything by winning the lottery."

"The lawyer advised you to declare bankruptcy?" I said in a quiet voice.

"Yeah. I don't know what I'm going to do. I've got no money, I've got unbelievable debts, my wife isn't talking to me, and now this lawyer tells me to file for bankruptcy." He shook his head again. "I'm not doing it. I've been a failure my whole life, and I am not going to do this."

We sat in silence for a moment. "You bought the lottery tickets after you saw the lawyer?" I said.

"Yeah."

"When did you think about buying them?

Mark looked at me. "I knew I was going to buy them the second he told me to file for bankruptcy."

"Do you remember what you were thinking then?"

"Yeah, I remember. I thought, 'Fuck it! I'm going to buy those tickets.' "

I nodded. "Did you have any other thoughts about the scratch tickets after that, before you actually bought them?"

"Well, yeah, I thought I would win big and get out of this rat hole." Mark paused. "Then I thought how stupid that was." He shook his head. "But then I just said fuck it."

"Say some more about that feeling."

"It's just . . . it's what I said. When he told me to file for bankruptcy, that was it. I had no goddamned place to go. I've been busting my hump trying to get even. I figured this lawyer might help me out. Instead, he tells me I'm stuck. There's one way out, he says, and there's no fucking way I'm going to take it."

After a moment, I asked, "How does the gambling help?"

"There was just nothing I could do! Maybe it was stupid, but I had to do something." Mark sat still a minute. "It was something I could do."

Now it seemed to me we had come right down to it. The advice Mark received from the lawyer had made him feel trapped as a failure, again. Even more important, he could see no way out of this trap. Confronted with such helplessness *about an area that was so desperately important to him,* he had to do something. We already knew that his gambling was an effort to be recognized, to feel as though he was a winner, to be somebody valuable. But now we were staring at the powerful other side to this coin, at his rage over being trapped at the bottom. It appeared that for Mark, who had been so passive in pursuing other goals, the one situation in which he *had* to do something was when he felt helplessly stuck in his old role as a failure.

This was what made his gambling burn so white hot. It was driven by a compulsion to act against an old helplessness. As with every addiction, he displaced his reaction against feeling helpless— to gambling. And as with other addictions, his compulsion to act arose at the moment that he felt trapped, when he was in the lawyer's office.

Once we understood his addiction better, we could better understand what we had already discovered—that Mark gambled to feel more valued. On most of the occasions when he gambled there had not been a major crisis such as his visit to the lawyer. But Mark's sense of being trapped as a failure were constantly with him, an ongoing feeling that lay just outside of his awareness. Imprisoned by this, he regularly sought to take action against it. His efforts to feel more important, like "a winner," were then inextricably linked to the intense fuel of his refusal to be a loser.

Over the following weeks Mark remembered many more times that he had felt powerless as a child to be seen as capable or worthwhile. Eventually we realized that it was this need to be important and valuable that had motivated his hours of playing at being a general in his basement, leading his armies to victory after victory. And we both felt again the sad irony that this withdrawal had been interpreted by his family as a sign of his *lack* of motivation, that his isolating himself this way had only made his situation worse.

———

Mark gradually became skilled at recognizing the many situations in his current life that could lead him to feel like a failure, and lead to his urge to gamble. He also became adept at finding nongambling ways to deal with these situations. For example, on one occasion Mark ran into one of his friends to whom he still owed money. He did not have the money to repay him, and he was flooded with thoughts of gambling. By this time, though, Mark was able to stop and think about it when this happened. He realized from his urge to gamble that being confronted by his debt brought up old feelings of being a failure. At the same moment, he recognized that this was the real reason he had avoided discussing his debt with this friend, and other friends he owed—not, as he had thought, just his concerns about his finances. Armed with his awareness, he did speak with his friend about what he owed him. They were able to agree to a further moratorium on repayment for a length of time that they both could accept. Mark felt a great relief that he had finally talked about this, and he did not gamble.

He had turned the tables on his addiction—using it as a signal of what was blocking him, and what else he could do instead.

FIVE

# *I Have to Do* Something

As Mark's case illustrates, the critical moment in trying to manage an addiction comes at the point that you feel the overwhelming need to do *something*. Each of the people in the cases I have described so far—Ted, Marion, and Mark—all ultimately learned to recognize this key moment for what it is: the point of feeling an overwhelming helplessness and, therefore, the need to do something to reverse it. Once they recognized how this pattern applied to *them*, rather than repeating an indirect, displaced solution to helplessness—their addictive behavior—they could look for an action that directly addressed what was behind the urge. Finding this specific action is quite important, and I will give several more examples of it later in this chapter.

First, though, it is worth looking at some important conclusions about the nature of addiction that follow simply from the fact that they are always displacements—substitutions for another, more direct act. Probably the most striking conclusion is that if addictions were not displacements, they would not exist at all. Without displacement, responding to overwhelming helplessness would mean taking a direct action. This might be helpful, as when people find useful specific solutions to their addictive feelings in the way I have been describing, or the direct response might be unhelpful, such as flying into a destructive rage. But helpful or not, without a displacement, there can be no addiction.

The fact that addictions are displacements also explains why people can shift so readily from one addiction to another. They are simply moving the *focus of their displacement* to a new activity. For example, I recall one man I saw for treatment of compulsive gambling who told me, "I used to be a drug addict in my teens, then I quit and started drinking out of control in my twenties. Now I'm thirty-four and I've stopped drinking. Gambling is my last addiction, and I'm not sure I can give it up. It's all I've got left." Despite the superficial changes in the *form* of his addiction, nothing had really changed. Twenty years after he began addictive behavior, he still had an addiction. In fact, if it were not that people usually give each addiction its own name, it would be perfectly reasonable to say that he had the same addiction. Whatever specific factors had led originally to his addictive behavior, there is no reason to think they had changed just because he shifted the focus of his displacement.

———

This man's story, like that of so many others who have replaced one addictive behavior with another, underlines the fact that despite their particular form, all addictions are related. They all have the common psychological roots that I have described. In fact, this is why I am able to speak of a general psychology of addiction—and why it is possible to write a book about all addictions.

The underlying unity of addictions also leads to a new perspective on their names—they are simply the names of displaced focuses. "Alcoholism," for example, is the title when the purpose and drive of an addiction is displaced to the behavior of drinking alcohol. When the same factors shift to buying lottery tickets, we rename the problem compulsive gambling. This view can be helpful in understanding what is occurring if you find yourself taking up a "new" addiction. It is not that you have another problem to deal with, just that the original problem is still with you. Likewise, even if you have been able to keep yourself away from one addictive activity, you are still at risk of starting another. On the other hand, once you understand the underlying psychology of an addictive behavior of yours, that understanding will apply to any others that you are drawn to.

Knowing that all addictions are related also helps in being prepared for seeing disguised or hard-to-recognize new forms of an addiction if they should occur in your life. There is no law that restricts the focus of a displacement in addiction to the forms we all usually recognize. So, if you suffer with an addiction, it is a good idea to watch for repetitive behaviors that do not look like an addiction but may still be displacements that express its underlying drive and purpose. In chapter 15, "When Are Compulsions Addictions?" I will discuss some of these more unusual forms that addiction can take.

Awareness of the unity and the displacement nature of addictions has still another advantage. It helps to undermine the current tendency to assign multiple diagnoses to people with addictions. A person whose addictive focuses include drinking alcohol, smoking cocaine, binge eating, and compulsive shopping can be, and often is, given four diagnoses. Not only do people understandably dislike being told they have multiple illnesses but this is fundamentally incorrect. Most important, this practice interferes with looking closely into the one underlying problem the person does have. (The official *Diagnostic and Statistical Manual of Mental Disorders*, the "DSM-IV,"[1] is notorious for labeling behaviors as separate diagnoses without considering the single unifying psychological basis that might explain them.)

There is one final word that should be said about the unity of addictions. While their underlying psychology is the same, *people* are all different. It would be wrong to conclude from the fact that an underlying psychology of addiction can be understood and described, that everyone who suffers with addictions is the same. On the contrary, as I have been trying to show, everyone is unique in the specific concerns and problems that he or she deals with through addictive behaviors. This is why any approach to self-understanding or treatment must be individualized, and why programs that treat everybody the same are so limited.

------

Knowing that addictions are displacements has another deeply significant consequence. It means that *addictions are inherently psychological compromises.* The very fact of performing an addictive act means that, for reasons that are emotionally important to you, you did not allow yourself to take a direct action. The addictive act is a compromise, therefore—between doing what you would have been inclined to do if you had allowed yourself, and doing nothing at all. Hence it is a compromise that is imposed by your own internal prohibition against performing the direct act.

So, this is still another reason why no one should feel ashamed about having an addiction. Unlike the common wisdom that addictions are a form of pleasure-seeking, the fact that they are self-imposed compromises indicates how much they are the opposite. Rather than being the simple enactment of an impulse toward pleasure, addictions are a sign of *inhibiting* an action that would have directly expressed your wish in that moment. Walter's story, below, illustrates this point.

------

Walter Millis was a hardworking man. He built up a restaurant business over most of his adult life, and now had four locations that were doing well. The business had grown so much, in fact, that it was a source of relief for him when his nephew, Jeffrey, graduated from college and came to work with him in the office. The increasingly complicated financial details of the business had never been Walter's first love, and they had especially tested his patience in the past few years. So, Walter turned over most of the day-to-day financial matters to Jeffrey and focused on the operational side of the restaurants.

Walter's success had come despite his long history of alcoholism. There were several factors that contributed to this positive result. From an early age, he had developed strong relationships with other people in the industry, and these personal contacts with suppliers had enabled his business to survive despite Walter's absences on drinking binges. At the start of a binge, Walter would usually call to ask for an extension on payments or a change in the time he was supposed to have a meeting, and almost always the person he called was willing to make the change. Walter had proved himself over many years to be very conscientious, and his willingness to work long hours when someone else needed a favor was famous. So his friends were glad to return a favor to this generous man, and his business thrived.

But he was not happy. He often ground his teeth, and he suffered with enough pains in his stomach that he had taken to eating antacids by the handful. He worried a lot, about nearly everything. Although business was going well, he worried about it. His wife Harriet's health had not been good recently, and he worried about that. But especially he worried about his nephew, whom he had taken in and brought up after his sister's death when Jeffrey was just two years old. Jeffrey had never put much effort into school, and he had been in a couple of minor scrapes with the police in eleventh and twelfth grades—once getting rowdy at a party, another time being accused of shoplifting from a clothing store. The charge was later dropped when Walter talked with the town's chief of police, who was a personal friend, but Walter in fact believed that his nephew had taken the sweater in question, despite Jeffrey's denial. There had also been some trouble in college, with accusations of cheating. So, when Jeffrey finally squeaked through and got his degree, Walter knew Jeffrey might have had trouble finding a good job if Walter had not invited him into the family business.

It was in the midst of his many concerns that I first met Walter. He had been drinking in binges, about once a month when we began, but as we started to understand the kind of helplessness that lay behind his drinking, he had managed to remain sober for six months—until the day I received a call from him canceling his appointment. As soon as I got on the line, I could hear the slurring in his voice.

"It's me, Doc. I won't be making it in today."

"What's happening?"

"I'm up at my cabin." Walter owned a small cabin in a rural area and I knew he sometimes went there during a binge.

"Are you drinking?" I asked.

"Yup."

I tried to convince him to arrange for a ride back to his home, but he was adamant that he was going to stay at the cabin for a few days. He said he had called Harriet, and she knew where he was. He assured me that she wasn't worried, and that I shouldn't be worried either. When I continued to be concerned, he reminded me that he had done this many times, and that though it was new to me, both he and Harriet were used to it. Finally, characteristic of him, he said he would call Harriet and ask her to call me, more to reassure me than because he thought it was necessary. Later that day Harriet did call me, and as Walter had predicted she was not pleased, but she was also not terribly concerned.

A week later, Walter came on time to his appointment. He had not had a drink for the past three days. When I asked him what led to the binge, he told me this story.

"Things were going okay until eight days ago, the day before we were going to meet. Then I found out some bad news. You know, I don't do the company's books anymore, so I haven't been on top of money things for a while. But that day, Thursday, I got a call from the bank. 'You're overdrawn on the business account for the payroll,' they said. I couldn't believe it. We haven't missed a payroll in twenty years." Walter fixed his gaze on me a moment and there was some fire in his eyes. "And there was no reason for that to happen—business has been very good." Then he shook his head and stopped speaking for a long minute. "I looked into it. It was Jeffrey. He's been taking money from the business. A lot of money."

I waited for Walter to go on, but he sat still. "What did you do?"

He shrugged slightly. "I didn't do anything."

I regarded him with surprise. "What do you mean?"

He paused before he answered. "Look," he said, "I've been running a business for a long time. I'm no fool. We've had thefts from the business before, and I know how to handle it. I treat my employees well, but they know that if they steal from the company, they're gone."

There was another silence before I said, "But you told me you didn't do anything."

Walter's jaw had been clenched, but now his face loosened and he suddenly looked older. Quietly, he said, "If it had been anyone else I would have fired him. Hell, I would have pressed charges." His voice grew softer. "But this was my sister's boy." He looked down. "You don't fire your own."

———

Through the years, whenever Jeffrey had been in trouble, Walter's view of what to do had never wavered. Even when Walter felt Jeffrey's actions were deeply wrong, Walter was clear that it was his job to defend his boy. For a long time this had caused tension with Harriet, who would have doled out more punishments to Jeffrey while he was growing up if not for Walter's unshakable views about what was morally right for him to do. Walter's reaction to Jeffrey's thefts was just the most recent example of this very old pattern.

Walter and I began talking about the thefts. When he first learned about them, he was furious and stormed around the office asking people what they knew about it. Notably, he did not think about drinking then. It was later, when he found out it was Jeffrey who had embezzled the money, that he first had the idea of taking off for the cabin. Indeed, Walter was aware that he had felt helpless at that point, and knew that the idea of going on a binge soothed him. But he had attributed his sense of helplessness to his financial crisis.

The more we talked, though, the clearer it became that it was not the business loss that made Walter feel so powerless. The clue was in the fact that he began to think about drinking only after he learned it was Jeffrey who had taken the money. His sense of being trapped was the result of his being unable to act on the course directed by his fury—to fire his nephew. Hence, his helplessness was the result of an internal inhibition arising from his lifelong sense of what was morally right.

Of course, when he gave up firing his nephew he didn't—he couldn't—give up taking *some* action; he couldn't be utterly helpless in the face of this catastrophe. So, he did what he always did when he experienced this sense of being trapped—he drank. The drinking expressed his rage at being trapped and was a victory over his helplessness. At the same time, it was a displacement of his feelings from the action he could not allow himself to take.

And this is the point. Although Walter was unaware of any conscious conflict about having a binge, the deeper truth is that the binge was precisely the result of a conflict—between his moral qualms about firing his nephew, which led him to do nothing, and his refusal to accept this powerlessness that those qualms imposed on him. He solved this inner conflict by making a *compromise*—and his binge was the compromise. On the one hand, it expressed, in a rather violent way, his need to restore his sense of empowerment and integrity. But on the other hand, it redirected this furious energy away from his nephew, whom he felt he had to spare.

Not surprisingly, some of Walter's coworkers viewed his drinking binge as a pure self-indulgence, a kind of tantrum after his loss. And in fact it was true both that he was enraged and that the drinking binge expressed this rage. But Walter's story shows how mistaken it is to think of addiction as a self-satisfying excess. Walter was acting on his rage, yes, but this was not about his monetary loss; it was about the enraging helplessness he felt in the face of a terrible inner trap. Rather than being a self-indulgence, his binge was the result of inhibiting himself from acting directly on his feelings.

———

Walter's story brings back the issue of finding a better solution when faced with the overwhelming need to do *something* that precedes addictive acts. What else could Walter have done? Certainly if he had understood what the binge was about, he would have been in a strong position to find another solution. For example, most simply, Walter might have rethought the wisdom of keeping his nephew in the company. That is, he might have used his urge to drink as a signal of how greatly conflicted he was about his decision to keep Jeffrey. Recognizing this, he might have given more weight to his mix of feelings and concluded that retaining Jeffrey was in neither his own nor his nephew's best interests (it did Jeffrey no good to be in a position to embezzle money from Walter). Or, if after becoming aware of the issues he was still determined to keep Jeffrey on, he might have altered Jeffrey's access to the company's money, or changed his role at work, or arranged more supervision for him. The point is that Walter would have easily come up with such possibilities himself, if he had been aware of what the drinking urge was about. And such solutions are likely to have worked to replace his drinking because the drinking was, to begin with, a replacement for a direct act.

Of course, it usually takes a little time to identify what the specific issues are behind your own addictive urge. But it is well worth the effort. Trying to manage an addiction without awareness of its psychology is like trying to subdue a tiger while you are wearing a blindfold.

Indeed, people who have not been aware of how addiction works have generally had trouble coming up with alternate actions that work. Without an understanding of the psychology of addiction, various nonspecific forms of advice have become popular—and they tend to be of doubtful value. The AA injunction to avoid being tired or hungry or angry is an example of such nonspecific advice. Avoiding being tired or hungry might be useful to some people by giving them a sense of well-being, which could possibly help them feel less overwhelmed when the conflicts and situations to which they are sensitive arise. But once you understand the way addiction works, it is clear that avoiding noticing when you are angry, or trying not to feel angry when you are, is just the kind of thing that can launch the drive toward addictive behavior. In fact, this bit of advice might be one of the worst recommendations one could offer to anyone suffering with an addiction.

———

I mentioned that it can take a little while before you become adept at finding truly specific alternative solutions to addictive behavior. Walter's story is an example. When he was in the throes of his reaction to Jeffrey's thefts, Walter was caught up in a long-standing set of his feelings and ideas about the way a man should treat children in his care. Walter and I later discovered, to the surprise of neither of us, that many of his ideas about this had originated in his relationship with his own father, who had shown similar strong feelings about standing up for Walter. As a young child, Walter had magnified his father's ideas about what was proper and improper into absolute principles, which had then always constrained him in responding flexibly to his nephew. Walter's ideas at the time of Jeffrey's thefts, therefore, had been present nearly all of his life, and were powerfully embedded in his thinking. Further, when he was caught up in these ideas, Walter tended to lose track of other factors in his situation. This is what happened when he learned of Jeffrey's thefts—the issue for Walter became narrowed to doing the right thing by his nephew, and he did not consider other alternatives that were available to him.

When anyone is caught up in an old and personally meaningful set of thoughts and feelings, however out of step these are with the current situation, it is difficult to put them aside and regain perspective. And, since addictions are characteristically a response to forms of helplessness that are deeply meaningful, addictive actions often arise in just those situations that invoke old and important issues.

This creates an additional hurdle to finding better solutions when you feel the intense urge to repeat an addictive act. Even when you identify the underlying conflicts that are producing an intolerable helplessness in that moment, you will still need to combat a tendency to follow the old patterns of dealing with those issues. For Walter, this meant he needed to think through long-entrenched feelings about his relationship with his own father, as he also tried to identify the ways this relationship cropped up in his current life—and led to renewed urges to drink.

Naturally, the more you can work out the old conflicts that lie behind a present tendency to repeat an addictive act, the better off you are. Fortunately, though, you do not have to have everything worked out before being able to master an addiction. Just by knowing the kinds of things that are the sources of your feelings of helplessness, you are in a better position to find alternative solutions. Here is another example of this.

———

Nancy was a twenty-eight-year-old teacher who addictively used the tranquilizer Xanax, a medication she could get in almost limitless supply from her physician father. She used enough Xanax for a long enough time to become physically addicted to the drug. She also had an intense psychological attachment to taking it that had frustrated all of her own attempts to wean herself.

Nancy had been living with her boyfriend, Mitch, for the past two years, but their relationship was not good. One of the first things Nancy told me when we met was how much Mitch was absorbed in his career as an architect and how little attention he paid to her. Yet, just as quickly, she made it clear that she was afraid to leave him. She did not want to be alone as she had been before meeting Mitch, and she worried that, despite Mitch's problems, she might not find anyone else who had as many of his good attributes.

Not long after we began meeting, it was apparent to both of us that she used much more Xanax when Mitch was preoccupied with his work and was ignoring her. At these times, she was tortured with conflicted feelings. She wanted nothing more than to scream at Mitch, yet she was terrified she would destroy the relationship. Feeling that she could not speak up, she turned to her addiction to manage the helplessness.

At the heart of Nancy's concerns was a very old loneliness. She had been left to fend for herself many times during childhood, by parents who seemed preoccupied with their own lives. As an adult she had difficulty tolerating separations, particularly from people who seemed too busy for her (she went to stay with her sister whenever Mitch was away on business trips). She needed to resolve this deeper problem, and we worked on it for a long time. But long before she worked this out, just knowing the source of her feelings of helplessness enabled her to respond in new ways when she felt the urge to use Xanax.

Her powerlessness in the past, when she was left alone by her parents, really had been beyond her control. As a child, there was realistically little she could do about this, and it was no wonder that it had overwhelmed her. Looking at these feelings now, though, she could consider responses to feeling abandoned she had never thought possible. Although she had never been able to talk to her parents about her feelings, she became less fearful about confronting Mitch when he withdrew into his work. Again and again she found that when she spoke up, she did not use Xanax. And when, despite her pleas, Mitch continued to disappear into his home office every Saturday morning—a regular Xanax time in the past—Nancy made her own plans to meet with two close women friends on alternate Saturdays, and Saturday became Xanax-free.

Nancy was still working on the very troubled relationship she had with her parents, and its ramifications in the ways she saw herself, well after she took control over her addiction. Over a longer time, too, she broke up with Mitch. But she had found ways to take control over her addiction long before then.

And here is one more case with a very different kind of solution.

———

I met Susan Nickerson, a tall and slim twenty-four-year-old woman, soon after she was arrested twice within six weeks for Driving Under the Influence of alcohol. Her second charge was aggravated by driving without a license. Susan was referred to me by her attorney, who was candid in telling me that he hoped that if she were in treatment, the court would look more favorably on her case.

She told me an intriguing story in our first meeting. Before her recent arrests, she had two previous DUI convictions in other states, two and four years ago. Strikingly, all four arrests occurred in either April or May. Then Susan told me another oddity. First, she was quick to say that she knew she was an alcoholic and that she was well aware that her drinking was out of control. Her most recent DUI had occurred during a blackout, and she did not even recall getting behind the wheel. But then she added that most of the time she did not drink at all. When I asked her what she meant, she explained that after the middle of May she stopped drinking each year until the following spring. At that point she drank heavily and often, as her series of arrests suggested.

This mystery did not last long, however. Susan soon began to talk about herself and her life, and her thoughts moved away from the arrests. I just tried to listen carefully. With a lot of feeling, Susan began to talk about how horrible it was for her when her mother died from cancer five years earlier, just after Susan turned nineteen years old. I noticed that her arrests for drinking began the following year, and putting that together with her unusual drinking pattern, I made the obvious guess.

"What time of year did your mother pass away?" I asked her.

Susan nodded. She knew the connection. "She died May seventeenth," she said.

Her mother's death had been a devastating blow to Susan. She had almost completed her freshman year in college and hadn't been home since Thanksgiving. That first year away from home was stressful, and Susan had often called home—especially to talk with her mother. A few years earlier it would have been different, as Susan and her mother seemed to fight all the time. But since she had gone away to school, they had become closer again. Then, in the spring, her mother was diagnosed with metastatic cancer. The illness was totally unexpected, found on a routine checkup. Despite very aggressive medical treatment, within two months Susan's mother was dead.

Looking back on that time, Susan knew that she had been overwhelmed. She remembered crying at the funeral, but could not bear to talk or even think much about her mother afterward. She recalled telling herself that she "had to go on," and she found that if she kept busy, she could put away her sad thoughts indefinitely— except when the anniversary of her mother's death occurred.

Since Susan and I knew the precipitant for her drinking, it didn't take long for us to make sense of the purpose and drive behind the drinking. Susan had never been able to fully grieve her mother's death. And behind her inability to grieve lay a terrible fear that if she ever faced the sadness, she would be overwhelmed again just as she had been immediately after her mother died. Susan was also vaguely aware that thinking about her mother's death brought up a great, helpless rage at the injustice of her mother being taken from her so early. Unable to deal with both her helpless rage and her fear of being drowned in sadness, Susan was in an emotional cage.

When her mother had died, Susan could do nothing but experience the shock. But in each of the following years she was determined that she was not going to be completely helpless. She could take control of her emotional state, by drinking.

As Susan recognized this, she was able to focus for the first time on whether there might be other solutions to her helplessness. Always before, she had told herself that her feelings were best avoided; after all, she couldn't bring her mother back. But we discovered that she had never been to the cemetery. She had also never looked at the old photo albums she kept, in which were preserved pictures of her mother as a child, her mother with Susan when Susan was a little girl, and her mother with their family all the way up to the last Thanksgiving.

So, it turned out that there were things that Susan could do about her feelings. Of course, like all grieving, these ways of remembering her mother were for Susan both comfort and pain. But at least they were things she could do, things within her power to address her sadness in a way that was not overwhelming. And she found there were also many other things to do. She had avoided talking about her mother with her husband and her two brothers, and she began to do that a little bit. Although religion had not been a central part of her life for a long time, she sought out people in her church to talk with and found this to be a comfort. Finally, she and I also talked a long time about her grief, and she remembered with sadness and release many memories of herself with her mother. She also talked about the great anger she felt at the unfairness of losing her mother. In doing all of these things, Susan noticed an easing of the pressure to drink.

Of course, she did not leap into doing these new activities. She had protected herself from feelings for years and did not find it easy to do anything that would open up the unhealed wound. But understanding that her disastrous drinking was a way to manage her helpless feelings about her mother's death was very meaningful to her. For years, she had known that she drank around the anniversary date of her mother's death, but she had not truly understood it. When she recognized the purpose of her drinking, she also saw that there were alternative ways to deal with these feelings.

SIX

# Hooked by the Mind: Physical and Psychological Addiction

Many people take for granted that addiction is a physical problem. The very words used to describe addictions—that one is "hooked on" drugs, or even the less colloquial version of this, that one is "addicted to" drugs—suggest that drugs somehow physically capture people. Adding to this impression are movies and television shows almost everyone has seen in which people are shown in physical agony withdrawing from narcotics, or feeling desperate to get a "fix" of their drug to prevent withdrawal effects. This desperate search looks as though it must be an important factor at the very core of addiction.

But surprisingly, it isn't. I am aware that you are likely to find this view controversial. In order to explain it, first I have to consider the nature of physical addiction.

———

The human body physically reacts to a few kinds of drugs, like alcohol or heroin, by adapting, changing itself in order to balance the effect of the drug. For instance, levels of chemicals—neurotransmitters—in the brain may be altered to compensate for the drug's effects. As a result of this adaptation, the drug soon no longer has the effect it had when it was first used. The body has found a way to *tolerate* the intrusion of the drug and still maintain its usual state. This phenomenon is therefore called "tolerance." Once a person's body adapts in this way, he or she must take more of the drug to produce the effect the drug had when it was first used. So, people who use tolerance-inducing drugs tend to take higher and higher doses to re-create their initial experience; if you have used these drugs, you are very familiar with this.

One important consequence of tolerance can be seen when a person abruptly stops using the drug he or she has learned to tolerate. The body is left in an unbalanced state: because it has adapted to the drug, the body is in effect pushing back against the drug's effect, but now there is no drug effect to push against. This causes physical symptoms (known as withdrawal symptoms) that are, in general, *opposite* in direction from those that the drug created. For example, withdrawal from drugs that sedate the nervous system, like alcohol or heroin, produces overexcitement of the nervous system, manifested in symptoms such as shaking, sweating, diarrhea, hallucinations, and seizures.

*Physical addiction* is a state in which both tolerance and withdrawal are present. The drugs to which the body reacts by developing tolerance, and subsequently withdrawal, are said to be "physically addictive" drugs.

———

To return to the original subject, why is it that the popular conception of physical addiction being at the core of the general problem of addiction is false? It turns out there are many reasons for this.

To begin with, there are a large number of serious addictions in which there is no physical addiction at all. The simplest examples of this are nondrug addictions, such as addictive gambling or addictive sex. I realize that it might seem unusual to include nondrug addictions in a discussion of the role of physical addiction. But there is not a sharp distinction between drug and nondrug addictions. The fact is that many people with addictions routinely switch back and forth between drug and nondrug addictions, or perform both addictions at the same time. It is estimated, for example, that

30 to 40 percent of compulsive (addictive) gamblers suffer with alcoholism, and, likewise, several studies have shown high rates of compulsive gambling among substance-abusing patients. It is also common for people, over a period of time, to leave drugs entirely and move to a nondrug addiction. You may recall, for example, a man I mentioned in chapter 5 who shifted over the course of his lifetime from addictive use of street drugs in his teens, to alcoholism in his twenties, and finally to compulsive gambling in his thirties. Back and forth switches of addictions like this, involving alcohol, gambling, sex, eating, and more, are frequent events. If people with unquestionable drug addictions, often *including* physical addiction, can switch from drug to nondrug addictions, this strongly indicates that physical addiction is not fundamental to the nature of addiction.

In addition, there are many people with purely drug addictions who use drugs of entirely different pharmacological type—such as cocaine and alcohol—at the same time, or alternately over a period of days or months. This switching would be impossible if physical addiction to one drug were essential to the nature of their problem. If physical addiction were the major problem, they could only switch between drugs that were capable of *physically* substituting for each other. (When drugs can do this they are said to be "cross-tolerant." An example of this is heroin and methadone, both narcotics.) The fact that it is common to find in one person addictive use of pharmacologically unrelated drugs further indicates that the essence of addiction does not depend on physical attachment to a particular drug. Rather, it suggests that the drive behind addiction is a psychological compulsion to perform a particular *action*, such as using a drug, regardless of type.

Then there are also people with addictions who use just one physically addictive drug, but never become physically addicted to it. This is the case, for instance, with people whose pattern is to binge drink. They may drink in a way that ruins their lives— nobody would doubt that they have alcoholism—but they may never drink for a long enough period to allow their bodies to develop enough tolerance to produce a withdrawal reaction when they stop. They have alcoholism but they never become physically addicted to alcohol.

Finally, there are also many people who addictively use a drug that is biologically incapable of producing physical addiction, such as marijuana or LSD. Addictions using these substances are quite real, though there is not a genuine physical addiction with these drugs.

It is clear, then, that there are many addictions, including some drug addictions, in which physical addiction plays no significant role.

But what about those people with addictions who regularly use just one drug that does indeed produce tolerance and withdrawal? How important to *their* addiction is physical addiction?

The first thing to be said about this is the most obvious. Detoxifying (withdrawing) people who are physically addicted to their drugs does not cure them. Not only do people often relapse immediately after detoxification, but it is well-known that addictive behavior frequently returns even many years after the last drug use. Clearly, the essence of the addiction exists separately and independently from the presence of physical effects brought about by the drug itself, or by withdrawal from the drug.

There is also another kind of evidence about this question. When American soldiers were in Vietnam, many of them used heroin or other narcotics both because they were readily available and because they were in an extraordinarily stressful setting. Heroin and similar narcotics, of course, are famous for being physically addictive, producing tolerance, physical withdrawal symptoms, and cravings for the drug, which are part of the withdrawal process. Of the soldiers who used these drugs, many took enough to produce physical addiction. The interesting thing is what happened to these men when they returned to the United States. When they were studied, "usage and addiction essentially decreased to pre-Vietnam levels."[1] Indeed, even among men who continued to use some narcotics, "the susceptibility to addiction declined dramatically. About one half of all narcotics users in Vietnam had become addicted, whereas only 7% of users after return became addicted at any time during the post-Vietnam period. This . . . produced addiction remission rates of 95% for those who had been addicted in Vietnam, rates of remission unheard of among narcotics addicts treated in the United States." How did these soldiers escape being "hooked"? The narcotics were certainly strong enough.

At the time these results were published, they were astounding to many people who had worked in heroin detoxification centers. Nobody had predicted this result, because detoxifying people from narcotics in the United States had been so ineffective. Practically none of the patients in these programs stayed clean from drugs after detoxification.

In comparing the results of the veterans study with the results from heroin detoxification centers in the United States, one conclusion seems evident. Since both groups used the same substances, the difference in results must have been because the people were different. What this means is that nearly all of the returning men who had used narcotics did not continue to be addicted because, while they had used large amounts of physically addictive drugs, *they* were not predisposed to addiction.

The results of this study of Vietnam veterans underscores a basic point. *Addiction is a human problem that resides in people, not in the drug or in the drug's capacity to produce physical effects.* For the returning soldiers, even when they had used drugs as physically addictive as heroin, and even in the face of the cravings known to be associated with withdrawal from this drug, once they were out of their abnormally stressful setting, addictive behavior could not be created in them. It was the abnormal setting that had encouraged the drugs' use, but even though they had been physically addicted to them, they did not continue to use them addictively because they did not have the psychological predisposition for it.

This should not be surprising. Not everyone, of course, has the psychological makeup to utilize a drug, or another activity, for the meanings and purposes I have been describing in addictions. Those people who have different psychological compositions find other ways to manage difficult feelings. And it is worth repeating that if you have an addiction, this does not inherently mean you are less healthy than other people who have found different, perhaps more easily concealed, ways to deal with troublesome feelings in their lives.

––––––

Some people, while agreeing that the problem of addiction lies in the person and not in the drug or its physical effects, would attribute the problem to genes, or to brain chemistry, rather than to a person's psychology. However, as an explanation for addiction, these ideas run into many of the same limitations that applied to physical addiction. For example, one hypothesis that has been advanced is that the level of sensitivity of an individual's brain opiate receptors could influence the way a person reacts to the introduction of a particular drug into the brain, causing an excessively strong response to the drug and presumably leading to increased susceptibility to addiction to that drug. But even if this occurred, as a model of addiction this mechanism could not explain the common phenomenon of people shifting from one drug to another, unrelated, drug, or to a nondrug addiction—where there is no question of brain sensitivity to a drug. Later in the book, I will return to the role of genetics and brain chemistry. For now, I will just say that the role of these factors in addiction has been greatly overstated in the popular press, and it is minor in importance compared with the psychological factors I have been discussing.

––––––

An addiction, then, is truly present only when there is a psychological drive to perform the addictive behavior—that is, only when there is psychological addiction. For this reason, I call behaviors in which this psychology is present *true addictions*, in contrast to cases in which there is only a physical addiction.

There is another large-scale natural experiment that makes the same point as the Vietnam study about the central importance of psychological factors versus physical factors in addiction. This example is the effect of education on cigarette smoking in this country. Nicotine is known to be capable of producing physical addiction with tolerance and withdrawal and cravings. Nonetheless, there are millions of Americans who stopped smoking cigarettes once they realized that smoking was dangerous to their health. Many were physically addicted to cigarettes, yet, like the returning soldiers from Vietnam, they were able to quit. How could they do this? The answer is the same as for the veterans. Despite having a physical addiction, these millions of people could quit because, although they had a physical addiction, they did not have the psychology of addiction. When they finally realized it was dangerous for them to smoke, they could stop because they had to deal only with their physical addiction, plus an admittedly difficult habit. But it was only a habit. They weren't driven by the deeper psychological drive behind addictive behavior that I have been describing in this book, with which people who have true addictions suffer. (Of course, there were also millions of people who did not stop smoking. Did all of them have true addictions? Probably not. I will return to why they kept smoking, in chapter 9 ["When Is Abuse Not Addiction?"]. I will also return there to the responsibility of cigarette manufacturers for the dangerous overuse of their products.)

The fundamental point here is also illustrated by the experience of thousands of medically ill patients with significant pain. Because of their pain, these patients were given narcotics in high enough doses and for long enough time to produce physical addiction. But, almost always, they did not abuse drugs once withdrawn from narcotics. Unfortunately, doctors have not always recognized that producing physical addiction is very different from producing true addiction. As a consequence, for many years patients were denied needed narcotic pain medication out of a fear of "hooking" them forever.

What can be deduced from all this? If unquestionable addictions can be present without any physical addiction—as with binge drinkers or compulsive gamblers—and if physical addictions can be present without any true addiction—as in the medically ill patients I just mentioned—then it must be that physical addiction is neither necessary to nor sufficient for an addiction. It can truthfully be said, then, that *physical addiction is surprisingly incidental to the real nature of addiction.*

Of course, physical addiction does play some role in making it harder to quit. People become afraid to experience a physical withdrawal from drugs, especially if they feel they will have to endure it without medical help, and this can contribute to their continued use. Likewise, physical cravings can make it harder to quit. But this role of physical addiction in maintaining drug use does not factor into the *cause* of addiction. Physical addiction is simply an additional difficulty of quitting, though it is nowhere near being the central one.

Nor does physical addiction play a significant role in *relapse* to addiction after a period of abstinence, as with the large number of people who return to an addiction even years after being physically withdrawn from a drug. Yet, it is relapse that is the real practical problem with addiction. The old joke, "It's easy to quit, I've done it a hundred times," reflects the fact that nearly everyone who suffers with an addiction does stop at one time or another. But unless the emotional factors that originally led to the addiction are addressed, relapse is the rule. Indeed, the original causes of an addiction and the causes for relapse are fundamentally the same psychological factors—which is why exploring the reappearance of urges to perform an addictive act can be so helpful to understanding the roots of an addiction. And after the relatively short period of physical withdrawal, physical addiction has little to do with this.

If you have an addiction to a drug, it may have seemed to you that physical factors are more important than this because you have come to worry about whether you can get along without the physical effect of a drug. In other words, you may feel that you have been self-prescribing for practical reasons to function better—as in using alcohol to remove social inhibitions. In fact, people often take drugs for just this kind of reason, but this is quite different from an addiction. Self-prescription is not driven by the same intense qualities that are present in addiction and consequently is much easier to manage. I will return to the distinction between such nonaddictive self-prescription and true addiction in a later chapter (chapter 9, "When Is Abuse Not Addiction?").

———

Given all the circumstances in which physical addiction is present without psychological addiction, and vice versa, why have they been so blurred together?

The most obvious reason, of course, is that the term "addiction" has been used to describe both, without any sense of the distinction between them. It would be good if these often mutually exclusive conditions were described by different words. A helpful convention would be to use the word "addiction" to mean only true or psychological addiction, and to specify "physical addiction" when speaking of that very specific phenomenon. This is the convention that I use in this book.

Another root for the misplaced emphasis on physical factors in addiction has been popular reports about changes in neurotransmitter levels associated with certain commonly abused drugs. For instance, cocaine produces increased brain levels of the neurotransmitter dopamine, which leads in turn to a feeling of euphoria. After sufficient cocaine use, dopamine levels become depleted, leading to a depressed mood and cravings for more cocaine. This is the kind of thing that is often erroneously reported in the media as important in understanding the nature of addiction. However, it is simply a description of the physical addiction aspect of cocaine use; it is the old confusion of physical addiction with addiction, again.

Another basis for physical factors having been so overstated is the frequent reporting about localization of the effects of drugs in certain areas of the brain. With modern visualization techniques, it is possible to show exactly what parts of the brain are affected by the presence of a particular drug. One area that has attracted a great deal of attention, for instance, is a region of the brain called the nucleus accumbens. Popular articles that describe these localization studies often relate how a drug may affect biological activity in the particular area of the brain known to be affected—again, via altering levels of neurotransmitters that are active in that region. The new information arising from these studies, however, only describes where in the brain drugs work. It does not say anything about why people are compelled to take them, or why some people—whose brains are affected in the same areas by the drugs—do not use them addictively. Hence, while we are learning more all the time about the way drugs affect the brain, this does not provide any evidence for a physical, biochemical cause of addiction. Indeed, there is simply no evidence of any neurochemical or neuroanatomical deficit in people that accounts for their having or developing an addiction.*

There is also a historical reason why physical and true addiction have been so blurred: the most commonly thought of addictions have always been drug addictions, especially alcoholism, and frequently the people suffering with these drug addictions *also* have had a physical addiction. Perhaps if, centuries ago, the first conditions recognized as addictions had been nondrug behaviors, if people had first applied the word "addiction" to behaviors such as compulsive gambling, then physical dependence wouldn't have seemed so central to the problem of addiction.

But to see the link between drug and nondrug addictions, or to see the psychological basis for drug addictions, would have required a psychological perspective, a level of psychological sophistication about human behavior, that has not been available throughout most of history. Aside from the works of great writers, like Shakespeare, who have shown the depth of psychological conflict that can lie behind actions, viewing behavior in psychological

---

*Interestingly, however, one researcher reported the case of a man who used cocaine not because it made him feel more energized but because it made him calmer. This man appeared to be using cocaine to self-medicate an attention deficit disorder (ADD)—and he was able to substitute the similar medication methylphenidate (Ritalin) for the cocaine (Khantzian, E. The self-medication hypothesis of addictive disorders: focus on heroin and cocaine dependence. *American Journal of Psychiatry* 1985, 142:1259–64). This appears to be genuinely a case of overuse of a drug because of a neurological problem. It is quite different from a true addiction, though, as shown by the fact that once given a prescribed medicine, he could give up use of his self-prescribed "medicine." I will discuss the difference between this kind of overuse and true addiction in chapter 9.

terms at all is a very new development in the story of mankind. The serious study of human psychology is, after all, only about a hundred years old. Those who came before that development can hardly be blamed for believing that the physical effects that they could easily see were the basis for addiction.

Today, however, watching those movies in which people are craving alcohol or heroin and are obtaining immediate relief from their withdrawal symptoms when they get their drug "fix," we can understand that what is being shown is not the *cause* of the addiction. What is being shown is a *result*, an end product of the addiction that began with a need to perform an addictive behavior—in this case, using a drug.

There are other reasons for the survival of the notion that addiction is a physical problem. Indeed, if you suffer with an addiction yourself, you are very aware of what I am about to say. All too often people suffering with addictions feel that they are bad or weak because of their addiction. Moreover, we live in a culture that frequently treats people with addictions as if their problem were caused by a moral deficiency. The idea that addiction is a physical problem may, then, provide some relief from guilt and shame. Understandably, this serves as a powerful reason to hold on to this idea, even though, like the idea that addiction is a moral deficiency, it is not true.

Finally, another reason that some people reject a psychological explanation of addiction is because they think that to say something is caused by psychological factors means it is a question of willpower—and that they are being told they are lacking in willpower. The opposite, of course, is the case. The essence of human psychology lies in not simply what is in awareness, but also the unconscious thoughts, conflicts, and feelings that drive much of our behavior, *especially* actions that are problematic and irrational. Ironically, and sadly, when people reject a psychological explanation because they confuse this with a challenge to their willpower, they do not permit themselves the relief from unrealistic self-blame that would come with truly understanding what drives their addictive behaviors.

# SEVEN

# The Genetics of Alcoholism

When Fred Martin came to see me, the very first thing he said was "Doc, I'm an alcoholic, but you got to understand, everybody in my family is an alcoholic." He quickly listed all the Martin family members with this problem: two brothers (out of five siblings), his father, his father's father, one uncle (out of three), and a cousin. "I didn't have a chance," Fred said with a little grin.

"How do you mean?" I asked.

"Hell, Doc," he said, "I've got bad genes. It's like being cursed. I was sunk from the minute I was born."

———

The role of genetics has been among the most misunderstood areas of addictions, especially alcoholism. For this reason, I will briefly summarize here the complex and at times confusing evidence about this. I am addressing only alcoholism because nearly all the work on a genetic role in addictions has been about this one diagnosis. And since this will involve a somewhat lengthy journey, I will start at the end—with the main conclusions that I believe can be drawn from over fifty years of research in this field.

Illnesses in which there is a clear and predictable inheritance—what we think of as genetic diseases—are caused by a defect in a single gene or chromosome. Examples of this kind of genetic disease are phenylketonuria or PKU, Down's syndrome, and Huntington's disease. The most important finding of research into a genetic role in alcoholism is that there is no such thing as a "gene for alcoholism." Nor can you directly inherit alcoholism.

The reason for the confusion, however, is that while nobody has ever identified any specific genes for alcoholism, like many other complex conditions there probably are many genes that can indirectly influence the *susceptibility* to developing alcoholism, without there being a gene for alcoholism itself. This means that alcoholism is more like peptic ulcer disease or high blood pressure—conditions where there may be an indirect genetic factor for *some* people, but this factor must be combined with numerous others to produce the problem. In alcoholism, in fact, the majority of people with the condition have what one genetic researcher summarized as "minimal or nonexistent" contribution from genetic factors.[1] There appears to be a minority of people who have more of a contribution to susceptibility from genetic factors, although even for these people the indirect genetic factors still must play a role alongside nongenetic factors. A good summary of all these findings was offered by another genetic researcher who wrote, "A narrow 'medical genetic' model of alcoholism . . . would appear to be inappropriate."[2]

Before discussing the genetics of alcoholism in more detail, I should say a word about what genes are and how they actually work. Genes are small pieces of the DNA molecule, specifically a sequence of the four "bases" of which DNA is composed (usually abbreviated using the first letters of their names, A, C, G, T). Every group of three DNA bases gives a code for production of a specific amino acid. Amino acids, in turn, are what make up proteins. The whole gene, then, is a sequence of DNA bases that defines the amino acid sequence of a chain of a protein molecule.[3] Put simply, genes are the recipe for making proteins.

This is important because the proteins whose production is directed by genes go on to determine the way the chemistry of cells works. As a result, genes determine the basic structure and chemical function of the entire body and have at least an indirect influence on everything in it.

Most of DNA, however, is not composed of genes. Instead, the rest of the DNA molecule contains information, "switches," that controls when or if the genes are "turned on." These switches are often strongly influenced by nongenetic factors in the environment, such as emotions or events. As neurology professor Robert Sapolsky of Stanford University described, "a mother rat licking and grooming her infant will initiate a cascade of events that eventually turns on genes related to growth in that child. . . . Or a miserably stressful day of final exams will activate genes . . . that will suppress the immune system, often leading to a cold or worse."[4]

Once you understand what genes do (produce proteins), and that they are often influenced by nongenetic factors, you can realistically assess their possible role in illness and health. For instance, as I mentioned, and will explain in more detail below, sometimes a problem in a single gene can cause a disease, because the absence or deficiency of the single protein it manufactures is essential for health. But it is unrealistic to think that any single gene, producing a single protein, could determine something as complex as addictive behavior is known to be.

The obvious nature of this point brings up the question of why it has been so misunderstood. One factor has been a general sense that genes (or brain chemistry) will eventually explain everything about people and their behavior, a mythical idea that I will address in the next chapter. But contributing to this notion is another factor—the tendency in our culture to sensationalize scientific findings about the role of genetics not only in alcoholism but in many other, nonaddiction, conditions. An example of this was an article headlined, "A gene for genius: Smart DNA could explain how IQ is inherited."[5] It is not until the fourth paragraph that the article notes that the gene to which it refers, like all genes, only controls a protein that affects a specific chemical reaction in cells—in this case, controlling the docking of a particular hormone with cells, a reaction that may make the cell grow. This might, or might not, lead to greater brain growth, but the connection of brain growth with IQ is unknown in any case (other animals have larger brains than man, and IQ may have much more to do with the efficiency of the connections among cells than total brain size). In the fifth paragraph, the article finally says that many scientists feel that this "IQ gene" is meaningless and is like previous false "discoveries" of genes for novelty-seeking, and other traits. The disparity between the exciting headline and the sober disclaimers buried late in the article's text are, alas, typical of the way genetic issues are often presented, including those for alcoholism.

————

Conditions that are clearly genetic diseases are caused either by an abnormality in chromosomes (parts are not in the right place or are missing, or entire chromosomes are missing or added, as in Down's syndrome), or by an abnormality in a particular gene. One example of the latter is phenylketonuria (PKU). A principal aspect of this illness is mental retardation, caused in early life by the buildup of the molecule phenylalanine, a substance that is toxic to the brain when present in large quantities. Normally, phenylalanine is metabolized, broken down, into another molecule (tyrosine), which continues to be metabolized to still other chemicals. But this normal breakdown to tyrosine can occur only in the presence of a particular enzyme (phenylalanine hydroxylase). This enzyme is itself a protein, for which there is a gene in the DNA molecule. People who have a defect in this gene cannot make this enzyme, and therefore cannot break down phenylalanine. As a result, phenylalanine builds up in their cells and they develop the disease PKU. Hence, the disease is truly genetic.

Since it is caused by a single gene defect, the inheritance of PKU is straightforward and predictable. The disease is a recessive trait that occurs when a person inherits the defective gene from both parents.

Indeed, the only nongenetic, or "environmental" factor influencing the development of PKU is whether the child eats foods that contain phenylalanine. Fortunately, this one environmental factor also provides the means for treatment: PKU can be largely prevented by providing a newborn with a special diet in which phenylalanine is very limited, starting during the first month of life.

Many other illnesses that are not caused by any given gene also have some degree of genetic influence—for instance, peptic ulcer disease, as I mentioned above. The fact that quite a few conditions fit into this category is to be expected since genes affect—at least indirectly—virtually everything about a living organism. But because these conditions are not actually caused by a single genetic defect, their inheritance patterns are a good deal more complicated than illnesses like PKU. Alcoholism, with an inheritance pattern that is quite complex, fits into this group.

How could genes producing proteins have any effect on alcoholism? The short answer is that nobody knows. No one has ever found a gene that increases the chance of developing alcoholism, so the closest example is some gene that might *decrease* its incidence. One idea has been to look at the role of enzymes (which are proteins) in the metabolism of the molecule ethanol, or drinking alcohol. It is known, for instance, that some people have a genetic abnormality in coding for two enzymes (ADH and ALDH) that break down ethanol. As with PKU, this abnormality causes a buildup of a toxic chemical, acetaldehyde. High levels of this chemical make people flush and feel sick (producing this reaction by blocking the metabolism of ethanol is the way the medicine disulfiram, or Antabuse works). A genetically caused enzyme defect in ADH or ALDH, then, could theoretically *reduce* the chance of having alcoholism by making people feel sick if they drink. However, research that looked specifically at the effect of these enzyme defects found that neither enzyme was associated with less preference for alcohol.[6] In any event, this is an example of how people have tried to think of a way that genes could influence rates of alcoholism.

I will summarize below a number of the key studies about genetics and alcoholism, dividing them as has been done in the scientific literature, into types of research. In reading these results, you should know that when researchers study genetics, they usually group together all nongenetic factors under the term "environmental." This category, therefore, includes psychological factors, social factors, physical aspects of the environment, and events in people's lives that have influenced their behavior.*

## FAMILY STUDIES

This research looks at the incidence of alcoholism in families. These studies have shown that while there is a tendency for alcoholism to "run in families," only about a quarter of fathers and 5 percent of mothers of people with alcoholism have alcoholism themselves.[7] In addition, genetic factors alone would predict a higher rate of alcoholism in closely related first-degree relatives (parents, siblings) of people with alcoholism in comparison with less-related relatives. However, when first-degree and second-degree (less-related) relatives were compared, three studies did not find any significant difference between them,[8] and in one of these studies second-degree relatives were even more likely to develop alcoholism than first-degree ones.[9] As one researcher put it, "Equal rates [of alcoholism] in the first and second degree relatives are inconsistent with virtually any genetic model."[10] This does not mean there is no genetic influence on susceptibility, only that it was too insignificant or reflected in too small a number of people to show up in these studies.

---

*I am grateful to Harvard professor Richard Gelber for his help in thinking through the statistical issues discussed in this chapter.

## TWIN STUDIES

People who are identical twins have exactly the same genes, so they are good test cases for the role of genetics. If genes were the only or principal cause of alcoholism, then in the great majority of identical twins, either both should have alcoholism or neither of them should have it. This, however, is not the case. When registries of twins were examined, the correlation (also called agreement or *concordance*) of alcoholism between identical twins was found to average about 40 percent, when nine different twin studies are combined.[11] Not all of this 40 percent can be due to genetic factors, however. These twins were raised together, within the same families, and were presumably treated similarly and had similar experiences. The combined influence of the psychological, social, individual life experience, and physical environmental factors that these twins shared for a lifetime also contributed to the 40 percent correlation between them.

Studies have also been done looking at same-sex *fraternal* twins, who have only, on average, half their genes in common. Several of these investigations have shown less correlation between fraternal twins than identical twins. However, this difference has not always been significant,[12] and it has tended to be less than would be predicted based on genetic factors alone. Indeed, there are many nongenetic factors that would lead to lower correlations in fraternal, compared with identical, twins.

Fraternal twins are no more alike than any two brothers or sisters. They may not look, act, or respond any more similarly than any two brothers or sisters, and these differences can be apparent from birth, as every parent knows. To add to this difference, by the time fraternal twins grow up and are studied, they have lived their entire lives with their different qualities—in appearance, athleticism, talents, skills, and so on—which in turn will certainly have had an effect on their self-image, self-esteem, relatedness to others, and emotional lives. This is an example of how differences in genetic factors, which, by themselves, have nothing to do with alcoholism, can lead to a myriad of intervening nongenetic experiences that could in turn influence occurrence of the condition—and affect the difference in inheritance between identical and fraternal twins. Several studies of these nongenetic factors have indeed supported this view. One[13] found that, at the time they were questioned, identical twins had significantly closer contact than fraternal twins, suggesting the greater degree of shared experience that one would expect in identical twins. Another study[14] found that 83 percent of identical twins reported that they usually shared the same peers when growing up versus 52–54 percent for fraternal twins, and 68–78 percent of identical twins were usually or always in the same classes at school versus 47–55 percent for fraternal twins.

The significance of all this is in interpreting the differences in rates of alcoholism between identical and fraternal twins. One group of researchers summarized this issue when they wrote, ". . . the classic twin study method [is] valid only if several key assumptions are met. In particular, greater MZ [identical] than DZ [fraternal] concordance implicates a genetic influence only if we assume that the environmental similarity of the two types of twins is comparable. . . . [but] recent observations suggest that MZ [identical] twins are environmentally more similar than DZ [fraternal] twins and that this greater environmental similarity may contribute . . . to greater similarity" in rates of alcoholism for identical twins.[15]

Of interest, this same group of researchers concluded, "heritability analyses . . . showed genetic factors to have only a modest influence on overall risk in both sexes . . . approximately 0.35 for male subjects and 0.24 for female subjects,"[16] with the remaining 70 percent or so of heritability due to nongenetic factors. The authors reached this conclusion despite the fact that in calculating their results they assumed that increased concordance between identical twins was due simply to genetic factors. If the study had taken into account the nongenetic factors that separate identical from fraternal twins, the heritability due to genetic factors would have decreased farther. (Incidentally, the lower statistical correlation among female twins has been found in a number of studies, further muddying the waters.)

## ADOPTION STUDIES

Adoption studies are designed to address the nature-nurture question in another way. These studies have looked at children of men with alcoholism who have been adopted away from home to see if they develop a higher incidence of alcoholism, compared with control cases of children who are adopted away from nonalcoholic biological parents. A measure of the role of genetic factors would be an increase in alcoholism in the biological children of an alcoholic parent, even though they are raised separately from the environmental influence of their biological parents.

The findings of adoption studies have been inconsistent. Some have showed no evidence for increased risk of alcoholism in adopted-away children of alcoholic parents,[17] or no significant difference between these children and children of nonalcoholic biological parents.[18] Other studies have found a correlation between adopted-away male children and their biological fathers, although the conclusions of by far the largest of these[19] were limited by the fact that children were not removed from their biological mothers directly after birth. (The average age at adoption was eight months, leaving a significant time for nurturance by the biological mother. Interestingly the researchers discovered that, compared with earlier adoption, later adoption increased the chances of developing alcoholism to a highly statistically significant degree. This suggested how potentially hurtful it was to the child to disrupt the connection with the biological mother once the infant had established this connection. The higher incidence of alcoholism in these adopted-away children was, therefore, not simply due to genetic factors.) In addition, later reevaluation of two of the major adoption studies found that environmental factors, especially heavy drinking by the adoptive parents, marred their conclusions.[20] In general, adoption studies have fit with the findings of other work in suggesting a minor to insignificant role for genetic factors in the majority of people with alcoholism, and a more significant role in susceptibility in a smaller group (one paper put it at 24 percent of the total).[21]

## DIRECT GENE STUDIES

The most direct attempt to look at the association between genes and alcoholism is to measure the correlation of alcoholism with a single gene whose location on a particular chromosome is known. The idea here is that if alcoholism is linked with a known marker, that would point toward a specific area on a specific chromosome where there might be a gene affecting alcoholism. However, the results of these many studies have failed to find any consistent linkage of alcoholism with any such markers.[22]

———

I began this chapter by listing the conclusions that could be drawn from all the information I have described. To recapitulate, genetic factors appear to be minimal for the majority of people with alcoholism, but for a hard-to-pinpoint subgroup there is probably a more significant genetic role in their susceptibility to alcoholism. The mechanism by which multiple genes may contribute to the increased incidence in this subgroup is unknown, but in any case it is an influence on susceptibility (a recent article called these "susceptibility genes"),[23] rather than there being a "gene for alcoholism."

———

Since any genetic role would operate via this indirect effect on susceptibility only, such an effect is easily compatible with the psychology of addiction that I have been describing. One way this might work, for example, is that while the psychology that lies behind addiction explains the compulsion to perform addictive acts, an increased genetic susceptibility to alcoholism in some people could influence the *focus* of their addiction toward the use of alcohol—rather than, say, compulsive gambling. Alternatively, some day we may learn that the role of genetics in the minority of people with alcoholism for whom it is more significant is through some indirect influence on emotional factors, such as decreasing frustration tolerance. For people in this subgroup, the psychology I have described would explain why, and how, such a decreased frustration tolerance would lead to an increased susceptibility to developing an addiction.

But no matter what "susceptibility genes" are eventually discovered, it is already clear that having alcoholism is not determined by your genes. So, if you understand how alcoholism works psychologically then you are in the position to master it.

EIGHT

# Myths of Addiction

The last chapter looked at what might be called, "the myth of a gene for alcoholism." This is but one of many widely believed misconceptions about addiction—I have already alluded to a number of others. Below, I will consider some additional generally accepted ideas whose mythical nature can be easily seen from the perspective of the psychology of addiction that I have been describing.

## MYTH 1: YOU ARE ADDICTED TO THINGS THAT ARE "ADDICTIVE"

This myth is related to the overemphasis placed on being "hooked" on drugs that I spoke of earlier. I mentioned that the customary use of the term "to be addicted to" something—a drug, a behavior, an activity—is one part of this problem. This unfortunate phrase suggests that it is the *object* of the addiction, the drug or activity, that magnetically attracts you, rather than that addiction is a psychological process that arises within a person. In point of fact, a quality of "addictiveness" in the object has meaning in only one limited sense: the craving sensations that can be produced during withdrawal as part of physical addiction to a drug. But if you remember the experiences of Vietnam veterans and of people with medical illnesses who were given high narcotic doses for pain yet were able to stop using their drugs, you will recall that even strong physical cravings are unable to create an addiction in a person who does not have the psychology for it. Even for physically addictive drugs, then, the "addictiveness" of the object—the drug—does not explain true addictions that target these drugs.

The false idea of addictiveness arises with many behaviors, however. The mythical addictive quality of the object of these addictions is generally attributed to a trait of the object that is especially appealing. Candy, for instance, is "addictive" because it is sweet, games such as bridge or Tetrus are "addictive" because they are intriguing or challenging, and so on. In these cases, the confusion does not come from overestimating the effect of physical addiction. The error is more fundamental—a notion that people can be helplessly drawn toward objects without the primary role of their own emotional lives.

Of course, objects of addiction are not chosen randomly—their properties do matter. A good example of this is the popularity of "scratch tickets" sold by state lotteries. These tickets provide immediate feedback because scratching away their surface reveals a message telling you whether you have won or not. In contrast, weekly or twice weekly jackpots require waiting until the day of the drawing to find out if you've won. Since their introduction, scratch tickets have become more popular than the original lottery jackpot games, a difference that has been credited to their ability to provide instant results. The tickets' attribute of *immediacy*, then, influences their use as an addictive object. And predictably, some people have concluded from this that scratch tickets are more "addictive" than other lottery games.

But this is not true. The popularity of scratch tickets indicates that there are people who find it frustrating to wait for a weekly drawing, so they choose scratch tickets as the focus of their addiction. For them, the ability of these tickets to give an instant result is attractive. But attractiveness is not the same as addictiveness. Objects' attractiveness for the purpose of being an addictive focus may in fact may vary over time, leading people to shift their addictive behavior from one activity to another, as you know. Their addiction remains the same, though different potentially attractive objects are utilized as the focus of an addiction at different times. The attractiveness of objects to become a focus of an addictive displacement, then, does not mean the objects are themselves addictive. I will say some more about the myth of objects' addictiveness in chapter 10.

## MYTH 2: YOU HAVE TO HIT BOTTOM BEFORE YOU CAN GET WELL

"You'll stop when you hit bottom" has been said of people suffering with addictions so many times that it has acquired a ring of truth through repetition alone. But it is a myth that is both silly and destructive. The silly part, of course, is that the "bottom" is knowable only in retrospect. Your "bottom" is wherever you were when you stopped an addictive behavior. It might be at a point when your life was near total collapse, or it might be after only a few minor setbacks. Since it can not be predicted in advance what situation will constitute your "bottom," and since nobody can define what is meant by the "bottom" for you until after it has occurred, "hitting bottom" as a concept is worthless.

It is also harmful. The myth of needing to hit bottom is frequently used as a thinly disguised way of moralizing, suggesting that only when you have suffered enough can you get it through your head that you need to stop—only then will you have learned your lesson. Implicit in this is that you are stupid or unable to learn from experience. Like many other false beliefs about addiction, this one is based on the idea that addiction is a conscious process that is allowed to continue through weakness of will. People who subscribe to this myth may be quietly judgmental of those suffering with addictions, including themselves.

Another problem with this myth is that it gives the message that things must inevitably get worse before you can be well. Of course, this is untrue. Once you learn the emotional basis for your addiction, there is no need to "hit bottom" in any sense, before taking control of your life.

## MYTH 3: IF YOU HAVE AN ADDICTION, YOU ARE SELF-DESTRUCTIVE

Many people believe that self-destructiveness lies at the core of addiction. They think that people suffering with addictions have a problem with wanting to hurt themselves, and that their addiction is evidence of that. As I hope is clear by now, this notion is precisely backward. Addictions are an attempt to preserve control over your feelings and your life and respond assertively to helplessness. The fact that they are almost inevitably self-destructive is only a disastrous side effect—caused by factors that are inherent to the psychology of addiction.

One of these factors is that, as with any compulsive action, addiction takes over your functioning at the expense of your better judgment. Considerations that would ordinarily be important to you for your health or well-being are temporarily ignored while you are driven by the compulsive need to act in the moment. It is no wonder that this often leads to unintended detrimental results.

The fact that addictions are displacements also contributes to their harmful effects. As displacements, addictive behaviors inevitably are a failure to directly address a problem that might have been repaired if it had been approached head-on. A consequence of this is to produce the appearance of being intentionally self-destructive, because more helpful actions—which may be obvious to others—are not taken.

Since a lack of self-destructive intent, even unconsciously, is clear once you understand the psychology of addiction, it follows that on the rare occasions when people with addictions *do* have a conscious or unconscious need to hurt themselves through their addictive behavior, this should be understood to be—and dealt with as—a separate problem from the addiction. Finally, like other myths, this one is harmful. It labels people with a problem they don't suffer from, and it distracts attention from understanding the true nature of addiction.

## MYTH 4:  YOU NEED TO SURRENDER

The idea that you must surrender your will before you can give up your addiction arose from the twelve steps of Alcoholics Anonymous, particularly Step Three, which advises turning over your will to a higher power. This step is based, AA says, on the belief that, "Our whole trouble had been the misuse of will power."[1] Step Three urges you, therefore, to surrender that power.

While some people can make use of this idea, it is clearly not for everyone.* However, along with other AA concepts, the "surrendering" notion is often described as the only way to address alcoholism or other addictions—and that is a myth that is both wrong and hurtful. The "surrendering" idea is, as the quotation above from AA indicates, explicitly based on the notion that alcoholism, or any addiction, is a sign of your failure, so you should give up on the belief that you can manage your own life. It is another idea that is backward, based on a misunderstanding of the nature of addiction. It does not understand that alcoholism, like any addiction, is a displaced effort to exercise a necessary, healthy power against helplessness, and is a sign of *inhibition* of the direct exercise of power. Accordingly, the appropriate solution is not to shamefacedly admit that you cannot manage your life, but to take over more management of your life—by understanding yourself and your addiction better so you can use that understanding to take power more directly in place of the addiction. The last thing you want to do is give up on taking control of your life.

---

*I will return to those people who can make use of this idea later, in chapter 18, "Treatment."

A corollary of this is the idea that you should try to distract your-self from thinking about your addiction. Again, quite to the contrary, if you avoid noticing your thoughts about repeating an addictive act when they occur, you will make yourself *more* vulnerable to enacting an addiction, because you will not have taken the opportunity to learn from each of these occasions about the issues that lie behind your addictive urge.

## MYTH 5: YOU SHOULD COUNT YOUR DAYS OF SOBRIETY

This is another AA tradition that works for some but is hurtful to many. As you probably know, after a day, a week, a month, and each year, AA groups award a small token to indicate that this much time has been achieved without drinking. The idea is to reward accomplishment and be a reminder of what will be lost if you do drink—your count will return to zero and you must start the long climb upward again.

Restarting from zero is the dark side of this tradition, and why it is a myth to think it is a good idea. In common with some of the other AA-based notions, the counting of sober days has a strong moralistic overtone. You are rewarded for success, but if you "fail" then you must suffer the punishment of losing everything you gained. Of course, this is infuriating and discouraging for many people who have been trying to stay sober.

It is also nonsensical. The fact is that if you have been doing well in your efforts to remain abstinent and have a slip, you are still basically doing well. Although slips are not desirable, they should not be a surprise—especially while you are working out your understanding of the sources of the feelings of helplessness that lie behind the addiction. Indeed, even though they are clearly not a positive event, slips can and should be viewed with thoughtful consideration—as something to learn from about yourself and the conflicts that you are dealing with through addictive behavior.

It is both punitive and unrealistic to encourage people to think of themselves as returning to zero because of a slip.

## MYTH 6:  YOU SHOULD BE TREATED BY SOMEONE WHO ALSO HAS AN ADDICTION

The idea behind this myth is that only someone who has gone through the same problem as you is qualified to deal with it. To the extent this has any merit, it would be because some people have trouble trusting anyone who has not gone through the identical experience. But in general this myth is another sign of not understanding what addictions are about.

Knowing that addictions are solutions to specific psychological conflicts, it follows that the people best suited to treat them are those who are trained and knowledgeable about the psychology of addiction. Of course, people with addictions who have obtained such training are as suitable for providing treatment as anyone else. But unfortunately, as is well known, there are many people presenting themselves as therapists or counselors in the addiction field who have limited or no training. Their principal qualification in their own minds is their personal status of being in the process of recovery from alcoholism or another addiction. Too often, they believe this credential suffices to provide professional assistance to others. Consequently, what they offer consists of little more than sharing their personal experience, or of a review of the twelve steps of the AA program. Naturally, it is good to hear of others' experiences, and when AA is helpful, mutual support is a major reason. But if you are seeking professional treatment, you deserve a lot more— someone trained to help you learn what you need to learn about yourself. And beyond this, sometimes such peer counseling is directly harmful, as when people are badgered to accept the one way that worked for the counselor.

On the other hand, therapists who are expert in the psychology of addiction have no more need to have an addiction themselves in order to help you than your medical doctor needs to have a cold in order to treat your cold. Naturally, any therapist should be compassionate, respectful, and empathic. But that has nothing to do with whether the therapist has an addiction himself.

This brings up another troubling part of this myth: it is an insult to people suffering with addictions. Believing that one has to be treated by a fellow sufferer implies that people suffering with addictions are so different from the rest of the human race that anyone who does not share the problem could not possibly understand them! What an awful idea. The truth of course is far from this. Addictions are human conditions like many other common problems with which nearly all of us suffer. It is perfectly fine to seek treatment for them from someone without an addiction.

## MYTH 7: ADDICTION IS BASICALLY A PROBLEM OF BRAIN CHEMISTRY

This myth arises from a number of misunderstandings. I have already mentioned some of them: confusing physical addiction with addiction; belief in a gene for addiction (which would have to operate by a biochemical route); and misinterpretation of the meaning of brain imaging studies that show *where* drugs work, not why some people use them addictively.

A different kind of basis for the brain chemistry myth is the mistaken idea that people take drugs or do other activities because it gives them a "high." Recent research that has shown that various drugs, including alcohol, increase brain levels of the neurotransmitter dopamine, has sometimes been misunderstood to support this idea. But the notion that addictions are a way to seek a neurotransmitter "high" is just the ancient mistake that addictions are essentially pleasure-seeking, dressed up in modern terms. Attributing the "high" from addictions to neurotransmitters does not make this idea fit the facts any better. It takes very little time listening to people with addictions before one learns that addictive behavior is an unhappy compulsion, not an effort to seek rapture. And a brain chemistry model of addiction also does not fit well with the widely known ability of some people to stop using alcohol, or another drug, as soon as they embark on a talking treatment, whether it is psychotherapy or a group support treatment.

A final reason for the brain chemistry myth is more general—a widely accepted idea in our culture that everything human, including addiction, will eventually be explained through either genes or biochemistry. This notion raises the question, to quote the neurologist Robert Sapolsky again, "What will happen to our cherished senses of individuality and free will?"[2] In answering this question, Professor Sapolsky pointed out that in fact behavior cannot be pre-ordained by genes—there are just too many complex environmental factors contributing to it.

This reasoning applies equally to brain chemistry. No matter how well we may end up understanding the biochemistry of the brain, we will never be able to predict complex human behavior such as addiction, or human psychology in general, simply on that basis.

Yet, many people believe just that. Sure, they say, they understand our emotional lives are complex, but just wait until we know more about how the brain works. Then addiction, and all aspects of human psychology, will be reduced to biochemistry. Depending on your outlook, you may be delighted by this idea or horrified by it. In any case, it is not true.

The clearest explanation of why this is not true comes from a surprising source—modern physics. In recent decades, physicists have come to appreciate that you cannot predict complex behavior of atoms, much less people, from knowing the building blocks of which they are composed. As M. Mitchell Waldrop noted in his book *Complexity*,[3] the Nobel Prize–winning physicist Kenneth Anderson said, "The ability to reduce everything to simple fundamental laws does not imply the ability to start from those laws and reconstruct the universe." As an example, Waldrop went on to speak about water. "There's nothing very complicated about a water molecule; it's just one big oxygen atom with two little hydrogen atoms stuck to it like Mickey Mouse ears. Its behavior is governed by well-understood equations of atomic physics. But now put a few zillion of those molecules together in the same pot. Suddenly you've got a substance that shimmers and gurgles and sloshes. Those zillions of molecules have collectively acquired a property, liquidity, that none of them possesses alone. . . . The liquidity is 'emergent.' . . . Weather is an emergent property: take your water vapor out over the Gulf of Mexico and let it interact with sunlight and wind, and it can organize itself into an emergent structure known as a hurricane. Life is an emergent property . . . the mind is an emergent property, the product of several billion neurons obeying the biological laws of the living cell." Quoting Anderson again, Waldrop concludes, " 'At each level of complexity, entirely new properties appear. [And] at each stage, entirely new laws, concepts, and generalizations are necessary, requiring inspiration and creativity . . . Psychology is not applied biology, nor is biology applied chemistry.' "[4] In short, no matter how well the underlying building blocks of the brain and its chemistry are known and understood, we will never be able to predict or understand on that basis the intricacies of the "emergent" property called human psychology. Personally, I feel that this is a very good thing.

## MYTH 8: PEOPLE WITH ADDICTIONS HAVE AN ADDICTIVE PERSONALITY

This myth confuses the use of a specific psychological way to manage certain feeling states—the psychology of addiction that I have been describing—with the concept of "personality." Personality refers to an overall manner of adaptation to both the outer world and to one's inner feelings, and is a pervasive quality that defines much of who you are. But people with addictions have every kind of personality. What they have in common is the use of an addiction to manage certain feeling states. Confusing this with an entire "personality" has at least two regrettable consequences. First, it incorrectly suggests again that people with addictions are different in a fundamental way from everyone else. And second, by suggesting that the issue in addiction is a problem of character, it is too close to the moralistic term "character defects" unfortunately used by AA to describe the problems of its members.

## MYTH 9:  PEOPLE WITH ADDICTIONS ARE IMPULSIVE

Here, the error is confusing the meaning of the words "compulsive" and "impulsive." As can be seen in the stories of the people I have described, addictions are generally not impulsive at all. They arise as a consequence of inner conflict at a particular moment but are frequently delayed until the addictive action can be put into effect. Indeed, since the urge to perform an addictive act always arises before the act itself—sometimes long before—I mentioned that it can be very useful to identify this critical moment, when you try to think back, in order to understand what *led* to a particular episode of an addiction. Likewise, if you can identify this moment when it occurs, you still have time to forestall the addictive act altogether and find a better solution.

Truly impulsive actions are the result of a breakdown of one's ordinary ability to think through a situation and act on some decision-making process. From a psychological standpoint they reflect mainly an absence of function. Addictions are very different from that—they reflect the *presence* of a rather complex function. (Regrettably, the Diagnostic and Statistical Manual of Mental Disorders, the DSM-IV, fails to understand this. Because it has a category for "Substance-Related Disorders" but no category for addictions, it has separated compulsive gambling—officially called "Pathological Gambling"—from drug addictions and erroneously placed it in the category of "Impulse-Control Disorders.")

## MYTH 10:  DENIAL IS A FAILURE
## TO RECOGNIZE REALITY

The most famous defense mechanism of people with addictions, denial is not what most people think it is. This myth arises from the surface appearance of denial—for example a man saying, "I'm not an alcoholic" in spite of every evidence to the contrary. It looks as if he is unable to recognize the obvious truth. But if we think about this from the point of view of the new psychology of addiction I am describing, a more likely explanation occurs.

At the heart of addiction is the necessity to defy helplessness. But when the man in this example is asked to admit that he has alcoholism, he understandably feels that he is *being asked to admit that he is helpless to control his own behavior.* This smacks directly into the problem with which he is trying to deal. In my experience, the so-called denial of a person in this situation is a problem with tolerating the *meaning* of what is being asked of him, rather than a problem with knowing reality. And I have found that when people come to see that addiction is fundamentally an effort to retain power, rather than evidence of weakness or powerlessness, this alters the meaning of the question for them. Now the question "Do you have alcoholism?" can be heard more accurately as asking whether a person uses the mechanism of addiction to express a fundamentally healthy sense of empowerment when he or she feels unable to act in any other way. There is little reason not to give an affirmative answer to *this* question, and indeed I have often found that "denial" suddenly disappears when there is no longer a need for it. It is a myth that people suffering with addictions have any more problem with knowing reality than anyone else.

# NINE

# When Is Abuse Not Addiction?

Many people take too many painkillers, or drink too much coffee, or chat on the Internet for longer than they wish they had. Do all of them have an addiction? What about cigarette smokers? In chapter 6, I mentioned that millions of people stopped smoking even though they had a physical addiction to nicotine, and that this was one piece of evidence for the relatively small role of physical addiction. But I said I would return to the issue of the other millions of people in this country who still smoke cigarettes. If addiction resides in the person and not in the drug, does this mean that all these smokers, or people who spend too much time on the Internet, or drink too much coffee, have true psychological addiction?

While there must be many people whose continued smoking or other excessive behavior, is driven by true addiction, it is unlikely that this is true for all of them. Behavior that is not good for you, including abuse or overuse of a drug, may, after all, occur for a variety of reasons besides addiction. *The fact that a behavior is unhealthy, as is cigarette smoking, does not in itself reveal what causes it.* For many destructive behaviors, including drug overuse, there is a combination of elements other than addiction that together can permit or encourage these behaviors to continue, despite their risks. Below, I will look at these *nonaddiction* factors that can contribute to drug overuse. (I will focus on drugs here, but many of these reasons apply to nondrug excessive behaviors as well.)

## PHYSICAL ADDICTION

First, I must revisit physical addiction. As I have described, anyone can become physically addicted to those drugs capable of producing physical addiction, if those drugs are used in large enough quantities over a long enough time. The risk of becoming physically addicted applies equally whether a person has a true addiction or not. And, as you know from the discussion in chapter 6, physical addiction cannot "hook" a person into having a true addiction. (Recall the experience of the Vietnam veterans who stopped using narcotics when they returned home.) However, the presence of cravings, or a fear of withdrawal symptoms—both due to physical addiction—while not "hooking" people in the popular sense of rendering them helpless, clearly does make it more difficult to stop using those drugs that are capable of being physically addictive. So, physical addiction, while not either necessary or sufficient to produce a true addiction, is one factor that contributes to continued unhealthy, destructive drug use. This is why it is a very bad idea to expose young people, especially, to drugs capable of inducing physical addiction.

The role of physical addiction is also one reason why cigarette makers must bear responsibility for inducing the habit of cigarette smoking in their customers. It has been reported that manufacturers have intentionally elevated levels of nicotine in cigarettes, which would encourage the development of physical addiction, making it harder to break the habit of smoking. While this is a separate matter from true addiction, that fact does not make the dangers to smokers any less, nor does it lessen the culpability of manufacturers.

## HABIT

Habit and learning also play a role in excessive behaviors. Habit is a more psychologically superficial phenomenon than addiction; it is not driven by deep inner issues of the sort I have described. Habit is simply a normal process in which a person acts automatically in situations that have been experienced before, without having to think consciously about what he or she is doing. In one form of this, cues in the environment lead to recall of sensations and feelings that were previously experienced in that situation. This in turn provokes an automatic, learned response. For example, a woman who has previously lit up a cigarette with her coffee each morning is likely to find herself the next morning recalling the pleasurable experience of the cigarette, and reaching unthinkingly for a smoke. Or the man who has stopped every day after work at his local pub will find, as he walks past the bar the next afternoon, the memory of a drink floating to his mind—and may notice his feet automatically turning toward the bar's door. The difference between habit and addiction is important because, as I will describe, habit is a lot easier to resolve than addiction.

## INTERPERSONAL PRESSURE

Like any behavior, the use of drugs can be partly a response to a need for acceptance by others. This is especially true for people in vulnerable interpersonal positions. For instance, someone in a relationship with a partner who has a drug addiction may feel pressure to join in the partner's use. The drug-using partner may actively encourage this use in order to feel less isolated. Or, the nonaddicted person may himself or herself want to feel connected to the drug-using partner's experience. People living with others who use drugs are often forced to balance their need to maintain their relationship against their desire to stop using the drug themselves—sometimes a painful choice. This same issue can also occur in larger groups or subcultures where drug use is the norm or is especially valued, as in some groups of adolescents. For teens, it can be hard to stop when stopping is uncool or risks expulsion from the group.

## SETTING

Somewhat related to interpersonal pressure is the influence of the setting in which one excessively performs an activity.[1] The example of soldiers in Vietnam was one instance of this, but even a temporary setting may contribute to overuse. Gambling casinos, for example, traditionally exploit the influence of setting on overuse by creating a festive environment in which both money and the passage of time can seem unreal (using chips only, and having no clocks or windows). Even without a gambling addiction, many a person has later regretted the amount spent in the midst of flashing colored fluorescent lights and exciting bells going off. Holiday parties and family celebrations are likewise settings in which people sometimes drink much more than they would at other times.

## INTENTIONAL EFFORT TO RELIEVE TENSION

Another factor in unhealthy drug use is the conscious use of drugs to relieve stress. Here, the drug is "self-prescribed" in order to help get through difficult circumstances. Under stress, the need to soothe oneself may temporarily overwhelm long-term considerations of good health ("When my plane was delayed, I *had* to have a cigarette to calm down."). This may look like an addiction, but it differs from it because the choice to use a drug is basically just a conscious decision, rather than being driven by deeper factors. I will describe a case later in this chapter that will illustrate this.

## DRUG-INDUCED DRUG USE

Heavy drug use itself can produce enough alteration of mental state so that further drug use is due to loss of the ability to make a rational decision. For example, a person could be too drunk to use good judgment about having the next drink. In itself, this is not unusual, although when judgment is severely impaired, especially repeatedly, it is often a sign of having a true addiction. However, there are people without any addiction who have unintentionally taken serious overdoses of drugs, including prescribed medicines, because the drugs they've already ingested caused them to forget what they had taken (this is called a "drug automatism"). Altered mental state due to the drugs themselves, then, can be a factor in overuse of drugs. However, since this altered state can only occur once the person has begun to use a drug, it is of little significance with regard to the repeated relapses that are the real problem in ongoing overuse or addiction. It cannot explain the return to use again.

## LACK OF KNOWLEDGE

Lack of knowledge is a common factor in unhealthy and excessive behavior. It has been particularly important in cigarette overuse, as I mentioned in chapter 6. People stopped smoking by the millions once they became truly convinced that cigarettes were harmful. But there are still many people who don't think that smoking is dangerous for them, or who are unaware of how dangerous it can be, and as long as they don't realize this it is unlikely that they will quit. They literally don't know why they should. Recent court decisions that have found cigarette manufacturers to have withheld critical information about the dangers of their products point to a major reason for this lack of knowledge. To the extent that manufacturers have actively created ignorance, this is another reason why they must bear responsibility for the dangerous overuse of their products. Lack of knowledge is also a factor in some drug subcultures, especially among younger people, where there may be a mutually reinforced belief that use of their dangerous drugs is safe. ("Nick has been using drugs for years, and he says that Ecstasy is harmless.

Hey, everybody knows that.") Finally, we have all been ignorant in the past about the dangers of certain drugs and activities. Smoking cigarettes is one example, but cocaine was also thought to be harmless at one time (it was the original "coca" in Coca-Cola*), and many people still believe that playing the lottery is without risk.

## INSUFFICIENCY OF SELF-CARE

Sometimes use of drugs is only an example of people not taking good enough care of themselves in general. Some researchers have written about people with addictions suffering particularly with what they have called a "self-care deficit" (I will return to this idea in the next chapter). However, difficulties in taking good care of oneself are not restricted to people who suffer with addictions, of course. Other people, who do not have an addiction but who do have trouble with self-care, may overuse drugs just as they are inattentive to their well-being in all manner of ways. For them, their drug overuse is an instance of another problem, but is not a true addiction in itself—a fact that becomes important in treatment. For example, Deborah was a thirty-four-year-old woman who had becoming increasingly depressed over several months. During that time, she neglected to pay bills, leading to threats from the power company to shut off her electricity, failed to properly take the insulin she needed for her diabetes, overused prescribed sleeping pills despite her doctor's warning that it was hazardous for her, and resumed smoking. Her overuse of drugs was part of a pattern of self-neglect related to her depression, and her treatment was primarily directed toward her depression; her drug abuse was not presumed, at this point, to be an indication that she had a true addiction.

---

*Of course, cocaine has long since been replaced by caffeine in Coca-Cola, though decocainized coca leaves are still a part of the "natural flavors" in the beverage (Weiss, R., and Mirin, S. *Cocaine*. New York: Ballantine Books, 1987 [p. 6]).

## AUTONOMY

Overuse of a drug, or other excessive behaviors, may also serve as a kind of defiance—particularly among teenagers—without being a true addiction. Here, the behavior is not produced by a specific drive to perform an addictive act, as in true addiction, but is instead a sign of broader, often developmental, issues around refusing to be stopped or limited. "Don't tell me what I can or can't do," when applied to a repetitive, especially a forbidden, action may look like an addiction. Frequently, what is at stake is a struggle around emerging autonomy (I will say more about this when I talk about teenagers in chapter 13). Unfortunately, for teenagers especially, this struggle around autonomy often combines with a lack of knowledge about the risks of their actions and with inadequate attention to their own safety, to produce behavior that can be highly dangerous, even though it is not an addiction.

———

There are many factors that can lead to unhealthy drug use. And these factors become even more powerful when combined. For many of the millions of smokers in this country, for example, their continued overuse of cigarettes reflects the power of factors such as habit, physical addiction, interpersonal pressure, stress, and ignorance. Separately and together, these factors produce unhealthy behavior among people who do not have a true addiction.

It is important to be able to distinguish this overuse from addiction because it has different causes, different treatment, and a different prognosis. It will come as no surprise to you that it is easier for people to stop overusing drugs when the basis for their overuse is nonaddiction factors. For instance, people who have continued to use drugs mainly out of fear of withdrawal may find that a safe medical detoxification is enough to enable them to remain abstinent. Others, whose drug use is largely determined by habit, may find that practice in avoiding old patterns, such as sitting on the porch where they used to have a cigarette after dinner, results in a fading of the pressure to repeat the habit over time. Still others leave abusive relationships or unhealthy subcultures and can make new drug-free lives for themselves once they are away from the interpersonal pressure to take drugs. Just with the passage of time, most adolescents grow up and find out that it is safe to be different from the group, so they can give up drug use that was not psychologically necessary for them, but was only needed to be included with others. Other people stop using drugs by getting out of stressful situations whose stress they have consciously tried to manage with drugs, and making sure that they never return to them. Or, they find ways to make those situations less stressful, so they don't feel the need to resume use of drugs that they know is hazardous for them. And people become educated about the dangers of what they are doing, even if this learning must sometimes come through unfortunate experience.

In all these cases, those who harmfully but nonaddictively use drugs do not ever have to deal with the powerful, unconscious inner drive at the heart of addiction. This significantly improves their likelihood of spontaneous or self-willed recovery, or recovery with brief treatment.

Distinguishing nonaddiction bases for drug overuse is important also because it undercuts unfair moralizing toward people who really do suffer with a true addiction. If you suffer with an addiction, you may have heard something like this: "Well, Joe stopped with no problem. Why can't you?" Of course, Joe may not have had an addiction at all.

————

Matters can be complicated, however. At the same time as nonaddiction factors may be present, there may *also* be a true addiction. If you suffer with an addiction you know that, unfair though it seems, having an addiction does not immunize you to the other issues that contribute to drug abuse. You must deal with as many of these nonaddiction factors—peer pressure, habit, and so forth—as anyone else. And since the situation can be complex, it is not always easy to diagnose the presence of true addiction. The following case gives an example of this in a woman who was abusing drugs and was referred to me by her general practitioner because she was "addicted" to them.

———

When I first went out to the waiting room to greet Carol Josephson, she was crying. A neatly dressed woman in her mid-forties, she was seated, holding one crumpled tissue in her hand and dabbing at her eyes with another.

"Hello," I said as I looked at her with concern. She made a game effort to smile, and we shook hands as I showed her into the office. I already knew something about her, because Dr. MacIntyre had called me when she referred Carol. She was worried about Carol's difficulty in tapering off Valium and aspirin with codeine—drugs that had been prescribed for her back pain—and about the fact that Carol sometimes took more pills than were prescribed.

When Carol sat down her lip was still quivering. As gently as I could, I said, "Tell me what's on your mind."

"Well," she began, but then stopped and cried a little more. "Well," she started again, "I think, and Dr. MacIntyre thinks, that I'm a drug addict." She looked at me with wide eyes. "I think I'm like one of those street addicts."

I knew from Dr. MacIntyre that Carol worked as an administrative assistant at a law firm and had been a valued employee there for many years. She was married with three children and had lived in a small suburban community with her family for all the time Dr. MacIntyre had known her, about fifteen years.

"Why do you worry about that?" I asked.

"Well, I've been taking, I mean some of the time, I take more of the medicines Dr. MacIntyre prescribes than I should. The pain bothers me sometimes and I take extra pills. I told Dr. MacIntyre I was doing this." Carol looked at me again as if to be sure I understood that she wasn't trying to fool her doctor. I nodded. "And I can't seem to cut down on them the way Dr. MacIntyre thinks I should. So, she said I should come and see you." Carol said this with a hint of shame, as if being asked to see me were a sign that she was bad.

"When you say you take too many, what do you mean?"

"Well, I'm supposed to take no more than three or four of the Valiums in a day, and Dr. MacIntyre doesn't even really want me to take that many. She warned me that I could become addicted to them and also the aspirin with codeine, but sometimes I take one or two extra Valiums in a day, and an extra aspirin with codeine too."

"You must run out of pills, then."

"Yes, I do. Then I call Dr. MacIntyre. I think that's one of the things that's been bothering her. She doesn't like to prescribe more of the pills when I've used them up too fast. She told me that with these medicines if she prescribed more, so I would have more, I would just get used to a higher dose. Then I would have to keep pushing up the number of pills to get the same effect." I nodded again. Carol was describing a common problem with medicines that are capable of producing physical addiction. She continued, "And that's the opposite of what we were trying to do—get me off the drugs, so I wouldn't be stuck on them forever."

I asked Carol about her history of back trouble. About a year before, she had injured her back trying to move a heavy box while balancing her infant daughter on her hip. The awkward motion had produced immediate searing pain, which had continued in lesser form since then—although it was slowly improving. Tests had indicated that the problem was only a sprain, but that it was worsened by the fact that she had a mild congenital deformity of her spinal column, which made the nerves in her back easily prone to injury. Surgery had been briefly considered to relieve pressure on these nerves, and to reduce the risk of further injury from the deformity, but she had been advised that the chances of surgery making her worse were at least as good as the chances of it making her better. So, a conservative treatment plan had been worked out that included medicines for inflammation, pain, and muscle spasm—the medication Carol had been unable to reduce, and which she had in fact overused. Carol also said that she knew that she had contributed to the slow progress of her condition by continuing to do some heavy lifting around the house, including lifting up her children, and that she had reinjured herself to a milder degree several times.

As we discussed her experience with the medicines, I learned that when Carol had tried to reduce them, or when she actually ran out, she became jittery and anxious, and that these symptoms subsided when she resumed taking her regular dose. These symptoms appeared to be an early withdrawal reaction, especially from the Valium. She had been taking the medicines long enough, even at the prescribed doses, for them to have induced physical tolerance and withdrawal symptoms when they were removed, since she had not gone more than two days in eighteen months without taking them. Dr. MacIntyre had tried to wean her off the drugs by prescribing fewer pills, but this had never worked because Carol was unable to stick to the schedule.

I told Carol that while both medicines she was taking were capable of producing physical addiction, Valium was the more serious because its withdrawal reaction was more dangerous than withdrawal from codeine.

"I know," she said, "Dr. MacIntyre explained that to me. She even talked about my going in the hospital for a couple of days to get me off the pills, since I couldn't do it at home. I'm willing, but I'm afraid. I don't know what I'll do without them." Her eyes began to fill with tears again. "I'm so scared. That makes me a real addict, doesn't it, being afraid to stop?"

The way Carol had spoken of dreading being a "street addict," or a "real addict," made it sound as if she thought being an "addict" was something awful. I wanted to tell her that people with addictions weren't bad, that even if she had a psychological addiction, that didn't make her a bad person either. But with her eyes brimming, I didn't think this was the moment to address her low opinion of people with addictions.

"We should talk about what addiction means," I said gently. She looked at me as she held back more tears. "You may be physically addicted to one or the other of the medicines you're taking," I went on, "but that can happen to anybody. You've been taking these drugs for a long time and you've been taking them without a break. When you do that, with these medicines, your body becomes habituated to them. But your body's reaction to the drugs doesn't say whether your use of them amounts to an addiction."

"But I feel as though I need them. I feel as though I can't get along without them. I get so shaky when I try to stop."

"Yes, it sounds as though you have withdrawal symptoms when you stop taking the pills. It's understandable that this would frighten you, and that you try to avoid it."

"But that's what addicts do, isn't it?" Carol persisted.

"Some of the time, yes," I admitted. But I went on to explain again that her symptoms indicated only that she had a physical addiction, and to briefly describe the differences between physical and psychological addiction.

When I finished, she nodded thoughtfully. "I understand what you're saying, but what bothers me is that it's more than that I worry about getting shaky when I stop taking the pills. I'm also afraid that the pain will come back."

"Say some more about what you mean by that."

She shook her head at the thought. "When it was bad, at the beginning, it was horrible. Then, I kept hurting it again. Now, when I get a twinge, I'm frightened that it will get worse. That's when I sometimes take an extra pill."

I thought about what Carol was saying. I said, "You've been worried about this for a long time, then."

Carol nodded, then her body visibly relaxed, and she let out a breath. After a moment, she said, "I've felt so guilty about taking the extra pills. I know it's hard for other people to understand. I've just gotten so used to taking them that I'm afraid to stop."

———

In order to understand Carol's overuse of her medicines, she and I had to carefully investigate her thoughts and feelings to know whether her overuse, and her trouble tapering off the medicines, was a product of the kind of deeper internal issues that drive addiction. As it turned out, for her there was simply no evidence of an emotional issue with helplessness, or rage at helplessness. Her difficulty was related to nonaddiction factors. She had a physical addiction and was afraid of withdrawal symptoms. She had used her medicines in a conscious attempt to lessen her anxiety about her pain returning. And we discovered another nonaddiction factor when, as a result of our talking out her fears, she gradually allowed her daily medicine dosage to decrease. It was particularly hard for her to give up her morning dose of Valium, for instance, because she had become accustomed to having what she considered to be a little "lift" in the morning. For the first week or two when she eliminated this dose, she felt worried and out of sorts, not so much because of physical withdrawal but because she was missing an experience that she had anticipated. She was, in other words, giving up a habit.

Eventually, she was able to take a lower dose of both of her medicines. She stayed with the decreased doses both because she knew she needed to, and because psychologically, with just a little help from treatment, she could. She never required a hospitalization for detoxification. Indeed, Carol was not difficult to treat. Although she had overused her medicines, was physically addicted to them, had developed strong habits of taking the medicines at certain hours, was afraid of withdrawal symptoms, and had utilized the pills in a conscious attempt to deal with anxiety, she did not have the powerful unconscious drive present in true addiction.

# The Internet, Shopping, Exercise: How Can You Tell If It Is an Addiction?

Carol Josephson did not have an addiction, even though it looked as if she did. As I described in the last chapter, people do a lot of things that are commonly and casually called "addictions" but which may not be, because they are driven by nonaddiction factors. In this chapter, I would like to look at the other side of this coin— some less traditionally "addictive" behaviors that *are* addictions, and how to diagnose them for yourself.

## OBJECTS OF ADDICTION

To begin with, is it even possible to have an addiction focused on something like the Internet or shopping? Yes, certainly. After all, an addiction may be directed at nearly any object or activity, so long as the object or activity can serve as the displaced focus for the drive behind their addiction. The Internet or shopping are perfectly good candidates. So are eating, exercising, playing sports, or many other activities. The key point here is to keep in mind the "myth of addictiveness"—virtually anything may become the focus of an addiction because it is the *person* who endows the object or activity with the property of being "addictive." And, you will recall, this endowment is usually accompanied by an explanation of what quality of the object makes it so addictive. In truth, however, what is being described is not "addictiveness" of the activity at all, but attractiveness. The "addictive" quality of an object or activity is that aspect of it that makes it attractive *for the purpose* of the person's addiction. I gave lottery scratch tickets as an example of this, in chapter 8. Here is another example.

———

Charlie was a short and slender man whose pale skin and somewhat large eyeglasses gave the impression of bookishness. His problem, he explained to me, was that he was wasting too much time at his computer.

"Of course, I work at the computer all day, that's not what I mean," he added. "But I work from home, so I can do what I want and I'm always goofing off."

"Goofing off on the computer?"

"Yes. I get on the Net and play games."

"Oh? What do you play?"

Charlie told me several games with which he was deeply involved. As he described them in detail, his eyes lit up and he became more animated. All of the games sounded similar to me—variations on war games of a fantasy type, in which the object was to kill as many other players as possible to accumulate their assets, without getting killed yourself. Charlie explained that these games went on indefinitely, over weeks or months, because your character could be repeatedly reborn, though with fewer capabilities on account of having been killed.

"You're playing against other real people, right?"

"Oh yes. They can be anywhere in the world, you know. You get to know who's who if you play long enough."

What Charlie meant, I soon learned, was not that he knew the people who were playing, but he knew their game characters. He went on to describe some of these characters whom he had come to know intimately as bitter enemies—figures he had killed on

many occasions and who had often tried to kill him, also sometimes
successfully.

Charlie found himself drawn to these games with an intensity
that he did not understand. He had lost sleep staying up late to play
them. During the day, the hours he spent playing on the Internet
had caused him to miss several deadlines because of uncompleted
work. Even when he didn't stop to play, his mind wandered to the
events and strategy of the games, interfering with his concentra-
tion. Recently, his boss had commented on a deterioration in the
quality of his work.

"I'm addicted to them," he said about the games. "I can't stop
playing, even when I know there's no time for it. I keep telling
myself, 'Just five more minutes, just five more minutes,' and before
I know it I've pissed away two hours."

I asked Charlie what he thought attracted him to the games. He
described the sense of invigoration he felt while playing, the powerful energy with which he was engaged in the struggle. But he said
he could not put his finger on the thing that was at the core of what
drew him to them.

It was not until several meetings later that Charlie and I began to
piece together what his addiction was about. It began to become
clear when he told me about his brothers. Where Charlie had
always been slight in build, his two older brothers were huge, at
least as Charlie saw them. And as the youngest of three boys in a
family given more to action than to talking, Charlie was often the
object of his big brothers' aggression. He told me about the many
split lips, the bloody noses, the broken wrist. His parents were of
the opinion that boys will be boys, and rarely stepped in.

Charlie was unable to defend himself, then. But he had become
an expert at killing his enemies now.

When Charlie came to see why there was so much at stake for
him in playing his war games, he also saw why these games had
become the object of his addictive drive. To add to the meaning of
these games, we later learned that Charlie had an idea in the back of

his mind of what his enemies—the actual people controlling the characters—looked like. He had never thought about them very clearly, but when we talked about these people he looked as though he had just heard a thunderclap as he suddenly realized that he had pictured them very much like his brothers.

———

Charlie's story illustrates how all sorts of objects or activities may become the focus of an addiction. Were his Internet games "addictive"? No—they were just especially suitable as a displacement for expressing his rage at an old helplessness, and redressing it. His addiction underscores again the fact that an object of addiction does not magnetically attract you—*you* are the one who supplies the magnetism. The good news about this, of course, is that it means you also may control the process once you understand it.

Other people's use of the Internet as a focus of addiction will reflect their own individual purposes, just as Charlie's use reflected his. Internet chat rooms, for example, may be attractive to people as a focus of addiction for a variety of deeper reasons. Some people may express a drive to prove to themselves that they can make friends or seduce others, some may take on a new identity over the Internet to live out an aspect of themselves that they are driven to express but cannot do otherwise, and so forth. The Internet's convenience and twenty-four-hour availability make it attractive for many purposes as an object of addiction. It is not that it is addictive, but that it provides a new vehicle for old issues.

What would have happened to Charlie before there was an Internet? Most likely he would have found another object or activity that was *attractive enough* to become the focus of his addiction psychology. This different focus might have been less well matched to his emotional issues than the Internet games, but the need to express the underlying issues in an addiction is more important than the availability of any specific addictive focus. This is why people so readily switch from one focus of addiction to another when their first choice is unavailable. Sometimes, however, the alternative focus is not easily recognized as another addiction, which makes it important to be able to recognize "hidden" forms of addiction. I will return to this topic later in this chapter, and more fully in chapter 15.

## DIAGNOSING ADDICTION

It is clear that just knowing the object of an intense interest—such as a drug, a game, running, or shopping—does not tell you whether the behavior is an addiction. Nor can you necessarily tell if a behavior is an addiction from its intensity, since many actions that are the result of nonaddiction factors may be quite intense, as in Carol's story from the last chapter.

This uncertainty may be a very practical concern to some of you who worry about a behavior that you think you do excessively. I have developed a short questionnaire based on the new ideas in this book that will give you a preliminary idea about whether your behavior is a true addiction.

You may already know about the traditional questionnaires that have been developed for assessing alcoholism, for example. They focus on the effects that drinking has had on a person's life: medical illness, interference in relationships with family or friends, trouble at work, legal and financial difficulties, and so on. The most famous brief questionnaire is the "CAGE." Its name is an acronym, referring to the key words in the four questions: Have you ever tried to *cut* down drinking? Do you become *annoyed* when asked about drinking? Do you feel *guilty* about your drinking? Do you ever have an *"eye-opener"* (drink in the morning)? Of course, this is only a very coarse screen. There are many people with alcoholism who do not drink in the morning, and many who have not yet suffered enough bad effects to have either tried to cut down drinking or to feel guilty about it. But even other, longer questionnaires that rely on asking about the effects of drinking are limited by the fact there are too many potential consequences from drinking to ask about them all, and—more fundamentally—by the fact that determining whether a behavior is an addiction depends on what motivates it, not what results from it.

Indeed, if you see alcoholism, and addictive behavior in general, as a fundamentally internal, emotional problem, it becomes possible to diagnose it in an entirely different way—from the inside out rather than from the outside in. This is diagnosis based on the emotional factors that produce it. Looking at alcoholism and other addictions this way may also allow you to identify the problem *before* there have been a series of disasters, before you get to the point that you are consumed with guilt or that you must start the day with a drink. And, of course, the sooner you can diagnose the problem, the sooner you can begin to address it.

Here is the questionnaire. Although the questions are about alcoholism, they apply just as well to other addictive behaviors, so substitute the behavior you are concerned about. (For the sake of clarity, after each question I have noted the reason for its inclusion in the questionnaire.)

## ALCOHOLISM QUESTIONNAIRE*

1. Do I drink sometimes when I really don't want alcohol, but feel I have to do *something*, and there seems nothing else I can do to relieve my tension? (This question focuses on the compulsion to redress a feeling of helplessness that underlies true addictions.)

2. Even if I like drinking, is there an intensity to my drinking—a kind of grim determination—that can't be explained by liking it? Do I sometimes feel I "have to have a drink"? (This focuses on the difference between the deep compulsion of true addictions versus the more superficial feelings underlying a habit or a purely conscious decision to perform a particular act.)

---

*I have published an earlier version of this questionnaire, on the Web site, "The Psychoanalytic Perspective on the Problematic Use of Alcohol," *www.cyberpsych. org/alcohol*

3.  If I am blocked from drinking by circumstances or by another person, do I become unusually angry? (This addresses the rage at helplessness in the psychology of addiction.)

4.  Do I feel better just knowing I'm going to have a drink, even before I drink it? (This addresses the fact that true addiction is a psychological not a physical process.)

5.  Are there certain situations that I know will lead me to drink (not physical situations like walking into a bar, but emotional situations like feeling frustrated, defeated, or helpless, or trapped into doing something that I feel I *should* do)? (This asks about emotional precipitants of the psychological process that underlies addiction.)

6.  If I cannot get a drink quickly, do I sometimes substitute another activity (taking a different drug or gambling or eating) that feels as if it is accomplishing the same thing? (This focuses on the displacement nature of true addiction.)

7.  Does my drinking seem to substitute for a relationship with a person—for instance, do I tend to drink if I am lonely? (This is one particular form of the psychology of addiction; I will discuss it in the next chapter.)

8.  Do I drink when I feel bad about myself? (This is another form of helplessness that may underlie the drive toward addictive behavior.)

9.  Does drinking seem to solve emotional problems, at least while I am doing it? (This is another way of asking about the psychological nature of the behavior.)

10.  Does drinking help me feel more in control of my feelings and my life, at least while I am doing it? (This focuses on the restoration of power against powerlessness in true addiction.)

None of these questions is absolute, but if you find that as a whole they apply to the behavior you are concerned about, it is probably worth investigating with a professional in the field. I will take up how to find such help later, in chapter 18, "Treatment."

———

You may have noticed that one of the CAGE items is close to one of the items in my questionnaire—the one about feeling annoyed when asked about drinking. I believe this is a significant question because it addresses a defensiveness, expressed as annoyance or anger, that often indicates an effort to protect the drinking and, more deeply, the drive that lies behind it (a drive that is very worthwhile to defend). Hence, it is the only CAGE question that speaks, albeit in this indirect way, to causes rather than effects of drinking. (The CAGE question about guilt, although it also concerns an internal state, has to do with a reaction to the effects of drinking, and the question about cutting down is also about a reaction after the behavior has occurred.)

What is interesting is that, in my experience, the annoyance/anger question is the CAGE item that may be the most often subscribed to by people with alcoholism. Obviously, the other questions may not be affirmed simply because many people with alcoholism do not drink in the morning, and because many have not yet suffered enough adverse effects to have either tried to cut down or to feel guilty about their drinking. And some people *can't* feel guilty, because they are so ashamed of their behavior that if they allowed themselves to feel guilt they would be devastated. But aside from these considerations, I have always been struck by the fact that the one CAGE question that deals, even indirectly, with feelings that are not specifically connected with the results of drinking seems to be the one most people find easiest to acknowledge, if it is true. This suggests that asking about underlying feelings rather than effects is not only a more direct way to know whether a behavior is an addiction, but it may be also easier to think about.

## THE EFFECT OF DIAGNOSIS ON THE
## "SINGLE DRINK" QUESTION

Diagnosing addictions from the inside out is also helpful in under-standing one of the more confusing areas of addiction: how to think about the "single drink" question. It goes this way: "Why does everyone say that, if I have an addiction, it is dangerous to have even a single drink [or drug or place a single bet or visit a single chat room on the Internet]?" The standard answer to this question is that the single event will "set you off." Either it will trigger the desire to continue, or it will lull you into thinking that, if you tolerated the one drink or the one wager, you can have a second, then a third, and then the sky's the limit. Both of these concerns have merit. But there is also another reason why having "just onc" is a problem, and it is related to thinking about addiction from the inside out instead of the other way around.

If you diagnose addiction from its effects, then you are stuck with the limitations of this approach—if a behavior does not cause problems, it is hard to recognize it as an addiction. But if internal factors are paramount in identifying addiction, then *any single episode may be understood to be an addictive act whether or not it causes any ill effects.* (This is the other side of the coin from the issue I explored in the preceding chapter—that certain behaviors that *do* cause problems are, nonetheless, not addictions.) This way of looking at the question gives new reasons to avoid even a single drink.

First, if even one drink may be an example of the addiction, then far from being unimportant or harmless, that single drink may well be a sign of internal turmoil and of a destructive failure to act in a more direct, useful way. Left unaddressed, this turmoil is likely to produce a more pronounced relapse, in which an *addiction cycle* can occur: an initial underlying helplessness produces the addictive behavior as a restorative response, but in turn the addictive behavior leads to more helplessness. The new helplessness—produced by the addictive behavior—is the result of both the destructive effects of the addictive act itself and problems resulting from failure to take a more appropriate action in the situation. In turn, this new helplessness leads to more addictive behavior. Conversely, paying attention to the desire for even a single drink in the way I have been describing throughout this book may allow recognition of the inner basis for the urge and may provide an opportunity to figure out something important about what is happening to you.

There is also a second way that diagnosing from the inside out may be helpful to you in thinking through the "single drink" question. Many people are told that they cannot ever safely have just one drink simply because they have a disease called "alcoholism." The effort here is to convince people that alcoholism or any addiction is like an infection—let the bug in once and it will eat you alive. You will inevitably lose all control, you are told—not because of some understandable series of emotional events such as I described in the addiction cycle, above—but because that is the nature of the "disease." However, this standard thinking frequently produces a backlash, because the people being given this advice often have had just one drink many times without it causing them trouble. Consequently, they discredit the warning and the adviser, paradoxically supporting their belief that the single drink was safe. But if you understand the psychology of addiction, you may find that abstinence makes more sense to you.

## DIAGNOSIS OF ADDICTION AND OVERALL EMOTIONAL HEALTH

Diagnosis of addiction brings up some related issues. As I have tried to show, self-destructiveness and addictions are not at all identical. In the last chapter I noted that there are many behaviors that are self-destructive and look like addiction, but are not addictions. And even though addictions are self-destructive, having an addiction does not mean that *you* are self-destructive. But let's say you are a person who feels sure you would resist doing something that is self-destructive— it is a strength of yours. Does this matter in assessing whether you might have or develop an addiction? The answer is yes, and no.

The "no" part is easy. Since addictions are a compulsive activity, by definition they tend to overwhelm other parts of your thinking and judgment at key times, even if your usual ability to avoid being self-destructive is quite good.

But there is no doubt that it is helpful to have a strong sense of self-preservation, an investment in taking care of yourself. The importance of this is not that, in itself, a strong sense of "self-care" can prevent addictive behavior. However, if you do have an addiction, good self-care can be one factor in helping you to seek treatment earlier, and in giving you the motivation to learn as much as possible on your own about the nature of your addictive behavior (I will say some more about the "self-care" concept in the next chapter).

———

A more general issue arising from a diagnosis of addiction is this: What, if anything, does having an addiction say about your overall level of emotional health? I said in chapter 2 that if you have an addiction, it does not mean that you are more troubled psychologically or less mature than anyone else—and this is absolutely true. I also mentioned in the chapter on "Myths" that the notion of an "addictive personality" is false. In particular, I underscored the fact that having an addiction is not a sign of a pervasive difficulty in dealing with life, as is the case when people use the term "personality disorder."

But what about the fact that addictions centrally involve a sensitivity to certain kinds of helplessness? What does this say about psychological health? In thinking about this, it is helpful to know that when people knowledgeable about human psychology speak of levels of mental health, they are often thinking in developmental terms. Problems that arise earlier in childhood are generally more problematic because they affect more basic aspects of the way one views oneself and others—as well as affecting subsequent developmental stages. Likewise, problems that originate in even slightly older children—who are now in a new stage of normal development—involve emotional issues that are farther from the bedrock.

In addition, problems that occur in later stages of development will generally not undo the accomplishments of the stages of growth that came before.

The key in this for the new way of thinking about addictions is that *the sensitivity to helplessness that I have described as at the heart of addictive behavior may arise at any developmental level.* This means, therefore, that *in itself, having an addiction says nothing at all about your overall level of emotional health.* For example, some people with addictions are struggling to reverse feelings of helplessness around developmentally earlier feelings of abandonment, while for others their addictions are an effort to deal with helpless feelings around rivalries with parents, siblings, and peers that arose later. The effort not to be emotionally overwhelmed or helpless that I have described in addiction is basically the same across this spectrum of difficulties; it is the kind of specific issues at stake for different people that are different. But since having an addiction does not define the kinds of conflicts that underlie it, it also does not define anything about your emotional health.

Indeed, the effort in addiction to control one's own emotional state, rather than be overwhelmed, is necessary for a sense of security, safety, and autonomy. Just consider the opposite. While we all have had experiences of feeling overwhelmed, if such a state continues for more than a very short time we tend to describe it in terms that reflect the trauma of such an experience—using words such as "panic" or "breakdown." Correspondingly, the ability to control oneself against these states is a critical aspect of a sense of stability and of a capacity to function confidently in the world.

And this brings me back to what I said much earlier: at heart, addictions are an effort at emotional health. They are attempts, though misdirected, to perform the essential function of maintaining a sense of control over oneself, preventing a destructive state of inner helplessness.

So, the relationship between addictions and overall emotional health may be encapsulated by saying that one cannot presume anything about the latter from the former.

## ORIGINS OF ADDICTIVE BEHAVIOR

What I have described may, however, provide food for thought about the emotional origins of addictive behavior. Clearly, there can be no idea of attributing addiction to any single time of development, since the kinds of issues important in addiction can arise at any point. But it does seem reasonable to guess that a vulnerability to addiction may be related to repeated experiences of helplessness in childhood. Faced with this personal history, it makes sense that a person would develop some mechanism to deal with it. Furthermore, the presence of such repeated difficulties would be expected to lead to a vulnerability to be *reinjured* by subsequent experiences of helplessness that would be tolerable to someone else.

You might object that feelings of helplessness are common in childhood, so how reasonable is it to link them with the single problem of addiction? There are several answers to this question. First, it is of course not just feeling helplessness that is important, but repeated, especially painful experiences of this sort. Second, it is quite true that there are other mechanisms people develop to deal with this kind of experience. Indeed, even if you have an addiction you may at times respond to the issues underlying the addiction in another way. For example, one woman with alcoholism developed the symptom of losing a certain letter that she was supposed to mail.[1] First she lost it, then when she found it, she lost it again. This behavior (technically called a "parapraxis," referring to an unintended act) was another way to manage her feeling of helplessness about having to mail the letter—which was her husband's and represented to her the kinds of chores and subservience he expected from her. The parapraxis was a brief substitute for her drinking—it served basically the same function. But the fact that people also develop other mechanisms to deal with the same underlying issues does not negate the role of these issues in creating addictions.

Finally, while it is true that painful experiences of helplessness are common in childhood—from loneliness and rejections to experiences of humiliation and terror—so are addictions in adulthood.

Indeed, they are more common than is usually recognized, because there are many behaviors not usually *labeled* as addictions that, from a psychological perspective, *are* true addictions. I have mentioned this before, and I will discuss it in some detail in chapter 15, "When Are Compulsions Addictions?"

———

Before closing this chapter, I should say a word about the commonly used term "dual diagnosis." A person is said to have a "dual diagnosis" when he or she suffers simultaneously with both an addiction, such as alcoholism, and a major psychiatric disorder, such as schizophrenia. The significance of the term is that it identifies the fact that there are two critical problems, both of which must be addressed in treatment. In recent years, it has become fairly common for hospitals to have "dual diagnosis" inpatient or outpatient facilities, which are expressly designed to attend to both areas.

However, the term "dual diagnosis" is also often misused. Instead of describing the combination of an addiction with a distinct disorder such as schizophrenia or bipolar (manic-depressive) illness, it is applied to situations in which an addiction occurs along with related feelings of depression or anxiety. Referring to this state as a "dual diagnosis" perpetuates the error of viewing addictions as somehow separate and unconnected to the rest of a person's psychology—as if the addiction were unrelated to the important emotional factors that lead to feeling depressed or anxious. As I mentioned in chapter 5, unnecessarily dividing people's troubles into separate diagnostic categories is not only upsetting for people who must think of themselves as having several diagnoses, but more important it obscures understanding the unifying underlying factors that lead to all of them.

# ELEVEN

# Efforts to Understand

My ideas about addiction have arisen from two sources. Primarily, I learned from listening carefully to the people I have seen in treatment. But I have also learned from many colleagues whose insight about the problems of addiction have enlightened and challenged me as I developed my own thinking. In this chapter I will review and give examples of some of these other ideas about addiction, and look at how they fit with my view. All of the ideas I will mention were originally described in reference to substance abuse, but I believe they may be applied to any addiction.

## THE SELF-MEDICATION HYPOTHESIS

This is the most famous of the psychological ideas about substance abuse. It states that people take drugs in order to treat or self-medicate themselves for their emotional distress. A number of authors[1] have described how people select certain drugs for an addiction because those particular ones are best suited for dealing with their particular emotional problems. For example, the use of stimulants, like amphetamines or cocaine, was suggested to be a self-medication for states of boredom and depression, narcotics were seen as self-treatment to manage states of rage or loneliness,[2] and hallucinogens, like LSD or mescaline, were thought to be used to self-treat states of emptiness and meaninglessness.[3] When it can be shown that there is this kind of direct correlation between a drug of choice and an underlying emotional state, it provides a clear link between the addictive behavior and its underlying meaning. Hence, when it is present, it is important to identify.

The only problem with the self-medication idea is that it often breaks down in practice. There are many people who do not have a strong preference for one drug, but will, more or less interchangeably, use several that have entirely different physiological effects. A number of different drugs may go with the same feeling state. And, of course, people often use the same drug—alcohol, for instance— for any number of different feeling states. The idea of a specific drug-to-feeling-state correlation has, therefore, only limited explanatory value and applicability.

However, one can also interpret the self-medication hypothesis more broadly—as a general statement that the use of drugs is a way to self-treat or manage an internal psychological problem—without invoking the specific drug-to-feeling-state equation. This broader version is certainly true.

The self-medication idea, in either its "narrow" specific version or as a broad general statement, fits very well with my view of addiction. In its "narrow" form, it is basically saying that if you have a drug of choice, you have selected it because it seems to best alleviate your most intolerable emotional state. And the very idea of an intolerable emotional state means a condition in which you are threatened with feeling emotionally overwhelmed—internally helpless. So, choosing a particular drug because it is the best antidote to this most intolerable feeling is equivalent to doing one's best to restore internal equilibrium and potency.[4] Selecting a drug of choice, in other words, is simply trying to act in the most precise way possible to reverse helplessness.

Finally, the "broad" form of the self-medication hypothesis—

that substance abuse represents a psychological mechanism to deal with emotional distress—is, of course, inherent in my understanding of addiction.

## ADDICTIVE BEHAVIOR AS A SIGN OF A DEFICIT IN SELF-CARE

Some researchers, thinking about the destructive results of addictive behavior, have raised the question of whether this might indicate some lack of capacity for taking good care of yourself—a "self-care deficit."[5] They described a group of functions that are normally present in people, including anticipation of danger, valuing yourself, self-assertion, skills in relating to people, and selecting safe relationships that they called "self-care" functions. (Interestingly, in one paper, the authors were studying not addiction but accident-proneness in children. They found that those children who tended to have accidents were lacking in these "self-care" skills—rather than that they were consciously or unconsciously trying to injure themselves.[6])

The question about addictions raised by their work was whether at least some people with addictive behavior might also have a deficit in their "self-care" functions. Over the years, observation has shown that this is in fact true for some people suffering with addictions. However, as I mentioned in the last chapter, any insufficiency in self-care functions can only help explain the extent to which self-destructive behavior *continues* before a person seeks treatment. It does not address the origins of addictive behavior. So, a self-care deficit may stand alongside the psychology that drives addiction that I have been describing.

## ADDICTIVE BEHAVIOR AS A REBELLION AGAINST A PUNITIVE CONSCIENCE

This idea is also in accord with my view of addiction, as may be seen in the following example.

———

Dr. Michael Durgin was a very competent veterinarian, but it had been a terrible day. Early in the afternoon a woman brought in her badly injured cat, hit by an automobile. He had taken the animal into surgery immediately, and was in the midst of an exploratory operation to check for damaged internal organs when the front door to his clinic rang three times in quick succession. He knew his receptionist would handle it, but he had a sinking feeling that nobody would beat on the doorbell that way unless there was another animal in serious distress. A minute later, the receptionist came into the operating room and told him what he feared. A dog had also been run over. Two emergencies. He rushed to put the little cat back together enough to hold while he went to see the collie. For the next forty-five minutes, he tended to the dog in a futile effort to save it. Then, when he returned to the cat, it was barely alive. He worked on it for an hour, and when he left it in the hands of an assistant to watch, the animal was alive but not doing well.

On his way home, Michael went over the choices he had made again and again. Should he have stayed with the cat, seeing that the collie was too seriously injured? Maybe he was right to try to save the dog, but certainly he should have given up sooner when any fool could see it wasn't going to make it. But maybe if he hadn't fussed at the end making sure the cat was stable he could have gotten to the dog more quickly, and saved it.

His thoughts went on and on as he drove home. He was sure he had screwed up. He couldn't really see how, but a dog was dead, and the blame had to go somewhere.

Michael had suffered with alcoholism for many years, though he had been sober for two years. But on the way home, he went into the liquor store and bought a bottle of vodka. Over the next few hours, he drank half of it.

———

Severe, unrealistic self-criticism is a very common precipitant of addictive behavior, as in Michael's case. His use of a drug to deal with the self-condemnation of such a punitive conscience has been described as a way to create an identity free of the "tyranny" of this internal hanging judge.[7]

This view of drugs is actually a prime example of the way I have described how addictive behavior works. In this case, your own conscience produces an internal flood of guilt or shame. This can result in exactly the sort of overwhelming helplessness that I have been saying addictive behavior is an attempt to reverse. Although, typically enough for him, Michael blamed himself for his drinking the next day, telling himself that he had been "escaping" and trying to drown his troubles in alcohol, this missed the point. His drinking was in fact a displaced effort to reassert control over his emotional state—rather than helplessly suffer at the hand of his crippling conscience.

## ADDICTIVE BEHAVIOR AS A SUBSTITUTE
## FOR A PERSON

A passerby walking downtown rounded a corner and saw a man sitting on the curb, leaning heavily against a parked car. Walking over to see what was wrong, he noticed that the man was unshaven and was holding a bottle of cheap wine. The passerby was a decent man, and in a kind voice he said to the seated gentleman, "Why don't you go on home with your family or your friends, and get a good night's rest." The other man slowly looked up at him and lifted the bottle in the air. In a quiet voice he said, "This is my friend."

———

Mary was sixty-eight years old when she came to see me because she was depressed. I soon learned that she had also been drinking heavily, and that one reason she stayed in her house nearly all of the time was that she was too drunk to go out. She explained that she had been a social drinker throughout her life and had never had any problem until the past few years. Of course, I asked her what had changed a few years ago.

"Oh, that was when my Carl died," she said. They had been married for forty-five years.

———

In situations like those above, a drug appears to replace a longed-for or needed person who was lost or never available. In my view, an important aspect of this idea is also the complete control one can have over the drug, or any addictive activity, because it means you can count on it being there when you need it—and not going away. The helplessness of the loss is reversed by having this substitute object, and this is why the object is compulsively used.

For some people, like Mary, the addictive use of a drug or another activity is evidently associated with managing feelings about someone recently lost. For others, their addictive behavior seems to deal with feelings about a much earlier loss. When the lost person is from early life, an addiction sometimes reflects an important aspect of that early relationship.

———

Martin was a compulsive gambler who spent most of his time at the dog track. His parents had been divorced when he was quite young, and he saw his father mainly on the weekends, when his mother dropped him at his father's apartment for the two-day stay. Almost every weekend, Martin's father took the boy with him to the dog track. It was the same track Martin haunted later in his life.

For Martin, who badly missed his father, the time they spent together at the track was of extraordinary value. The fact that his father paid more attention to the races than to him was secondary to the boy, and a sign of how desperate he was for a relationship with his dad.

When Martin returned to the same place much later in life, his addictive object—the dog track, and his gambling there—stood in for his relationship with his father through its meaning in memory as the place that they were close. It gave him a sense of attachment to the father whose attention he could never fully have.

———

The concept of drugs, or other addictive activities, as substitutes for important people represents an interpersonal version of what I have been describing. Having an object over which you have complete control is an external form of the need to reestablish power against helplessness. Martin found an object that was linked, for him, with his father, while Mary used drinking to restore a sense that she could be in control in her life in the face of her utter helplessness to be able to control its most important aspect. The man on the curb related to his bottle as if it were a friend, reversing his actual helplessness to hold on to those he had loved.

## ADDICTIVE BEHAVIOR AS A COMPLETION OF THE SELF

In this view, instead of an addictive act replacing a relationship with a person, it provides a needed sense of self-esteem or of a basic sense of oneself.[8] Here is an example.

———

Jennifer was a senior in high school whose weight had been steadily increasing for the past six months. She neither binged on food nor vomited, but she ate seemingly nonstop, and she gained thirty pounds. She was depressed and horribly unhappy about her appearance, but she could not stop eating.

Jennifer's weight gain was particularly unusual for her since she had been a star athlete and by far the best member of her school's swimming team, often winning local and even regional meets. She had been practicing and swimming competitively for years, and had been a "pool rat" who could be found in the water every afternoon after school. Inside, she had secretly harbored Olympic dreams, though her coach had pointed out more than once that, as fine a swimmer as she was, this was not realistic.

Everything changed when she broke her ankle at the end of her junior year. She was in a cast for a couple of weeks. But even after it was removed and she had made a good recovery physically, something was different. She did not return to the pool. And she began to eat.

Whenever she was asked about what had changed, Jennifer said that she could no longer swim, so it didn't matter whether she ate or not. Her parents and coach had repeatedly told her that this was completely untrue—there was no reason she could not swim as well as before the accident. But Jennifer was convinced. Her depression persisted while her weight climbed.

When Jennifer came to see me, it did not take long to ascertain that her eating was a deeply driven compelled behavior. Indeed, in the end it was the fact that it was an addictive behavior that was the clue to understanding her problem. If she had an addiction, then did she feel terribly helpless about something? And if so, what? Her eating had begun after she broke her ankle, but now she could swim perfectly well. It seemed the helplessness she may have felt during the brief time she was unable to swim could not possibly be the basis of an addiction now.

Or could it?

As Jennifer began to open up about her feelings, her thoughts turned to her Olympic hopes. Although in her own mind she had never given up on the idea of making it to the Olympics and, if the truth were told, winning a gold medal, she now talked about this as an impossibility. All the counsel she had received from her coaches and parents had never stopped her belief in this future. But when she could not even go in the water, it was as if something crashed inside. All at once, it hit her that it was never going to happen. In her thinking, she had been on a straight track toward her dream. But this single injury, which in her mind interrupted her steady progress toward her goal, broke through her rejection of her coach's attempts to gently discourage her.

The fact that Jennifer had denied her limits for years was also a clue. Her hopes had been more than the dreams of many young athletes. We gradually learned that she had *needed* to believe she would be an Olympic star. It came clear that, for all her accomplishments, Jennifer lacked a basic sense of personal value. As far back as we could tell, she had never felt the kind of good feeling about herself that ordinarily develops early in life. Becoming an Olympic star was therefore more than achieving excellence in a field of endeavor. It was a solution for her very fragile self-image, which, once shattered, threw her into depression and an addictive search to recover a sense of solidity, of groundedness, about herself.

For Jennifer, the helplessness she was trying to manage through her addiction was of a deep nature. When she ate, she felt she was making herself more substantial, more whole. In addition, through eating she could literally nurture herself and not depend for her emotional self-sustenance on the external, unreliable fate that had made her less than an Olympic athlete. With issues involving such fundamental aspects of her sense of herself at stake, her treatment took a long time. It involved helping her to see the buried fantasies of her worthlessness, which had been for years kept out of her awareness through her single-minded focus on an eventual redemption as the best in the world in her field.

———

As you can see from Jennifer's story, this view of addictive behavior, in which an addiction serves as an effort to reverse and repair the overwhelming helplessness of a shattered identity, is also an example of the perspective on addiction that I have been describing.

## ADDICTIVE BEHAVIOR AS THE ONLY WAY TO BE SOOTHED

This idea is based on the experience of some people who seem unable to permit themselves to care for their own needs. As an example, one researcher[9] described the case of a man suffering with physical complaints who felt that the only way he could manage them was to use food or drugs addictively. It turned out that the man felt an inhibition about caring for himself—because he had grown up thinking it was a parent's right to make such decisions and was forbidden to himself. Consequently, he felt he could only turn to an external agent, like a drug, to take care of him. While unusual, this story may be grouped with others in which there is an inhibition about acting on your own behalf, then looking to an object to provide the comfort that is needed. This object becomes, therefore, the focus of an addiction.

This concept should be distinguished from the idea of a "self-care" deficit I described earlier. In the latter case, an incomplete learning (or internalization) process has occurred, leading you to fail to notice when you are in danger, or to fail to care enough about yourself to take adequate steps for self-protection. This new idea, however, involves a specific *inhibition* of taking care of yourself, resulting in a search for an outside source of care.

While this idea has some usefulness, it overlooks one important point—that the addictive act is itself an action to take care of yourself! Of course, this act may not involve caring for yourself in an externally realistic way, but you are familiar by now with the fact that addiction is about managing an internal helplessness—even if doing so fails to address external needs, as it often does.

However, there are some useful ideas that can come out of this way of thinking about addiction. One is, if you *do* feel that you are powerless to act in your own behalf to take care of yourself—as may be the case, for instance, if you are feeling discouraged—and find yourself turning to a drug or another addictive act with the feeling that it will "take care" of you, it is helpful to know that this is an illusion. *You* are taking care of you, or at least trying to, via the addictive act. You are attempting to empower yourself—and since you are actively doing this, you might also think through what might have made you feel helpless and what other active ways you might have to reverse it. You certainly do not need to believe you are capable only of "passively" seeking nurturance, as the man described above told himself.

Another useful conclusion is this: not only is it an illusion that having an addiction means you are powerlessly seeking soothing, it is an illusion that the object of any addiction has the power "over" you to place you in such a passive position. This is a corollary of the myth of "addictiveness," that I spoke of earlier. I said that if you suffer with an addiction, it is not the object that is addictive, rather it is that you *create* the object's "addictiveness" by using it as the focus of an addictive drive. The same reasoning applies to seeing the object as a seductive caregiver: it is you who is attempting to care for yourself by using the object.

Sometimes, the idea that drugs (or any addictive activities) have power to place you in a passive position may actually be a kind of emotional defense—a denial of the *active* nature of addiction. The need for such a defense can arise if you do not understand your addiction, and, therefore, feel ashamed of it. Understandably, then, it feels less shameful to attribute the requirement for the addiction to the object—to say it has power "over" you. Unfortunately, however, looking at addiction this way both interferes with understanding the problem, which, of course, is neither passive nor shameful, and carries with it its own embarrassment—that you have been rendered powerless by the object. So, if you find yourself falling into the idea of an addictive object controlling you, it is good to remember that this idea is exactly backward.

This is also important because people commonly use the idea of addictions being self-soothing as a pejorative description. Without doubt there is some truth to the idea that addictions are self-soothing, but there is nothing wrong with that. Like fighting to reempower yourself, self-soothing is a normal and essential function. Indeed, it is a problem when people are unable to be self-soothing, for instance not giving themselves time to rest before plunging back into work. But those who use this description pejoratively do not understand that addictions are much more complex, a psychological process with specific underlying drives and purposes. Said another way, the popular notion of addictions as self-comforts misunderstands their intensely active, driven nature for purposes far removed from being "comfortable." To the extent that addictions are self-soothing, it is a soothing via the feeling of having regained control of your emotional state, specifically at a time when you have just felt helplessly out of control. That is very different from soothing for the sake of a simple gratification.

# TWELVE

# *Puzzling Cases*

Sometimes when people read about the stories of others they have the thought, "Yes, I can see that, but my situation is more complicated." Indeed, diagnosing, understanding, and treating addictions can be puzzling, with unexpected discoveries and at least temporary mysteries. However, if you suffer with an addiction you should know that no situation is so complex that it cannot ultimately be understood. If you keep in mind the psychology of addiction and adopt the sort of exploratory approach to yourself that I have been describing, there is a strong likelihood that you will eventually be able to understand even the most confusing aspects of your addiction. Below, I will describe the somewhat more complicated stories of two people suffering with addictions.

## ROBERT

Robert appeared at first glance to be a fastidious man. When I met him, he was carefully attired in a gray suit with matching maroon tie and handkerchief, the latter folded to show a small double triangle in his breast pocket. He had a neatly trimmed moustache and his shoes were shined. His words were a little surprising, therefore, when he sat down and began to speak.

"My life is totally out of control, that's why I came to see you. It's a complete mess. Or, I should say, I've made a complete mess out of it."

"How do you mean?"

"I must have an addictive personality. I can't control myself in any way." He looked at me. "I have two addictions. I can't deal with either one of them. I think I'm an alcoholic. I drink way too much, and it's ruining everything. Sarah—that's my wife—she's furious at me all the time because I'm up late drinking or I'm drinking on the weekends." He shifted in the chair. "She says she never sees me, or we don't have enough time together." He made a dismissive gesture with his hand.

There was a brief silence. "The whole marriage is falling apart," he went on. He sat for another moment. "It's not like I haven't tried to stop. I try all the time. And I *do* stop, but she never notices. I've been able to stay away from drinking for a week at a time, but then something happens and I'm back to it." He made the same dismissive gesture, then was silent again.

"So, you think you have alcoholism?"

"Yes. I tell myself it's not, because I can stop. I've proved that to myself." He let out a sigh. "But I always start up again."

"Well, if you have alcoholism, it's good to know it."

"I guess. But that's not the only problem."

"Yes, you said that there were two addictions."

"Uh huh. The other one is harder to talk about."

I waited for him to continue.

"It's personal, you know? Sort of embarrassing." He took a breath. "Okay. I have a problem with phone sex. I call those 900 numbers, and, you know, talk to the girls." Robert scratched the back of his hand, then scratched his head. "It's a big problem for me. For one thing, it gets very expensive. I mean I'm spending a lot every week on this stuff. And, it's bad for our sex life. That's the other thing Sarah is mad about. She knows about the calls, and they really upset her."

I nodded. "You consider that to be an addiction too?"

"Well, yes, I think so. I try to quit, and I can't do it. I promise myself that this one is the last call, but . . ." He shrugged and shook his head. "And it's destroying my marriage. They both are—that and the drinking. Plus, it's no good for my work. I'm a real estate broker, residential and commercial properties. I've got to be available at odd times to show a property, and I haven't been. Sometimes I've been too drunk. And I hate to tell you this . . ." He stopped for a moment. ". . . but sometimes I'm on the phone, you know, with the 900 number, and I don't pick up the business line. I just let it ring. Then, when I'm done, I listen to the message, but, you know, I just don't feel like going out."

I nodded again. I thought to myself that he was right—it did sound like he had two addictions. But before asking more about them, I asked him to tell me about himself.

"Well, first of all, I'm thirty-four but I only got married eight months ago. I was sort of a confirmed bachelor." He smiled a little. "I was going out all the time, lots of different girls. But don't get the wrong idea, I wasn't a jerk. They wanted to have a good time too. It wasn't, you know, love 'em and leave 'em. I wouldn't do that. Everybody knew the score. It was just a lot of fun.

"Then, I got married. Jeez, that sounds bad too. I don't mean it that way. I like Sarah, maybe I love her. But, it's just, you know, I was having a great time being single. But, I was getting older, and all my friends were married. And they bugged me all the time: 'C'mon, Rob, when you going to tie the knot? When you going to tie it around your neck?' They kidded me a lot, and I'm not saying that's why I got married. It's just, they were right. The time had come, and I liked Sarah maybe better than anyone I'd ever gone with. So, I got married."

Robert looked at me and paused. The order of people's thoughts is rarely random, and I was sure that the details he was telling me about how he became a husband were important, and were related to the problem of the two addictions he had come to see me about. So, I was prepared to just listen some more when, as if he had read my mind, Robert made the connection himself.

"Well, that's when the phone sex began." He shook his head. "Look, I'm not a pervert. I was pretty much a ladies' man before I got married, but as I said, I wasn't a jerk and I wasn't into anything weird. And I never called a 900 number until after I got married. I mean, why would I?" He shrugged his shoulders. "I don't want to sound like I've got an inflated idea about myself, but . . ." He raised his palms, face up. "I just didn't need it, you know?"

"Then you got married."

"Yes. That's where it got bad. Sarah and I are perfectly compatible, you know? I mean sexually. That's not the problem. It's not one of those, 'we were great until we were married, then it was lousy.' It's still great. That's why I don't understand it. Starting about a month into the marriage, I began calling." He paused. "I do it two, three times a week. I masturbate, then I get the hell off the line, just hang up." Robert rubbed the back of his neck, then he shifted in his chair. "It's really embarrassing to talk about this."

———

Despite Robert's hesitancy, we were able to talk about his experiences with both phone sex and drinking. They appeared to go together much of the time. His pattern was to have phone sex, then drink later that evening or sometimes the next day. The phone sex and drinking never seemed to occur in the reverse order.

As Robert and I talked about his phone sex over the next few weeks, its connection with his marriage became more plain. When he married Sarah, he felt he had given up what he called "the good life." It was true he was fond of Sarah, or as he said, maybe he even loved her as well as he could, but he resented having lost so much from his former life. Often, he berated himself for his decision to get married. This was connected with his absolute determination to be faithful. Once married, he was never going to have sex with another woman. Therefore marriage was, as he put it, "being behind a locked door." Certainly, he called the 900 numbers—but he did not consider these phone liaisons to be cheating on Sarah. (She did, however—and he also resented her for that.)

So, it appeared that his phone sex was indeed an addiction. He dealt with being trapped with one woman forever by having long-distance relationships with other women. The force behind his addiction was not actually sexual at all. While he had been a "ladies' man" before marriage, he had never felt it necessary to have sexual intercourse on a daily or every-other-day basis. And after he was married, he and Sarah had a good sexual relationship. Hence, rather than a sexual drive behind the addiction, its force came from his not being able to stand being curtailed, trapped helplessly with no chance of seeing other women again, ever.

Of course, like other addictions, the issues behind Robert's phone sex had roots in his overall emotional makeup. In time, we had to look at what made it so intolerable for him to be with just one woman. But for the moment, we at least were coming to understand the addiction itself.

And as we discussed this, something else crystallized—the function of the second addiction. This became clear in the middle of a session after he talked about having made another 900 call. He had been making fewer of these calls as he came to understand their meaning, but the night before he had called again.

"On top of that, I drank again too. It was about two hours after the call. Sarah had gone to bed—well, it was late and I should have been in bed too, but I couldn't go to sleep."

"What kept you up?"

He shrugged. "I was keyed up. I don't mean excited. I was, I guess upset. I was upset about the call." Robert rubbed the back of his neck, then his cheek.

"What else comes to mind about that?"

"Well, you know, I felt bad about making the call. I mean, it's just not the sort of thing you go around telling people."

"But you're saying you felt bad just inside yourself," I said softly.

"Yes." Robert sat a little slumped in the chair.

"What are you feeling?"

He made a small shrug. "I don't know. Ashamed. I . . . I feel ashamed about it." He rubbed his arm. "What sort of loser calls up for phone sex?"

There was a pause. I said, "Is that how you felt last night—when you couldn't go to bed?"

"Yes."

Robert sat looking down at his shoes. Finally, I said, "Is that how you felt when you drank?"

"Yes."

We sat in silence a minute, then I said, "I guess that's why you drank."

Robert didn't look up. "Yes, I guess so. I wanted to escape."

"Well, I was thinking more that it was like the phone sex."

Robert raised his head and looked at me questioningly. "What do you mean?"

"Well, we know that you call when you feel especially trapped in your marriage. You said that when you drank last night you were feeling ashamed. I can see that feeling this way is painful for you, and I'm wondering if last night, when you felt this way, you felt trapped by your shame."

Robert thought a minute. "I know this sounds stupid, with my history and all, but I do care about doing the right thing. I mean, I never did the wrong thing with any of the girls I used to go with. Some of the guys, they'd laugh about how they talked some girl into bed. Not me. I always treated them with respect—even afterward, you know?" He paused. "I don't know why I'm saying all this."

"I think you're saying that it's important to you to act in a way of which you can be proud."

Robert thought again. "Yes. I can't stand it when I mess up."

"You felt you messed up last night, when you called."

Robert nodded.

There was another pause. I continued, "Maybe when you feel ashamed because you've messed up, that feeling is so awful that you need to do something to deal with it. Maybe you can't stand being stuck in that feeling."

Robert paused another minute. "Well, yes and no," he said. "I don't think I'm ashamed when I call the phone sex numbers. I mean, I can see that's how I feel afterward, but I don't think I feel that way before. Like we talked about, I'm mainly mad about being stuck in my marriage when I call up." He hesitated. "But I do hate feeling I've done the wrong thing. I think that's maybe worse than anything."

"Even worse than feeling stuck in your marriage."

Robert nodded slowly. "I think I see what you mean. I have to drink like I have to make the phone calls."

"I think so. By drinking you take control of your feelings, rather than being helplessly trapped in your shame—just as by making the phone calls, you take control against feelings of being helplessly trapped in your marriage."

Another minute passed, then Robert frowned. In an aggravated voice, he said, "But it's really stupid, you know? Then I've got *two* addictions to deal with."

"Yes," I said. "But they're connected. Your drinking follows the phone calls because it is a way to deal with the overwhelming shame caused by the calls. It looks like one addiction is a response to the helplessness caused by the other."

———

The idea of addictive behavior leading to more of the same addictive behavior is not unusual. Addictions usually lead to bad effects—external losses and internal feelings of shame and embarrassment—which are themselves a source of feelings of helplessness, in turn giving rise to more addictive behavior. This is the addiction cycle I mentioned in chapter 10 (where I described it in the context of avoiding this cycle by attending to the meaning of even a single drink). Robert's situation was unusual only because his efforts to deal with the results of his addictive use of phone sex involved drinking, a different addictive act. If he had used the same addictive focus, he would have appeared to have simply had an extended "slip" of his phone sex addiction.

The use of two, or more, addictive focuses by one person is not that unusual. Indeed, it illustrates that sometimes one focus is a more specific solution to a particular underlying issue and, therefore, is used when feelings of helplessness arise around that issue. This is an example of what I called the "narrow" or specific version of the self-medication hypothesis (chapter 11). Naturally, as I have pointed out, there are also many cases in which several different addictive acts may all serve the same purpose for a person. However, Robert's story is an example of why it is important to inquire about the specific emotions and issues associated with each addictive behavior, rather than to assume that the meaning of addictions should not be explored.

If Robert's story strikes a chord with you because you also suffer with more than one addictive behavior, consider whether they might work together as Robert's addictions did. A clue to this would be, as with Robert, that one addiction follows the other.

## DARYL

The corridors of the large law firm were busy, as usual, when Daryl stepped out of his meeting with one of the senior partners. He took a deep breath and started walking down the hallway. He had been thinking about this meeting for four weeks. But in another sense, it had been on his mind for the last couple of years, even though it wasn't until last month that he learned he would get the word today about whether he would be promoted to senior associate—the last stop before eventually making partner himself.

Daryl walked to the elevator, rode down the eighteen floors to the street, and strode directly out of the building. He got in his car and drove home to his apartment in a nice building downtown. Once there, he went straight to the cabinet where he kept his stash. He removed the little bag of cocaine, and set things up. Very soon, he began to snort the first line.

What was odd was that he had gotten the promotion.

When Daryl came to see me, he was fifteen minutes late. He rushed in and apologized, telling me he had been at a deposition that was supposed to have ended an hour and a half ago, but didn't. He had a nervous energy about him, and he began to quickly tell me about his day, before saying anything about what brought him to my office. It seemed that he needed to talk out the energy he felt before he could turn his attention to this session.

"Here's the summary," he finally said after describing the two briefs he had due by Thursday and the motion that needed to be filed in court by five o'clock today, on top of the deposition that he had just hurriedly left. "I use cocaine. It's a problem, but I thought I had it under control. Then, last week, I started using a lot of it again. I want to get it stopped, and that's why I'm seeing you." Daryl looked at me with anticipation.

"Tell me a little about your use of cocaine."

A frown briefly creased his brow. "As I said, I used it last week, and actually I'm still using it. It interferes with my work. I usually work from about eight in the morning until nine or ten at night at the office, then bring home some work to do there. I know that coke is supposed to make me more efficient, get me revved up, but it doesn't work that way for me. I don't pay attention to the work when I'm high, then I stay up late and usually don't get enough sleep and I'm too tired to work efficiently the next day." Daryl looked at me again.

"You weren't using it recently until last week?"

Another slightly exasperated look crossed Daryl's face. "No, no. I use it a few times a month. I just used it a lot more the past week." Daryl sat still, looking at me again. The thought crossed my mind that he was about to look at his watch, decide that this had taken enough time, tell me that he needed the remedy now, and dash back to work.

I asked him, "What are you thinking?"

"Well, I'd like to get this solved. It's getting in my way." Daryl looked as if he was holding his breath for a second, then he slumped a little. "I'm sorry, I don't mean to be rude. I just have a lot to do, and my life is pretty well filled up."

"Yes, it sounds that way."

I asked Daryl to say more about his current life. He was a bachelor, living alone in an apartment downtown. He had some friends, a few dating back to his college years, but he said that even with the friends who lived nearby, his relationships had dwindled to quick e-mails. He had not been on a date for six months. In short, his life was filled, but it was nearly all filled with work.

Despite his impatience, Daryl agreed to meet to try to understand his problem. And the more Daryl told me about himself, the less nervous he seemed—but the more depressed. It was obvious that he pushed himself terribly, and that this made his life highly stressful. Because of this, Daryl at first reminded me of another man I had seen—Ted Baldwin, whom you may remember from chapter 2—the man who had no time for doing the things *he* wanted to do. Perhaps, like Ted, Daryl pushed himself relentlessly and, through an addictive act, angrily rebelled against this self-imposed helplessness in order to have his own time and his own life. But years of trying to understand people's troubles had taught me that it was never a good idea to think that two people were just alike. And as we continued to meet, not surprisingly I realized that Daryl was telling me something else. Indeed, the more we met, the more he seemed to be making it clear that beyond his considerable anxiety, he suffered with a much deeper sadness.

———

Because he was so focused on his many daily concerns, Daryl did not tell me right away about the promotion. When he did, I asked him what had gone through his mind when he heard.

"It was really strange. Well, I shouldn't say that, because I have this experience a lot. It's actually pretty awful. The instant I heard that I made it, I felt a kind of exhilaration inside. You know, I've been busting my ass for a couple of years to get this. I was really proud and happy. Then, two seconds later, I felt horrible. Just like that. I don't know why. It was like a dark cloud came over me. I suddenly started thinking about everything I'd have to do to make partner—that was some of it. But, it's . . . it's more than that." He struggled with how to say what he was thinking. "It's also that . . . it wasn't enough." Daryl looked at me with a pained expression.

"How do you mean?"

He raised his hands in a kind of helpless gesture. "This always happens to me. Making senior associate is great. But when good things happen, I usually enjoy them for about a minute."

"Then it's on to the next thing?"

"Well, yes, but not only that." Daryl paused a moment. "It's that even though I made senior associate, as soon as I did, I thought to myself, 'Big deal.' "

There was a silence.

"You always feel like this?" I said softly.

Daryl nodded. "As long as I can remember, it's always been the same."

We were quiet. Finally, I said, "That's when you used more of the cocaine. What does it do for you?"

"It makes me feel good—I get high. It's like a little vacation."

"Say some more."

He shrugged. "I work hard, so I figure I deserve it."

I thought a moment. "You work hard all the time, but you only use coke once in a while."

"Well, I use it usually a few times a month. But I used it more after the promotion."

"You deserved a vacation then?"

"Well, I felt so bad. Yes."

"Maybe it was a reward."

"Well, I deserved it!" For a moment, Daryl looked angry.

I nodded. "Especially if you didn't let yourself feel rewarded for more than a few seconds when you heard the good news."

Daryl sat back and looked at me. "Life sucks. It really sucks. You bust your ass to get somewhere, then how long can you really enjoy it? It's not just me, I don't think. I don't know how anybody stands it. Maybe it is just me. But every time you achieve something important, isn't there always something next? Okay, maybe if I won the Nobel Prize, I could say, 'Well, that's it.' But, you know, how long can you rest on your laurels? You've got to do something more, or you're doing nothing. You're wasting time. You're lazy. You're doing nothing with your life."

There was a minute of silence. I said, "Everyone needs to enjoy the triumphs of life. But you don't let yourself—at least for more than two seconds." I paused. "As you say, who could stand it? Who could stand giving up the pleasures of life when they come along?" There was another moment of quiet. I continued, "But you *don't* stand it. You use cocaine. I wonder if the days that you used it were days when you had a small victory. You gave yourself the rewards you deserved in this way, since you don't seem to allow yourself to have them in another way. When you got the promotion, it was a big victory that deserved a big reward—which you gave yourself with a week of cocaine."

Daryl sat a minute. Then he said, this time calmly, "I do deserve something. I really do."

———

Daryl's addiction seemed strange on the surface because he was driven to repeat it when things were good. But those were just the times that he was most helpless. He knew that with all the work he did, and with all the periods he felt pressured and down, he should enjoy the good times, and the fruits of his work. But for reasons that became clearer as we continued meeting, he could not let himself have that pleasure. Cocaine's ability to make him feel good gave him his only power against this helplessness—not because of its physical effects, but because of its underlying meaning as the one way he could let himself enjoy his life.

Daryl's experience may be familiar to you. There are quite a few people who have trouble with feelings—anxiety, guilt, or shame, for instance—that may be aroused by success. Like any overwhelming flood of feelings, this may become a precipitant of addictive behavior because such a flood creates the internal experience of helplessness—here, helplessness induced by success.

# THIRTEEN

# *Teens*

Teenagers are well known to be especially at risk for getting into trouble with alcohol and other drugs, as well as nondrug addictions. Recently, there has been a slight shift in drugs abused by young people, with overall usage of marijuana, amphetamines, hallucinogens, tranquilizers, and heroin about the same, but with increases in use of certain drugs, including the stimulant MDMA, or Ecstasy (methylenedioxymethamphetamine), and anabolic steroids (synthetic derivatives of the male hormone, testosterone).[1] Other substances that have become increasingly popular as "club drugs"—drugs used at dance clubs and parties ("raves")—are the hallucinogens LSD and ketamine, and the sedatives GHB (gamma-hydroxybutyrate) and flunitrazepam (Rohypnol, or "Roofies").[2] In addition, some drugs, such as inhalants (butane, glue, typewriter correction fluid, and dry erase markers), are particularly used by young people because they are common, legal, and inexpensive.

Of course, the use of these drugs does not necessarily mean that the person has a true addiction, as I described in chapter 9. Young people, as much or more than adults, are prone to many of the *nonaddictive* causes of drug abuse that I have described previously.

Among the factors that are particularly common in teens are peer pressure, lack of knowledge (thinking that a certain drug or activity is harmless—a view often supported by one's peer group), and use of drugs as a more or less purely conscious, noncompulsive choice to deal with stress.

However, there is reason to believe that teenagers have higher rates of true addiction as well. Several studies of teenage gambling, for example, have shown higher rates of pathological (compulsive) gambling among adolescents than in adult populations.[3]

That adolescents do more experimenting with, abusing, and addictively using drugs and other activities is not surprising. Adolescence is a time of particular psychological tasks and difficulties. (In this chapter I am using the terms "adolescence" and "teenager" interchangeably, but adolescence as a stage of life actually often extends into the twenties.) The special tasks facing a person in adolescence might be expected to lead to excessive behaviors of both nonaddictive and truly addictive sorts. The story below illustrates this.

———

Barbara's mother called me originally. She was worried about her daughter who, at seventeen, was getting drunk, using drugs, and, she said, "dressing like she was trying out for the job of street person." Her mother added that she could see that Barbara was very unhappy. I suggested to Mrs. Purcell that it would be a good idea for Barbara to call me herself to set up the appointment, so that she and I could arrange it ourselves. Mrs. Purcell was hesitant, saying that she was afraid that Barbara might not call if it were left up to her, but she said that she would ask Barbara. The next day Barbara did call, although it would be hard to overstate the lack of enthusiasm in her voice. But she agreed to come in to see me.

On the day of our appointment, I greeted Barbara outside the office. She was about five feet four inches tall and was significantly overweight. She wore torn jeans, a shirt, a vest, unbuttoned, and a kerchief that did not match either the shirt or the vest. While I did not consider myself expert about current teen styles, the shapeless and uncoordinated way she dressed appeared to obscure rather than enhance her appearance. Barbara did not say anything in response to my hello, but just stood up and walked past me as I was holding the door. She dropped into the chair, looked briefly around the office with no expression, then leaned her cheek on her hand and closed her eyes.

"When your mother called, she told me a little about your situation," I said. Barbara did not say anything. "Well," I said with a smile, although her eyes were still closed, "how can I be of help?" There was a pause. Barbara opened her eyes.

"My mother thinks I should see you."

I nodded, but it was too late. Barbara's eyes had closed again.

"Yes, I know that from her call. She seems to think you're not doing well."

She made a sarcastic sound.

"That mean you don't agree?" I said lightly.

There was another pause. "She can think what she wants," Barbara said. Her eyes stayed open, but she was not looking at me.

"Sure, but I'm interested in what you think."

Barbara looked at me with hostility. "Right!" she said.

There was a silence. "You don't believe me," I said matter of factly.

Barbara did not respond. We sat for a moment. I said, "So, your mother wants you here, but you don't want to be here." There was more silence. I continued, "Well, is there anything you would like to talk about?" Barbara shifted her gaze from my left to my right. There was another pause. Finally, I added, "Like current events, or politics?" She said nothing. I went on, "Or maybe Australian rules football?" Nothing. "Defects along the Great Wall of China? What about proper serving etiquette when entertaining a duke?"

Barbara started to smile, then caught herself. She continued to look to the right. Seeing her smile, I went on. "Perhaps you would rather *do* something more fun, like go to a movie, or have a root canal."

She looked up at the corner on the right.

I pressed on. "Or, swim with great white sharks, or be pelted with bricks."

Barbara rolled her eyes. "Look, I'm here because my mother told me to come. So here I am."

"Indeed you are, and allow me to say what a pleasure it is to have you."

Barbara laughed. Then she shook her head. "You're really weird, you know?"

I made a motion with my hands, as if to say, "Well, there's nothing I can do about it." There was another brief pause, then I said, "So, what's going on?"

She shrugged. "My mother is worried because I'm into drugs. So I've got to see you."

"Tell me about the drugs."

"It's nothing. I do what everybody does. Some booze, some weed, 'shrooms, uppers, the usual stuff."

I knew of course that weed was marijuana, and 'shrooms were mushrooms, which are hallucinogenic, but there were a lot of uppers, so I asked her which ones she was into. "Crystal," she said, meaning methamphetamine, a powerful stimulant.

"Maybe a lot of people are doing them," I said, "but that's quite a combination."

"Well, I don't use them all at once!" I had the clear sense that she had omitted the "duh" for my benefit.

I nodded. "How are things besides drugs?'

She shrugged again. "Okay, I guess."

"You don't sound too sure."

She didn't say anything.

"How are things with your friends?" I asked gently.

"I pretty much stick to myself."

"You get lonely?" I asked softly again.

"I don't know."

"How are things at home?"

Barbara just shrugged.

"Not so good?" I said.

"My mom is a jerk. She worries more about me than she does about herself."

"How do you mean?"

"She's a doormat. Whatever my father says, she does. And . . ." Barbara looked at me. "How much of this gets back to them?"

"None of it, without your permission."

Barbara considered this a moment, then went on. "My father doesn't exactly beat my mother, but he's pushed her. I've seen it, lots of times. And she's a big zero—she stays home and does the laundry, and takes care of my brother Billy, and straightens up, and she never complains." Her voice was more sad than angry as she said this.

"Your mother is a disappointment to you?" I said.

Barbara looked very sad for a moment, then she shrugged. "I don't care what she does," she said.

———

Over the next few meetings Barbara talked about her life, her drugs, her parents, her little brother. She could still be very guarded, but she seemed to have decided that it was at least somewhat safe to talk to me.

Our understanding of the meaning of her drug use gradually improved. One day we were talking about a conversation she had with a boy at school.

"Craig came over to me again yesterday. I wish he'd leave me alone."

"I thought you said you liked him."

"No, I don't. He's cute, but he's a pain."

"How so?"

"He's just always hanging around, wanting to go somewhere or sit in the caf and talk."

I raised my eyebrows. "And that's bad?"

"I don't want to bother with him." But as often happened with Barbara, her face showed something more than what she was saying.

"I don't understand," I said.

"I'm not into all that girl-boy stuff." She said this as though it was beneath her. I already knew from other statements she had made that she was not a lesbian, so this was not what she meant.

I said, "Oh? Why not?"

"Maybe it's because I know better!"

"What do you mean?"

"I see what it's like. Pretty soon it's all about the guy. I don't need that—I'm an independent woman."

"You've seen what it's like?"

"I've seen my mother! I'm not going to be like her! You think I want to spend my days doing laundry and catering to some man's every whim? Forget it."

There was a pause. I said, "So, you avoid boys?"

Barbara shrugged.

"That must be hard."

She didn't answer, but slowly her face began to give her away again as her eyes started to well up.

At our next meeting, Barbara told me that as soon as she left the office after our last appointment she had used several of her drugs. Of course I had been interested in hearing about her drug use, and I had asked her about it during previous sessions, but she had said little. Now, she was bringing it up herself.

"What do you make of your taking them right after we met?"

"I was upset, that's all."

"Do you know what upset you?"

"Not really."

I looked at her and said quietly, " 'Not really' is a little different from just 'no.' "

Barbara shrugged. After a moment she said, "I don't like talking about my mother, and boys, and stuff."

"Well, you were saying that there's a connection between them." Barbara didn't say anything. "Did the drugs help?"

"Yeah, sort of."

"How did they work?"

Barbara hesitated, then she said, "I feel like I'm being more myself when I use them. I can do what I want. I'm my own woman."

I thought for a second. "Do you mean, rather than being your mother's daughter?"

She answered immediately. "Yes! I'm free of her, and my father too. They're living in their own stupid lives—they don't understand anything. I have my own life to live."

"Free of following in your mother's footsteps."

"Yes." Barbara nodded her head vigorously, but there was a little girl quality to it, and I thought that she was nodding hard to shake off the confusion inside.

———

Barbara was faced with some of the most common and difficult issues for adolescents. Before returning to her story, I will briefly outline some of these issues.

As a stage of life, adolescence requires people to give up a degree of the certainty and safety of their former childhood identity, at the same time as developing significant new aspects of identity, including feelings about oneself as a sexual person, new ways of relating to peers of both sexes, new ways of thinking about existence and mortality, and a sense of oneself as an independent person. In going through this, there is an unavoidable struggle between retaining aspects of oneself that are identified with your parents, while also differentiating from them, particularly from the parent of the same sex. Because all this is uncharted territory, and often difficult and painful, adolescence is inherently a time of both great potential excitement and of great stress. And adolescents' behavior reflects their struggles, often fluctuating between, or simultaneously representing, wishes to regress to childhood, and insistence upon being seen and treated as already completely adult.

Feelings of powerlessness are also especially common during adolescence. At the same time as there is a powerlessness to be the adult one longs to become, there is also the powerlessness to return to old, known, and settled ways of thinking about oneself, one's family, and the world. Each of the major developmental issues of adolescence regularly produces feelings of vulnerability and uncertainty—around sexuality, peer relationships, strength and autonomy, having a cohesive sense of who you are versus fragmentation and confusion, and even around life and death. As one of the great writers on adolescence put it, "The adolescent's slow severance of the emotional ties to his family, his fearful or exhilarated entrance into the new life which beckons him, these experiences are among the profoundest in human existence. . . . The limitless future of childhood shrinks to realistic proportions, to one of limited chances and goals; but, by the same token, the mastery of time and space and the conquest of helplessness afford a hitherto unknown promise of self-realization."[4]

At the same time as being faced with feelings of weakness and vulnerability in so many areas of life, it is of great importance to teens to feel empowered. To be able to assert yourself as an independent person with your own place in the world, respected as an equal by adults, and able to fend for yourself on your own, is, after all, a good deal of what adolescence is about. The unavoidable discrepancy between this need to feel empowered and the powerlessness inherent in this stage of life makes teens ripe for the development of behaviors whose emotional purpose is to manage feelings of powerlessness.

Partly, this results in behaviors that are not true addictions, but rather are normal teenage experimentation. For example, teens often try out new identities, especially those that create a sense of separation from their old childhood identity, or from the identities of their parents. These new identities allow them to feel a needed strength, solidity, and independence. Of course, some of the activities associated with this effort may be excessive or outlandish, and be understandably difficult for parents to live with. But such behavior, while hard on those around the teenager, is not surprising, since part of the function of these activities is precisely to *be* outlandish, that is, to make a clear symbolic statement of how different one is from the way he or she was in the past, and how different from at least some of the values and mores of the parents. When you add to this a need to be accepted into a new group of other adolescents—one that is distinguished from the old family group— plus the factor of group-reinforced misinformation about the safety or appropriateness of certain activities, teenagers are at particular risk of all kinds of excessive behaviors as part of trying out new ways to be in the world.

Teens are also more at risk of dealing with their struggles through the development of true addictions: particular displaced actions that restore a sense of empowerment against the many aspects of their emotional lives that leave them feeling disempowered. A need for *displacement* may be especially necessary in adolescence, because direct actions that are available to adults may be very difficult or impossible for a teenager. A teenaged boy who is creating a defiant struggle with his father in the service of separating from him, for instance, generally does not have the option of physically leaving his home. He also may find a direct, appropriate negotiation with his father on equal terms to be emotionally impossible because of his own not yet matured ability to do this. And, sometimes, this kind of direct negotiation is not possible because a parent also is finding it emotionally hard to allow the separation.

I will return at the end of the chapter to the implications of all this for the prognosis for teenagers with excessive activities, either addictive or nonaddictive.

———

Barbara was a person who appreciated being listened to seriously. We were able to work together, in fact, because I had gradually been able to prove to her satisfaction that I was really interested in what she had to say—in contrast to her original expectations. When she agreed so vigorously that she did not want to follow in her mother's footsteps, I had the impression that she was glad I understood this important point about her autonomy, and about the specifics of her relationship with her mother. But I also could see from the apparently mixed feelings in her reaction that there was a lot more to what she was saying.

We had in fact come to a complicated and critical set of feelings. Barbara had used drugs after the previous session when we talked about her avoiding boys and about the connection between this and her not wanting to repeat her mother's subservience to her father. But as we explored this, we learned that the disappointment she said she felt in her mother was not only because of her sense of the submissive way her mother ran her own life. An even more significant disappointment for Barbara was that she had never felt her mother was satisfied with Barbara the way she was. Barbara, who had been an innately active child, had always felt her mother's disapproval for her inability to be enough like the relatively passive woman her mother was—at least as Barbara saw her. Barbara's aggressive style was so different from that of her mother, in fact, and so different from her father's expectation of females, of any age, that there had been tension between her and both of her parents for as far back as she could remember.

An important part of Barbara's confusion had to do with this. Underneath her contempt, she continued to love her mother and to look up to her. Indeed, her identification with her mother was intimately connected with her yearning to be an adult woman herself. But in her mind she was certain that to be like her mother meant becoming the "zero" she saw her mother to be. So, she avoided the very relationships with boys that she was desperate to explore, and she maintained her avoidance by dressing in a style designed to keep the boys away, and to deny her own femininity.

A consequence of the lifelong tension between Barbara and her parents was that she was left with the conviction that she was bad, and bad especially because of her anger. She saw herself as too angry to be acceptable to either parent. And while these feelings had gone on for years, matters came to a head in adolescence.

In grappling for a solution to her feelings, Barbara adopted a temporary identity as a tough, uncaring outsider. She presented a distant, sullen attitude to the world, one that expressed her superiority and contempt for others—rather than the enormously devalued and frightened feelings with which she lived.

And her solution included the use of drugs. She had said that when she used them, she felt that she was more herself, that she was her own woman. When we explored this, she did not say that the specific feeling of being high was being "herself." Indeed, this would have been difficult, since the mixture of drugs she used produced a variety of opposite effects. But what they all had in common was that she was in control of them, and therefore in control of the way she could make herself feel. This was in sharp contrast to her daily sense of being helplessly caught in the insoluble dilemmas of her life.

Barbara also had a particular reason to need a displacement for her feelings of rage at being in this trap. It had, after all, always been her *anger* that was a source of conflict with both of her parents, and a source of her feeling that she was bad. So, it had to be expressed indirectly.

————

Barbara did have a true addiction, which was fueled by underlying emotional issues that were lifelong. As often occurs, these old issues had been brought to the surface in a new way in adolescence.

Fortunately, however, Barbara was able to make a relationship with me in which she could think about her life and her addiction. This was helped by her gradually increased ability to talk about and see me as being different from her image of her father. Part of her initial hostility had been not only her general need to establish her independence but also her worry that I would be just another man who was trying to keep her in her place. As this concern subsided, she and I worked well together.

It is important to note that Barbara's parents had also tried hard to talk with her. Before her mother called me, both of them had done their best to help her talk about what was bothering her. But as is so often the case, Barbara did not feel she could open up with her parents. Confiding in the very people from whom she needed to separate felt to her like a return to childhood. This is part of what makes adolescence so hard to go through—with the entire thrust of development in the other direction, teens often cannot

turn to their parents even when what they most long for is someone close to talk to.

However, if you are the parent of a teen with an addiction, there
are a few guidelines that may be helpful in trying to talk with him
or her. First of all, despite the difficulty involved, it is important to
try to talk—to show your child that you are available whenever he
or she is ready. Second, it is a good idea to state in a matter-of-fact
(not lecturing) way whatever accurate information you have about
the particular excessive behavior you are concerned about—drinking,
taking drugs, gambling, having unprotected sex, and so forth.
Remember that teens often get their information from unreliable
sources, especially from each other, so you may be the only
provider of valid data. A word of caution, however: be sure that
your own information is accurate. As hard as it is to have your good
advice listened to, it may become completely impossible if you are
found to supply false information, especially ideas that reflect
mainly your personal opinion rather than the objective facts. Third,
do not require acknowledgment that your message is received. It
may be important for your teen to not disclose that he or she is
relying on what you say, even if—perhaps especially if—he or she is
doing exactly that. Fourth, while part of a conversation may involve
setting some practical limits, it is helpful to go out of your way to
be clear that you are doing this because of your concern, not to
prove that you still have power over him or her. Finally, since teens
often have trouble letting parents in particular guide them, you
may come to the point of telling your son or daughter that you
want to seek a good evaluation, both for diagnosis and treatment—
and that you will respect the confidentiality of the contact between
your child and the evaluator.

———

It turned out that Barbara's addiction was not one of the more difficult parts of our journey. She found it easy to see, from examples
like her taking drugs after we had talked about her strongest feelings, that her use of drugs was a way to support her sense of herself
as a strong and independent person against feelings of being help-

less and overwhelmed. Knowing this was important to her. Having an understanding of why she felt driven to use drugs made her feel stronger, and more independent. In fact, when she could catch herself before she used drugs, she described her feeling as being even more the way she had been hoping to feel from using the drugs— more the strong woman she wished to be. She was highly motivated therefore to use her new understanding about her drug use first to reduce it, then ultimately to stop entirely. Working together with Barbara in a way that valued her ability to comprehend herself fit well with the essential emotional goals of her life. Indeed, she was able to stop using drugs a lot sooner than she was able to feel consistently good about herself, which took quite a while longer.

––––––

With the likelihood of both true addictions and nonaddiction excessive or abusive behaviors so high among teens, what can be said about the diagnosis and prognosis for young people? Are teens with these behaviors more likely than adults to give them up when they get older?

First, it must be stressed that determining the difference between nonaddictive behavior and true addiction can be made in teenagers, just as in adults, only through individual investigation into the emotional life of each person. It is not a good idea to assume the diagnosis without careful evaluation (and even then, caution is always necessary when making long-term predictions about any teenager). The necessity for a good evaluation is important to keep in mind if you are the parent of a teenager and planning to talk with your child about his or her excessive behavior. It is better to focus on the behavior itself and its risks, rather than to prematurely label it as an "addiction" before the diagnosis has been established; otherwise, you run the risk of purveying false information, possibly alienating your child.

With regard to prognosis, you can see from the cases of adults I have described that the underlying roots of a sensitivity to a specific helplessness may often begin in childhood, though the first manifestation of this as an addiction does not occur until adolescence, or later. Therefore, some adolescents with excessive behavior are showing the beginnings of a true addiction. Their prognosis will depend on obtaining good treatment at an early point, or failing that, seeking good treatment later.

On the other hand, many teens may be like the Vietnam veterans I have mentioned. You may recall that they abused narcotics because they were in an extraordinary setting, but extremely few of them continued to use these drugs addictively, and many did not use them at all, once they were out of that setting, because they did not have the psychology of addiction. For many teenagers the extraordinary setting is their adolescence itself—a time of stresses that are not likely to be repeated later in life. The prognosis for these teens for outgrowing their excessive or abusive behaviors is good, just as it was for the Vietnam veterans once they left their specially difficult setting. Again, the difference between this situation and teens who suffer with true addictions is based on whether there is a deeper drive to perform the behavior, as I described in chapter 9.

In addition, even teenagers who do have true addictions often have the expression of these addictions facilitated by the special circumstances of adolescence. Because these young people do suffer with the internal psychology of addiction, they will remain at risk of future addictive behaviors when they grow out of adolescence. However, after adolescence, they may have a reprieve until, or unless, life circumstances restimulate the addiction. For instance, a woman whose separation conflicts in her teenage years led to intolerable feelings of helplessness, and who resolved them through an addictive behavior at that time, may have ended this behavior as she grew out of adolescence and perhaps entered a stable relationship in young adulthood. If this relationship failed later, she would be at risk of resuming her old, or a new, addictive behavior. But the good news is that even if this occurred, she would at that point be free of the other developmental burdens she shouldered during her adolescence. She could bring to bear all of her adult capacities to deal with the addiction, in the way I have shown in the many cases of adults throughout this book.

In saying this, I do not mean to say that teenagers cannot use the approach I am describing. As in Barbara's case, they can. It is just that the ability to deal with addiction, as with any emotional problem, typically increases when a person grows into adulthood. But there are, in fact, advantages for teenagers of the approach I have been describing. For one thing, it is respectful of a person's ability to use his or her own mind, and attentive to who people are as individuals—attributes that are at least as important to teenagers as they are to adults. Approaching addiction by understanding it also does not require a blind faith in precepts, or in the all-knowing wisdom of a counselor, conditions that are understandably often difficult for teens. Unfortunately, these difficult factors are commonly present in many addiction treatments, particularly AA-oriented approaches.

To sum up, many teens will have a good prognosis with respect to their excessive or abusive behaviors, either because these have a nonaddiction basis, or because they have true addictions that are brought emphatically to the fore by the special stresses of adolescence. Of course, this does not mean teens or parents should "wait it out" until adolescence is outgrown. On the contrary, whether the basis for a dangerous activity is addictive or nonaddictive, early attention to evaluation and treatment is critical.

# FOURTEEN

# *Couples*

If addiction is about powerlessness, rage at powerlessness and reassertion of power, as I have been describing, this hints at the ways in which a relationship will be affected by one or both partners suffering with an addiction. In turn, this opens the door for couples to use the way of understanding addiction that I have been describing to improve how they relate to each other. In this chapter, I will look at the stories of two couples.

## BETH AND ALAN

Beth was standing in the waiting room apart from her husband, who was seated reading a magazine, when I went out to greet them. After they came in, Beth began the session.

"Alan is an alcoholic. We're here because I can't stand it anymore, and we thought we should see somebody about it." Beth had been the one to call, and I had not yet spoken with Alan. He was looking at me appraisingly as his wife spoke. "Alan has been drinking for all of the time we've been married—it's been five years—and it's no better now than it was on day one. Every day he comes home half in the bag, then mixes a martini when he walks in the door. After a couple of those, he wants dinner, then he has what he calls a 'nightcap,' which is two or three more drinks, then he falls asleep in front of the TV. We really don't have a marriage. I'm fed up. I told him if we didn't get some help I was leaving." She did not look at Alan, and Alan continued to look at me. I turned toward him and said, "What do you think?"

"I do drink too much," he said without expression. I waited but he did not continue. Beth spoke, instead.

"He knows all about it. I've been telling him for years that he has to stop. I've been begging him, pleading with him, yelling at him." She waved generally in his direction. "It makes no difference to him. Last weekend we had friends over for dinner and he was drunk, as usual. After that, I took the liquor bottles and emptied them down the toilet. I did that before, but it doesn't make any difference, he just buys more." Alan continued to sit impassively. Beth shook her head. "I know you're not supposed to do that, throw away the bottles, and of course, it doesn't do any good at all, but I don't know what else to do. Sometimes I feel like killing him, I really do."

I looked at Alan. "You said you drink too much. It obviously upsets your wife."

He nodded slowly. "Yes. I know I should cut down."

"Cut down!" Beth said. "Who do you think you're kidding? You've tried to 'cut down' a million times. Don't give me that 'cut down' crap. You need to stop. You need to just stop buying the bottles, stop going to the bars before you come home, just *stop*. Just keep the hell away from liquor." Beth was nearly yelling, but it seemed to have no effect on Alan.

———

What was going on here? Alan may have been remaining quiet because he was embarrassed or ashamed about his drinking, or because this appointment was his wife's idea to begin with and he wanted nothing to do with it, or possibly because remaining quiet was a way he had developed to control relationships. But whatever the reasons, there was something notable about the way in which the couple was relating to each other. Alan was the one with the addiction, but Beth was the one who was upset.

The interaction between Beth and Alan demonstrates something often seen in couples where one person has an addiction. For a period of time after having performed an addictive act—and before the urge arises again—the person with an addiction has "solved" his or her immediate problem. A consequence of this is that commonly people feel better, less anxious, and certainly less angry after performing an addictive act. (Later, of course, guilt and shame often become paramount.) In Alan's case, although he had not just had a drink before the session, he was at the time of the session free of the urge to drink—that is, free of the powerful feelings that led him to drink. So, the strong feelings that were expressed in his addictive behavior were not in evidence in the session.

But what happens to the person in a relationship with someone who has an addiction? Because it is the nature of addiction to be compulsive, to be driven by internal purposes and drives as I have described, it tends not to be responsive to external factors. Consequently, just as the internal psychology of addiction drives it to continue despite loss after loss, this compulsive psychology also drives it past the objections, concerns, and even threats of one's partner. The repeated displaced expression of power through the addiction, which is unable to be altered by the partner, therefore leaves the partner with just the opposite result. He or she is rendered powerless by the addiction.

On top of this, because it is the nature of addiction to express rage, addictive acts are often *experienced* as rageful by those around the person with the addiction. Said another way, people in contact with someone with an addiction accurately pick up the rage present in addiction and, when the addiction affects them, they become enraged in return. This is an understandable response. When added to the powerlessness of the partner to affect the behavior, it is usual for partners to be furious with the person who has the addiction.

As it turned out, this is what had happened to Beth and Alan. Besides whatever personality tendencies Alan may have had to be reserved, his appearance and behavior also manifested the calm after the storm. He had already expressed his feelings in his addiction. But Beth now had the rage.

She described this in her own words in a session not long after. "I used to be so patient," she said. "Now, I'm on edge all the time. I know that Alan thinks I'm a nag, but I wasn't always this way. I've changed so much over the years. The truth is, I hate the way I am now, but I don't feel that I have any choice."

In working with Beth and Alan, this was one of the things that we dealt with from an early point. Alan did see her as a nag, or worse, because he felt that she gave him no leeway. He said, "I can go four days and not touch a drop, then have some drinks on Saturday, and she's on my case." He was not aware of how enraging his actions had been to her, no matter how long it had been between drinks, because he saw his drinking as a "bad habit." He did not appreciate the insistent, compulsive quality of his drive to drink. Beyond this, he also did not realize that he was expressing his own rage through his addictive behavior. It was not until he began to see some of the key factors that lay behind his addiction that he could start to appreciate how angry he was when he drank. And once he saw why he drank and why he drank when he did, this helped not only with his understanding his alcoholism, but with understanding the extent to which he had been preoccupied with managing his own internal issues, and because of that, ignoring the effect of his actions on his wife.

For her part, Beth also developed a different perspective on Alan's drinking. Her fury with him had been normal, as I said, but it was also based on a lack of knowledge. Like Alan, she thought that his drinking was a bad habit, with emphasis on "bad." Her view was that he was doing something wrong and should exercise his willpower to stop doing it. As I mentioned in chapter 6, the problem with this idea is that it assumes that behavior is entirely a matter of conscious choice. But this view omits most of what causes people trouble in their lives—emotional factors that are beyond their conscious awareness. Naturally, it would have been beneficial if Alan had sought help for himself, seeing the pain it was causing his wife as well as the destruction he was producing for himself in other areas of his life. But his behavior was not at heart a matter of being bad. And as Beth came to understand the real nature of her husband's addiction, she became less angry.

In the end, Alan and Beth continued to meet with me as a couple, and eventually Alan agreed to embark on a separate, individual treatment (with another therapist) for himself. (It is generally not a good idea for a therapist who sees a couple to also treat one of its members individually. The integrity of both the couples and individual treatment is compromised.) With their new awareness of the emotional factors that had arisen between them as a result of Alan's drinking, the couple found that they could continue to work together through the time he was becoming sober.

———

If you are the family member with an addiction, a message from Beth's and Alan's experience is that you may not have realized that the anger you might see around you is in significant part a result of the addiction itself. Like Alan, you may have assumed that you are just unlucky to have an unsympathetic partner—that on top of your trouble managing your addiction, you have to deal with a lack of support, as well. But as with Alan and Beth, it is important to realize that the nature of addiction is to produce just this kind of interaction, not only because of the detrimental effects of the addiction, which are usually pretty obvious, but because addiction inherently expresses an insistence, a rage, which disempowers and enrages others. So, it is not wise to assume that you would be able to manage better with someone different. On the contrary, if you recognize this pattern in time, you will have the chance to both address your addiction and keep your relationship.

If you are the spouse of somebody with an addiction, there are two useful messages from Beth's and Alan's story. One is that if you find yourself feeling terribly guilty for not being more patient with your partner, it may be because, like Beth, you have been *induced* by the nature of addiction to be less patient than you usually are. You should not feel that the loss of your usual for-bearance is a sign that you have become less tolerant as a person. It is frequently difficult to live with someone who suffers with an addiction, and it can help to understand that you are caught up in an emotional web that was not consciously intended by either of you.

The other message from this vignette, if you are the partner of a person with an addiction, is one you already know if you have read this far. That is that, rather than being a "bad habit," addiction is a compulsion based on deeply important emotional factors. Of course, you need to take good care of yourself, and you should. But often the best thing you can do for both you and your partner is to take a clear stand that your partner seek the help he or she needs and deserves.

## LAURA AND JIM

Jim was a compulsive gambler whose gambling had cost his family tens of thousands of dollars. When I met with him and his wife, he had already begun treatment elsewhere for compulsive gambling, and they had also already consulted a financial planner to help them deal with their enormous debt. When we met, I asked them about their deciding to come for couples therapy, in addition.

"Jim has had this problem for a long time," Laura said. "I understand that sometimes he can't help it, and now that we've gotten the money situation taken care of, at least I can sleep at night."

"We went to see this financial guy," Jim said, "and he got the debts consolidated. He told me to cut up my credit cards, and I did."

"Most important," Laura added immediately, "he helped us to arrange what he called a firewall for the money. I am the only person who has access to the accounts, and the house and car are in my name. Jim's paycheck is directly deposited to the bank, and he gets an allowance each week for expenses."

Jim nodded seriously. They had obviously talked this out before they came to see me.

"But the problem that is destroying our marriage hasn't gone away," Laura went on. "It's trust. I can't trust anything Jim says." She leaned forward for emphasis. "For years, he told me that he wasn't gambling, and he was. I found out when the bill collectors called the house, or when the dealership repossessed our car a couple of years ago." Laura sat back. "I can understand that gambling is an addiction, but I can't deal with the lying. I can't live with someone that I can't trust."

There was a short silence. "And it's still a problem?" I asked both of them.

Laura looked at Jim. "Well," he said slowly, "the truth is that I still gamble sometimes. I go in the store and buy lottery tickets. Of course, I don't have much money for it now, but, you know, maybe that's part of why I buy them. It sure would be nice to turn some of that allowance into real money." He perked up a little bit. "I did win money a couple of weeks ago, two hundred dollars, and I gave it right over to Laura to help pay our expenses."

"That's just what I'm talking about," Laura said to him with some exasperation. "You think that was great. Well, it wasn't great. I found out you had gambled when you handed me the money. Before that, you said you had stopped." She turned to me. "He won that time, but I know perfectly well that all of the times he gambles and loses, he doesn't say anything. I'm protected by the steps we took to insulate Jim from our money, but the lying just destroys the marriage anyway."

I looked over at Jim. He said, "I know she wants me to tell her, but I just can't. I can't bring myself to do it."

I said, "You figure if you lose, you better not say anything?"

"That's part of it," he replied. "That was a big part of it when I was betting a lot of money. Now . . ." He shrugged. "She gets so mad that I don't want to tell her."

"I've told you a hundred times," Laura said to him, "I'd rather *know* than have you lie about it."

Jim looked uncomfortable, but he didn't say anything. Finally he mumbled, "Yeah, I know."

Neither of them spoke for a moment. I asked Jim, "How do you feel after you gamble?"

"Terrible."

I looked at Laura. "You knew that, I suppose."

"Yes. I've been as supportive as I can be. As I said, I know this is an addiction. It has consequences, and we've dealt with them. I know it's hard for him to stop, but if he just told me when he gambles, we could get through this together."

I nodded. "Why do you think he doesn't tell you?"

"He's too proud, if you ask me. He thinks it's shameful, or a defeat or something. Too proud, and too stubborn."

"Is that true?" I asked Jim.

"I guess." He spread his hands apart in a gesture of futility. "It's just too . . . humiliating. What am I going to say? 'Oh, sorry, hon, I know we've only talked about this a million times, but guess what?'" He shook his head. "She says it would be okay, but I know it won't be okay. It's not like I've *never* told her. She tries to be calm, but I can see it in her face—she's hurt, angry, disappointed. She tries to hide it, but. . . ." He threw his hands up. "Then later, she can't keep it in anymore. So she'll say, 'Are you going to buy some more tickets tomorrow?' and I can see she's furious because I bought them today." He blew out his breath. "Look, I'm not blaming her. I fucked up and she has every right to be mad. I just don't see the point in telling her every time. The fact is, I gamble times she never knows about, and then I save both her and me from the grief."

"That's where you're wrong!" Laura jumped in. "Your lying is the *cause* of the grief. I wouldn't be nearly so mad if you were honest with me. You think I don't know that you gamble other times and don't tell me? *That's* why I get after you when you tell me— because I don't know if the next day you're going to gamble and not tell me about it!"

———

Keeping addictive behavior secret from a partner is one of the most common problems in couples dealing with an addiction. Once the addiction is not producing an immediate crisis, this issue frequently becomes the main bone of contention between people, for the reason that Laura said—it undermines trust. And Jim must have known this. Yet, he still was keeping his gambling secret. Why?

Partly, it is what he said—that he felt humiliated about his continuing addictive behavior, and he was afraid of his wife's angry reaction. In turn, her angry reaction was partly just what she said— a response to his lying about the behavior to begin with. But this bears looking into more closely.

Jim's feeling of humiliation, it turned out, was basically the *interpersonal* consequence of his feeling ashamed. His sense of humiliation meant that he felt exposed as the shameful person *he* believed himself to be. So, his keeping his actions secret in order to avoid feeling humiliated was really a reflection of his own sense of shame. Indeed, at heart, his anticipation of feeling humiliated was actually quite independent of Laura's reaction. This fact became important for Jim to understand, in order to make it easier for him to talk with her.

Likewise, if you suffer with an addiction, this is a good point to keep in mind when deciding whether to keep your actions secret. Your partner may be a lot gentler with you than you are with yourself, and it may be your own severe self-criticism that you imagine would be your partner's attitude toward your secret.

Jim's treating Laura as though she would see him as shameful, when in fact it was he himself who felt ashamed, is a process that you may know is called *projection*: thinking that others have thoughts that are yours. In itself, it is not abnormal—in fact, it is a routine part of everyday life. Without it, we would never be able to correctly guess what someone else was thinking. But it can have another consequence, as it did for Jim. By keeping his secret, he unwittingly *induced* Laura to be the stern taskmaster that he was with himself. This happened because by not telling her, or by lying to her about his actions, she, understandably, became more suspicious and angry with him. In the end, Jim unintentionally led her to act in the very way he was afraid she would act. As you can see, this is just like the way Alan unintentionally induced Beth to be angry with him, via expressing his own anger through his addictive act, then being unaware that her reciprocal anger had originated in him.

This sort of unintentional creation of behavior in partners by projecting one's own feelings into them, or by treating them in a way that is based on a projected idea of what they are like, is not unique to addictions. Indeed, it plays at least some role in any relationship (think of treating people with the assumption that they deserve respect, thereby bringing out the best in them). But the problem with addictions is that so often what is projected is one's harsh judgment of oneself. This is another basis, then, for the conclusion that if you have an addiction, you may yourself be unintentionally producing the harsh or judgmental behavior you see in your partner.

If you are the partner of a person who is not telling you the truth about his or her addictive activities, there are also some useful conclusions you can draw from Jim's and Laura's story. On the one hand, it is true that any relationship must be based on mutual trust, and certainly it is only reasonable for you to expect that in your relationship. But on the other hand, it is useful to remember that the issue for your partner may not be about trust at all. While he or she may be untrustworthy about telling you about an addictive behavior, this may be the result of his or her shame, as I have described—not the result of a basically dishonest relationship. Therefore, it may be sensible to tolerate a certain amount of this kind of secrecy, so long as it is not risking catastrophe for you or the family, and so long as your partner is pursuing treatment for the addiction. This may allow the two of you to do what Laura said she hoped to do—get through the problem together.

———

There are two other points that can be taken from Jim's and Laura's story. First is the familiar idea that, if you have an addiction, remembering the psychology of addiction as I have described it throughout this book will hopefully help you not to feel so ashamed to begin with—and, therefore, not feel such a need to keep your addictive behavior a secret. Addiction seems shameful only when it is not understood.

And second, if you have an addiction, sometimes you may feel that you have to keep your addictive activities secret because, like addiction itself, this becomes an important way to retain a needed sense of power and control. The ability to keep secrets, after all, is quite significant—a part of one's normal sense of self-control and autonomy. Telling someone that you have done something that you yourself find embarrassing, or worse, means giving up this boundary between you and the world. While the power to maintain this boundary is important to everyone, if you have an addiction, keeping your addictive acts secret may be particularly important for you, rather than feeling that this self-boundary is out of your control.

The message from this is to think through your motivation for keeping the secret. If it is like an addiction itself—a way to retain a sense of power against helplessness—then being aware of this, you may be able to free yourself from a sense that it is imperative to hold on to your secret. And if you are the partner of a person with an addiction, it can be helpful to understand that this basis for secrecy is just another aspect of the addiction psychology with which both you and your partner are suffering.

———

In connection with couples, I should say a word about the concept of "enabling." As you probably know, this refers to actions or an attitude by a partner (or a parent, coworker, or friend) that are thought to "enable" a person's addiction—generally by either blocking the negative consequences of the addiction or, more extremely, rewarding the addictive behavior. A commonly given example is a wife who calls in sick for her husband to his employer, when he is actually hungover. In sparing him the consequences of having to admit why he is not at work, she is said to be enabling his drinking. The idea behind this is a behavioral one—if a person suffers adverse consequences from a behavior, then the behavior is more likely to be extinguished. Does this make sense for addictions?

It does, to some extent. Repetition of any behavior, including addiction, is the product of many factors, one of which is what happened as a consequence of doing it in the past. However, as everyone knows, addiction is a prime example of behavior that is repeated *despite* its consequences—because it is an internally driven compulsion. It is simply not altered very much by its negative effects. Therefore, while reducing these negative effects from addictive behavior—"enabling" the addiction—is certainly not helpful, it is only a limited factor in the continuation of the addictive behavior. Consequently, the choice about whether to do something that may appear to "enable" the addiction should be carefully thought out in broader terms.

First, I will take up a related matter. For some people, "enabling" a person with an addiction carries a negative, moralistic quality. They feel that people with addictions should suffer the consequences of their behavior, they should get what they deserve for doing something bad—therefore, they should not be "enabled" any more than one would enable someone to commit a crime. Obviously, this attitude is destructive and inappropriate.

Such a rigid, moralistic view of the importance of not "enabling" can make it very hard for loved ones to know what to do in the often complex and painful situations that arise in trying to be helpful to someone with an addiction. I have often seen this in parents who are worried about a grown child. They wonder, for instance, if they should be continuing to send him or her money to live on if the child is on drugs and has no other means of support. Or, with regard to the wife in my example above—if she refuses to call in sick for her husband, and he loses his job, is that a beneficial outcome or not?

These are not black-and-white matters. In the end, the decisions must be made individually in each circumstance. It is important, though, to always bear in mind the overall goal: to try to get the problem treated. The best limit-setting, therefore, generally involves mandating that a person with an addiction seeks appropriate treatment. For instance, the wife in my example might decide to call in sick for her husband, but then tell him that, quite apart from this incident, she can stay with him only if he involves himself in treatment. The parents in the other example might likewise tell their child that they will support only the most basic expenses to allow survival, and require that the child seek treatment, which they will support fully and wholeheartedly.

In summary, if you are the partner in this situation, you should not feel that there is a rigid standard about "enabling" that you must follow in order to be doing the "right" thing. Struggling over the complex issues that arise when you love someone who is harming himself or herself is a difficult enough process without adding unnecessary guilt. Indeed, you may find it very useful to give yourself a chance to talk with a professional familiar with these issues, as you consider the choices you are facing.

If you suffer with an addiction yourself, the message here is to be aware of the dilemma facing the people who love you. Fortunately, the best thing you can do to ease their burden is also the best thing you can do for yourself—find a good treatment and stick with it (I will discuss treatment in the book's final chapter).

# FIFTEEN

# When Are Compulsions Addictions?

In the last chapter, I mentioned that Jim's keeping his gambling secret from Laura may have had some characteristics of an addiction itself. But could a compulsion to keep secrets be an addiction? And if that is possible, what other compulsions might be addictions?

To begin with, I must clarify that I am referring here to compulsive behaviors that have a psychological origin. These are common behaviors ranging from a need to arrange things neatly in order, to compulsively playing solitaire, to compulsively shopping. These activities that are of psychological origin must be distinguished from the similar-appearing but apparently biologically predisposed diagnosis of Obsessive-Compulsive Disorder, or OCD. All references in this chapter will be to psychologically based compulsions. I will return to OCD at the end of the chapter.

Compulsions are in fact strikingly similar to addictions. Just like addictions, they are repetitive, powerfully driven activities over which a person does not feel he or she has control. Indeed, some addictions are commonly named as compulsions, such as compulsive gambling. Yet, compulsions and addictions have traditionally been considered separately, as though they are completely different diagnostic entities. Are they?

In a paper I wrote a few years ago,[1] I quoted a case that was given in a classic textbook of psychology[2] as a prototypical description of a compulsion, as opposed to an addiction. In that case, a man—I will call him Philip—felt compelled to yell out in the middle of church services. I wrote that a principal reason that this case was defined as a *compulsion* was that the man strongly disliked what he was doing, even though he felt compelled to repeat it. He had a sense that he *had* to act—not that he wished to.

This quality of having to act against one's will has been a main reason for the separation between addictions and compulsions.* While compulsions characteristically are behaviors that are consciously *not* desired—in fact they are behaviors one would like to be free of—addictions have traditionally been seen as behaviors that *are* consciously desired. When a person with alcoholism walks into a bar, he or she is intending to have a drink. As you know, there is frequently a strong determination to perform an addictive act. This is in contrast with Philip's case, or, to give another example, a person who feels a compulsion to arrange and rearrange items on a desk. This person is not intending—wishing—to do this, but feels he must. On the surface, therefore, addictions and compulsions seem to be opposites.

But this distinction is something of an illusion. For one thing, of course, people with addictive behaviors regularly wish they could stop doing them. It is true that the drive behind the addiction is powerful and often leads to a conscious decision to perform an addictive act, but both before and after the fact, it is common for

---

*The other reason they have been seen as so different is that, unlike compulsions, addictions have not been considered to reflect an internal emotional compromise (shown by the need for displacement). Instead, addictions have been mostly thought of as either just self-gratifications or self-medications. The idea that there is a compromise *within* addiction—just as is the case in compulsions—was first introduced in my article I just cited above.

people with addictions to wish that they could stop. Even more to the point, as I have been stressing throughout the book, addictions contain an *internal* compromise within the addictive act itself. Far from being the simple enactment of a wish to perform an action, they are more deeply almost the opposite: a need to do something in displacement, because an original drive, or wish, is inhibited.

Addictions, then, both lead to conscious wishes to stop the behavior and are intrinsically the result of an emotional compromise. Their superficial characteristic of being consciously sought out is just that—superficial. It is not a fundamental attribute that should be held in contrast with compulsions.

From the other side, compulsions too can have the reverse quality from their characteristically unwanted state. It is fairly common for compulsive actions to become not just accepted, but valued. Consider for example the case of someone repetitively arranging his desk. Over time, that person might find some pleasure in keeping the desk neat. The person might even take pride in the careful, ordered way he or she does things. Or, a person needing to check the stove several times before leaving the house might feel this is a virtue—that you can't be too careful. He or she might go even farther, and feel a bit superior to those people who are less cautious. This sort of transformation of compulsive actions to being consciously desirable, rather than unwanted, is not unusual.

Besides this, there is a deeper and more important way that compulsions are like addictions. I have described the way addictions always reflect an internal emotional compromise. But compulsions have long been seen in just this way—as emotional compromises. Indeed, this is what creates them. For instance, consider the case of a man who had a compulsion about his alarm clock. When he went to sleep, he had to pull out the little knob that set the alarm, then push it back in, then pull it back out, and so on for many repetitions. He broke a number of alarm clocks this way. This man had a job that required him to arise at an extremely early hour, and he thought that he was checking the alarm because he wanted to be sure he would get up on time. But there was more to his compulsion than that. He also hated to get up at that early hour. Yet he could not let himself be fully aware of this feeling, in part because he believed he should be grateful to have such a well-paying job, and in part because it was important to him not to complain, even to himself. Since he both wanted to get up and did not want to get up, yet could not work this out in his mind because he kept himself from knowing how ambivalent he felt, he alternately expressed the opposite wishes about which he was unaware, by pulling and pushing the alarm setting. His compulsion reflected his wishes, even though consciously he was only aware that he disliked having to do them. Having a drive be unintentionally expressed in a compulsion is a very common situation. And as you have no doubt already noticed, this sounds a lot like the indirect, displaced expression of a drive in addiction.

————

To summarize, the traditional distinction between addictions and compulsions was largely based on one being consciously wanted and the other being consciously unwanted. But addictions may become disliked, and compulsions may become liked. In fact, whether one likes to do a thing or not is in general a rather superficial and changeable attribute, as both addictions and compulsions demonstrate. Beyond this, both addictions and compulsions reflect an internal emotional compromise. Neither is a simple expression of one wish. Finally, both compulsions and addictions reflect the expression of a powerful drive, and share an intensity and an overwhelming imperative to act. Having demonstrated all this, what is left of the difference between compulsions and addictions?

I have concluded that *there is no fundamental distinction between addictions and most compulsions.* (I will return to the one way that some compulsions are not true addictions, later.) This is, I believe, a very important point, because it says something critical about both the nature of addictions and the kind of treatment appropriate for them. Compulsions have always been considered one of the basic kinds of emotional problems of people, and they have traditionally been approached with an attempt to understand their psychology as deeply as possible. Furthermore, compulsions are not usually hard to relate to because nearly everybody has a touch of them, and even those people who have a more serious problem with compulsive behaviors are generally not judged as morally inferior. What a far cry from the way addictions have been approached, by both many professionals and nonprofessionals alike! Addictions have been segregated as though they were different from other human problems, as though they required a unique approach (as in Alcoholics Anonymous), and as though they could not be understood as emotional issues by either the people treating them or the people suffering with them. But if addictions and compulsions are basically the same, psychologically, there can be no reason to think of or treat them differently. Like compulsions, addictions are, as I have been saying throughout this book, in the mainstream of the human condition.

---

Philip's yelling in church was a compulsion and he disliked it. In his treatment, it was discovered that his behavior was connected with an early experience. When he was a boy, his father had been sick, and Philip was told to keep quiet, for his father's sake. Philip loved his father, and wanted to stay quiet. But he had other feelings too. Like many a child, his feelings about his parent were complicated and mixed. These led him to the thought that he also wanted to *make* noise, in order to—in his child's mind—hurt his father. The conflict expressed in these opposite ideas about making noise or staying quiet stayed important to him into adulthood, where they expressed themselves in a displaced fashion, in his compulsion. Quite outside of his awareness, when he felt the compulsion to yell in church, he was enacting the old drive to hurt his father—in effect, to yell in God's house as he had the forbidden wish to yell in his father's house. Since he could never allow himself to express this feeling directly with his father, he felt an apparently irrational urge to perform this displaced, substitute act.

Hearing the story behind Philip's compulsion, with its displaced focus of an intense drive to perform a forbidden behavior, you can see its similarity to the psychology of addiction. And in keeping with my point about the unity of compulsions and addictions, let me take this even farther. What if Philip's yelling were not disliked? What if he were like some people who enjoy yelling in public places—for instance, people who are amused by heckling others who are onstage? If his heckling were persistent, pleasurable, sought out, and had a driven quality, it would start to look like an addiction. In fact, if Philip repeatedly called out in church in a way that he consciously enjoyed, and continued to do it despite suffering harmful effects as a result, and insisted on doing this despite the concern and good advice from his friends and family to stop, then his yelling would match behaviors that are traditionally called addictions. The diagnosis would have changed from compulsion to addiction by simply changing Philip's conscious experience of liking or not liking his behavior. Remembering that people regularly do shift in their liking or not liking to perform both compulsions and addictions, this again underlines the sameness of the two conditions.

Indeed, Philip's condition even as originally described, fits well into the psychology of addiction as I have defined it. When Philip was a little boy, he wanted to yell, make noise, but he could not. The brief history provided in the original description of Philip's case does not explain why this was so important to him—what his anger toward his father was about—but we can assume from its lifelong consequences that it was significant to him. Philip was then faced with just the kind of helplessness that is present in addictions—he was blocked from taking a direct action to do something that was emotionally meaningful for him. As a child, some of this blocking was, of course, enforced by the adults around him. But, more deeply, he obeyed the command to stay quiet because he himself felt an inhibition against harming his father, whom he also loved. Consequently, his later compulsion can be understood as driven by his need to reassert his power against this self-imposed helplessness, in displaced form. In other words, his behavior was exactly the same as any addiction. Philip was aware when he entered treatment that he had a compulsion. What he did not know was that his compulsion was also an addiction.

Philip's story also raises another point. Initially, he was aware only of the side of his feelings that were opposed to his yelling—he was aware only that he was doing something that he did not want to do. It was not until he was treated that he discovered that behind this compulsive act was actually a (forbidden) wish—that he was actually doing something that he did want to do, at least in part.

On the other hand, in addictions, you are often aware only of the side of your feelings that finds gratification from the addictive act, so consequently you may *not* be distressed by it. You are likely to be unaware of the self-inhibition from acting directly that is always part of any addictive act. Said another way, you don't realize that you are keeping yourself from doing something that you *did* want to do. Again, this difference in the way you *experience* addictions and compulsions can be seen to be just a superficial matter of which side of your conflict you are initially aware of—the apparent difference between addictions and compulsions hides their sameness under the surface.

Because of the unity of addictions and compulsions, it is clear that addictions are no different from other common psychological difficulties, and that approaching their treatment by understanding their psychological basis is as appropriate for them as for any other emotional problem. In addition, if you suffer with an addiction, there is also a very practical consequence of knowing the sameness of addictions and compulsions, as can be seen from the story below.

———

Caroline Matson was thirty-four years old and had been overweight for as long as she could remember. Her mother said there had been a time early in her life when she was thin, but Caroline did not recall it. Before we met, she had also developed a history of bingeing and vomiting and in the past had taken an excessive number of diet pills to lose weight, though she had stopped that a few years ago.

Her behavior, we quickly learned, was a true addiction. When she ate, or vomited, she had a feeling that she was in control of her life. Over time, we found out that eating meant not only that she was choosing what and how much she took in but had the larger significance that she, and she alone, was in control of her well-being. When she vomited, she likewise felt she was in control not just of her gaining weight, but of how much of what she took in she would decide to "keep," or reject.

Caroline was an only child. Her parents' marriage was never good, and her earliest memories were of hearing loud shouting and being frightened. Her parents were divorced when she was four years old, and although she had a general sense of having been attached to her father, she never saw him again. She and her mother lived on Welfare for a year, during which they moved three times because of problems with the violent neighborhood in which they were living. The following year, Caroline's mother went to work full time, and Caroline stayed with her aunt each day until her mother returned home in the evening. This arrangement contin-ued after school let out when Caroline started kindergarten, and for years beyond, because the school day ended several hours before Caroline's mother could get home from work. As she described it, Caroline never felt comfortable all those years staying with her aunt. The aunt had three children of her own, ranging from three to seven years older than Caroline, and they generally did not include her in their activities. When her mother finally came to pick her up, her mother was usually exhausted and had limited energy for the little girl.

After Caroline had been meeting with me for some time, we had come to understand that her "eating disorder"—her excessive weight, bingeing and purging—was an addiction like any other. As a child, she had felt adrift and that she could not count on people to look after her. When she binged and purged, she had the sense that *she* was in control of whether she would receive what she needed—in control of her own sustenance. And the more we met, the more she saw how enraged and desperate she was to never again be helpless. The nature of her eating troubles as a displacement of this concern became increasingly clear to her.

Caroline began to get better. The binges and purges decreased. But as she did, she began to have a new problem. She started to spend much more money than she could afford, buying clothes and furniture and jewelry. Often, she returned items she had just bought, but a few days later she would be back in the stores buying something equally expensive. At first, I had no idea this was happening. Caroline would mention to me how beautiful her new sofa was, but not that she had overdrawn her account to buy it. Eventually, though, she let on that she was having some trouble paying bills, and I learned the story of her shopping sprees.

Naturally, it was not hard to figure out that Caroline had simply shifted some of the focus of her addiction from eating to shopping. She had even kept the same "binge and purge" pattern with her buying and returning items. And, the nurturant quality of food could easily be seen in her purchases for herself. As we explored this, Caroline's shopping addiction faded. She still continued to binge and purge on occasion, however.

Not long after the shopping sprees had ended, while we were working on the issues underlying her addictive eating behavior, Caroline told me about something else. Unlike the shopping, she told me about this new problem as soon as it cropped up.

"I think I'm going crazy," she said one day.

"Why do you say that?"

"Because, when I get up in the morning I clean the house. Then I go to work. As soon as I come home, I have to clean again. Then I have dinner, and right after dinner, I'm dusting, and getting into the little crevices of the appliances with a toothpick, and wiping the table, and the table's legs. It's driving me crazy. I was always neat, but there's something wrong with me. It never seems neat enough."

"How long has this been going on?"

"Since last weekend. It's horrible and it's getting worse. On Saturday I started cleaning the house, because I figured it's almost winter, and some people have a spring cleaning but I like to clean before each season. But I just started cleaning and cleaning, and the more I did, the more I saw dirt. I can't stop, and it's making me nervous."

"I see it upsets you," I said. After a moment's pause, I asked her, "How is the eating going?"

"Okay."

"You last had a binge three or four weeks ago, right?'

"Yes, I think that's about right. Not for a long time. That's not what's bothering me now, though."

"I know, I'm just trying to see how the cleaning problem fits with that."

She shook her head. "This is completely different. I can't stand this. The binges, well . . ." She shrugged. We had talked about her binges a lot, and we both were aware that as much as they, too, bothered her, there was a big part of her that insisted on having them. Her great rage against helplessness that was expressed in the addictive behavior was very close to the surface.

She continued, "I've got to find a way to get rid of this."

I nodded. "Tell me about how you feel when you clean."

"You mean usually, or now when it's driving me crazy?"

"Is it different?"

Caroline thought a moment. "Well, not really, just now it's very intense." She paused a second. "Well, usually I like to clean. I mean, I guess I don't really like cleaning, but I like the result. That's why I have a big cleanup four times a year. I like things neat and clean. I like to know where everything is, and that it's ready."

"Ready?"

"Ready to use."

I thought for a second. "Say some more about that."

Caroline squinted her eyes, which she sometimes did when she was thinking. After a minute, she said, "There's nothing more to say. When things are clean and neat, and I know where they are, then I know I can just go get them when I need them, and use them. I don't see what this has to do with my cleaning now. I told you, I'm cleaning up little cracks, cleaning along the baseboards—it's stuff that has nothing to do with anything. It's stuff that's completely unnecessary to do."

There was a pause, then I said, "Maybe there is something necessary about it. I don't think you would have such an intense urge to do it if it weren't important." Caroline squinted her eyes but didn't say anything. I went on, "You said that you clean things in order to have them be ready—available to you when you need them. That sounds like what we already know about the meaning of your bingeing and purging. When you do those things, it makes you feel that you have control over what and how much you take in. I think that your cleaning means that you, again, have proven that you're in control over having what you need."

Caroline looked off to the side and was quiet. "You mean this is like the shopping? Another way to do the addiction?"

"Yes, I think so."

Caroline was quiet again. "Well . . ." she said slowly, then paused and squinted at the wall. "This is really stupid, though. I'm cleaning things that don't help me in any way. They don't help me to be ready."

"Sure, but how sensible was it when you bought the sofa and returned it two days later? Your cleaning is excessive, as the shopping was, and as the bingeing and purging is. It's excessive because it's carrying the load of expressing something important. The feelings behind it determine how strongly you experience the urge to do it and how much you do—not whether the behavior makes sense."

Caroline was familiar with this thinking from our exploration of her eating troubles, and had just not thought about it concerning this new problem. She nodded, and we were both silent for a minute. Then she said, "But there is something different about this. I *wanted* to shop. I don't *want* to do this."

I nodded. "Yes, the feeling you have about this new activity is different—even though it seems to have the same meaning and purpose as the other forms that the addiction has taken." There was another pause. I thought about what Caroline had said. "You know," I went on, "you've been having more and more control over your eating. I wonder if getting better is hard for you."

Caroline looked a little surprised. "Well, yes it is. I didn't think to mention it, because, well, getting better isn't really a problem."

"It can be. Tell me more about it."

"Well, you know I've been working hard to stop the bingeing and throwing up. Mostly, I think I'm doing a great job. I can tell when I'm feeling out of control and that's why I have the incredible urge to eat. I've been trying to do what we talked about, to do something else that's more to the point of what's eating at me." Caroline smiled. "Sorry, no pun intended. A lot of the time, I can figure out something else to do. But it's hard. Sometimes I feel like I'm losing control, not gaining it. I always had my eating and vomiting to fall back on. Now, I don't."

I nodded. "Yes, you seem determined to make as much use of your new understanding as possible, to not do some addictive act."

"Absolutely."

"Well, maybe that contributes to the new form this addiction has taken. I think it would have been hard for you to do something you enjoyed, as a new addiction."

Caroline's eyes opened wide. "You know, that's probably true. I would have caught that immediately."

"I think you would."

————

Caroline's cleaning was a compulsion that she did not want to do, but when we saw through it, we could see the drive that it was expressing. Like Philip's yelling in church, her compulsion was truly an addiction. Recognizing this, she was eventually able to take control of it as she had with her shopping, and as she was still working at doing with her eating.

Caroline's story highlights the value of understanding that many compulsions are addictions. If you can recognize them for what they are, you are in a good position to be able to track the changes in an addiction, even when it transforms to unusual, compulsive forms. This is particularly significant since the addiction may not remain in its compulsive form forever, and may shift back to development of a "new" addiction. Without awareness of the continuity of the problem, you might feel that you had an unexpected relapse. Even more important, you might have not continued to pursue your understanding of the addiction when it had shifted to the "disguised" compulsion form. It would have been a shame, for instance, if Caroline's compulsion had been seen as a wholly new diagnosis, and its connection with her original problem were lost.

———

I said I would return to the one distinction between compulsions and addictions. It is this: some compulsions express almost exclusively a need to inhibit or *undo* a forbidden thought or act that has already been done, rather than to *do* the forbidden thought or act in a displaced way, as in addictions. A famous example is in Shakespeare's *Macbeth*, where Lady Macbeth has a compulsive need to wash her hands of imagined bloodstains, as an expression of her guilt over deaths she has caused. Her compulsion is driven by the need to emotionally *undo* her acts, differentiating it from true addictions.

So, compulsions may express undoing, or they may express doing—as in Philip's yelling in church or Caroline's cleaning—or they may express both. In my view, *all addictions are compulsions (of the "doing" form) and all compulsions of the "doing" form are true psychological addictions—i.e., reassertions of power in displacement.* It is only those compulsions that principally express the "undoing" side of a conflict that are *not* addictions. Put another way, in my view, addictions are a—very large—subset of compulsions.

———

A final issue is the significance of the well-publicized diagnosis of Obsessive-Compulsive Disorder, or OCD. If addictions are compulsions, does OCD have anything to add to knowledge about addictions? The answer appears to be no, for a quite simple reason.

As I mentioned before, although they share the same name, and can look alike, OCD is different from obsessional or compulsive *psychological* problems because it appears to be biological in origin, not psychological. This is not to say that OCD symptoms cannot have psychological significance, but their cause and treatment do appear to be different from primary psychologically based compulsions. Accordingly, medication treatment that is effective for OCD, namely the group of medicines known as SSRIs (selective serotonin reuptake inhibitors, such as Prozac) have not proven to be helpful for treating addictions. This does not mean that if you have an addiction, these medicines should not be taken. Although they are not useful treatments for addictions per se, it is perfectly reasonable to take them as prescribed if you also have the kind of depression for which they are effective, or if you also have OCD.

# SIXTEEN

# The Victors and the Vanquished: Compulsive Gambling

I have discussed compulsive gambling throughout this book, beginning with Mark's story (chapter 4), and continuing through Jim's and Laura's story in chapter 14, but in this chapter I will go into some aspects of compulsive gambling that are unique to this addiction.

Before looking at the internal, individual factors that are important in compulsive gambling, it is worth noting that the incidence of this addiction has been increasing in recent years. Its rise is correlated with the overall increase in gambling in the nation, and has especially risen among groups of people who have not historically been very involved in gambling—women and teenagers. Although illegal gambling on sports continues to be a vast and growing business, the increase in gambling, and in compulsive gambling, among new groups of people has arisen largely because it no longer requires an interest in sports or horse or dog racing. Gambling has become regularly available through both casinos and, especially, state lotteries. Since New Hampshire introduced the first state-sponsored lottery in the 1960s, nearly every state in the nation has created its own version. Besides the fact that these lotteries are readily available, including their well-known accessibility to under-age youth in spite of legal age limits,[1] states have heavily advertised their lotteries, at times even to the point of mailing out free lottery tickets to induce people to get started (reminiscent of drug pushers giving away initial free samples in the school yard).

State-sponsored and state-encouraged gambling has contributed to a societal shift toward viewing gambling as a routine part of the culture. Associated with this shift has been an increase in on-campus bookmakers at colleges and even high schools, which in turn has become another factor in the rise of both gambling and compulsive gambling among youth. The result of all these new forms of available gambling is that, while it used to be said that compulsive gambling was overwhelmingly a problem of (mainly adult) men, with estimates that they constituted 90 percent of all compulsive gamblers, this statistic is no longer tenable because of the rising incidence in women and teens.

The fact that compulsive gambling has increased along with gambling in general is largely a matter of exposure. Any time a new population is exposed to a potential addictive focus, those people who are vulnerable to using it as an object of addiction are at risk. For instance, consider the fact that there were no people with an Internet addiction twenty years ago, even though some of the people now using it addictively were already adults then. Their vulnerability became manifest once the focus was available.

This in turn raises the general question of whether people would suffer with an addiction if their "choice" of addictive focus never became available. Would the new group of compulsive gamblers have had any problem if it had not been for the advent of new gambling opportunities? My view, it will not surprise you, is that since the psychology of addiction resides within each person rather than in the object of an addiction, in the absence of any one addictive object, people will find another way to express the same important issues. One possibility, of course, is development of another clear-cut addiction. But another possibility is development of an equivalent behavior, such as one of the "hidden," or nontraditional addictions (compulsive behaviors) that I described in the last chapter. The point is that the absence of an addictive focus does not alter the need to manage the issues within any person suffering with an addiction, as is well known from the commonplace substitution of one additive focus for another when the first object is no longer available.

I must repeat, though, that the same logic that applied to cigarette manufacturers applies to gambling venues such as the state lotteries. The fact that addiction resides *within* people in no way exonerates lotteries from the problems with gambling to which they have contributed. As with cigarette manufacturers, they are responsible for promoting a hazardous product to the public without having provided sufficient accurate information and warnings about its risks. Furthermore, as with cigarettes, lotteries lead to harmful effects through nonaddictive overuse alone. The highest per capita spending (and losing) on state lotteries occurs, for example, in the least wealthy areas,[2] making them truly a tax on the poor and vulnerable. Finally, state governments, unlike private companies, have the additional liability that they are, of course, supposed to be looking out for the welfare of the public.

———

You may remember from Mark's story in chapter 4 ("The Secret General") that at the heart of his compulsive gambling was the meaning to him of winning and losing. Mark originally thought that he gambled to make money, but we discovered that money was only a tool to have what was really significant to him. Rather than simply trying to win, he was trying to *be* a "winner"—someone of value and importance, instead of feeling like a failure as he had always experienced himself. We also learned that fueling the fire of his gambling was an intense insistence, a rage, never to return to that old trap of being a failure in which he had lived much of his life. In the end, knowing this old helplessness that he was powerfully driven to reverse through his attempt to be a "winner," Mark began to find nongambling ways to manage his feelings of failure when they arose.

If you suffer with compulsive gambling, you may recognize in yourself something similar to Mark's feelings about the importance, beyond money, of winning and losing. Certainly it is very common in gambling addiction for winning to mean some kind of a reempowerment. For Mark, it was his overall value as a person that was at stake. But you may find that winning reasserts your power against certain specific forms of helplessness. For example, consider Roger's story.

————

Roger McDaniel had worked for a large computer company for twelve years when he was abruptly laid off at the age of forty-five, along with many others in the firm. When this happened he was understandably upset and worried, but he had always considered himself a "go-getter," and he lost no time after he was let go setting to work rewriting his résumé, contacting job search consultants, and looking for help-wanted postings in trade magazines and on the Internet. Indeed, in spite of his bitter feelings about what had happened to him, he was at first optimistic. After all, he had not been fired because he was incapable of doing the job. As he liked to point out, "The company performed poorly—I didn't."

But months passed and Roger had not yet landed a new job. His family used up almost all of their savings. Roger reluctantly concluded that he had to start looking for stopgap jobs until he could find something in the computer field. This deflated him. And as the time continued to drag on, he became increasingly depressed.

About five months into his unemployment, he began to buy lottery tickets. By the time I met Roger, several months later, he had run up thousands of dollars of debt playing the lottery. When I asked him about his betting, his thoughts were straightforward. "It's a way out," he said. "I need money, a lot of it, and I figure this is about the only way to get it." But the more he lost, the greater was his need for money, and the more he bet to recoup his losses.

As you probably know, Roger's pattern of betting more to win back what he lost is called "chasing your losses." Although its purpose appears self-evident—to recover what has been lost—when it is part of a gambling addiction, there is, as usual, more to it than its simple financial meaning. Ultimately, Roger and I had to come to an understanding of his compulsion to gamble before we could comprehend his destructive "chasing" behavior.

Roger's gambling was certainly a response to his helplessness to find a job, as his history suggested. For months after losing his job Roger had been able to tolerate his unemployment, because he believed that his "go-getter" attitude, on top of his experience and knowledge, would soon yield him another position. But as time went by, and none of his diligent work was paying off, he felt more and more helpless, and more and more enraged. This was the point at which he began to buy lottery tickets.

But beyond this, his gambling was a response to a particular old helplessness that had been revived by his job loss. When Roger had said that losing his job had been the company's fault—due to *their* poor performance, not his—he was doing more than stating the facts. He was emphasizing his conviction that what had happened to him was unfair. He found it enraging to have a stable position in midlife taken forcibly from him—one that he had worked and studied for, and that he had performed well.

This became more understandable one day when Roger was talking about why it felt so awful to him to be helpless. As a child, he said he had often been picked on by larger boys. When this had occurred, he said the worst part for him was having to go home and be asked by his father whether he had been beaten up again. Usually, he denied it, he said, because it was shameful to him to admit this to his father. As an adult, Roger continued to harbor a deep feeling that being someone's victim was intolerable. And losing his job had felt like that to him. His "way out" of his helplessness through the lottery was not, then, just to make money, but was more deeply his attempt to reverse the intolerable powerlessness he felt inside. This is why his gambling was so compelled—

why it was an addiction. When Roger won, he felt that he was not helpless at the hands of his former employers who had let him go— nor at the hands of his old bullies.

Once Roger and I came to understand this meaning behind his gambling, his "chasing his losses" became clearer. While his gambling was an effort to take action against his intolerable sense of powerlessness, it had a terrible, unintended result beyond the loss of more money. Because of the meaning behind his gambling, when Roger lost, he was thrown back into feeling precisely the same powerless, shameful way he had felt when he lost his fights as a child. Thus in losing, instead of reversing his helplessness, he had reproduced it. *This* is what led him to chase his losses. He was compelled to try to reverse his losses by gambling again and again, because there was much more than money at stake—and because he was not aware of what that meaning of losing was. It was only later when he understood this that he began to regain control over his insatiable need to gamble.

Roger's experience is not unusual. If you suffer with compulsive gambling, you may have found yourself that while winning can make you feel, temporarily, like a "winner" (in whatever sense is important to you), losing can just as much make you feel like a "loser," often with devastating results. After losing, many people with compulsive gambling describe horrible feelings of depression that cannot be explained simply on the basis of monetary loss. If you find yourself in this position, it is helpful to remember that the reality of losing at gambling is not the same as its personal meaning to you. Losing your bets only means that you have been trying to reestablish, through gambling, some control over an area of your life that is critical to you, and this displaced attempt at control has backfired. But no matter how much you lose in dollars, no amount of financial loss ever means that *you* are a "loser."

———

Chasing losses is in fact just an example of the addictive cycle that I have described previously, where the addiction itself produces a helplessness—in feelings or results—that must be responded to with more addictive behavior. While this cycle is present in virtually every addiction, it is especially pernicious in compulsive gambling because gambling inevitably produces losing, and generally sooner rather than later.

Another characteristic, although not unique to compulsive gambling, is especially associated with it. This is a tendency for the addiction to corrupt your otherwise good logic. If you are a compulsive gambler, or know someone who is, you are probably familiar, for example, with superstitious ideas about luck. There are "lucky tables" at casinos, "lucky decks" of cards, "lucky numbers" to play the lottery, and so forth. In themselves, these ideas are common and are not necessarily a sign of compulsive gambling, but they assume a quality close to *beliefs* for some people who suffer with the addiction.

Making use of the new way of thinking about addictions, a reason for the emphasis on luck immediately jumps out. Since it is critical in addictions to reassert control against helplessness, it follows that anything that will aid this sense of control will be eagerly sought. A major problem with gambling, after all, is that by its very nature it cannot be accurately predicted. When you gamble, the result may be exactly the opposite of what you are seeking. So, in compulsive gambling, in addition to its underlying function of reasserting a sense of power against helplessness, there arises the additional need to reassert power over the outcome of the behavior itself. Believing that you have a way to know what is happening, or what is going to happen, can provide this needed sense of empowerment. "Knowing" about luck is a way to achieve this.

"I played that table while it was red hot," one man told me, "then I got away from it when it started to turn cold." He felt that he had wisely played the invisible patterns of luck. Another person who needed to make sense of random events was a woman who told me that she knew she was getting "closer" to winning the lottery because she had correctly matched first two, then three numbers in successive weeks. A third person was certain that his luck would change soon, because he had so much bad fortune recently playing blackjack. "It stands to reason," he said, "it's the law of averages!" No attempt to discuss the idea that each day of playing was an entirely separate event, as uninfluenced by prior days as successive flips of a coin, was helpful to him, since he needed to believe that he could predict his luck. He could not rethink this until he saw for himself why it was so particularly important to him to be in control of what happened to him, rather than be at the mercy of an uncaring fate.

You may be familiar also with another form of thinking that reflects the need to feel empowered against the powerlessness of gambling, namely a belief in a "system" of betting. Here, what is important is the ability to assert intellectual mastery by having figured out a way to beat the odds, either through calculation or through superior knowledge. A common example is the belief that one can figure out which way to bet on a professional sports event by carefully studying information about the teams. This seems reasonable until you realize that the odds, or the point spread, on these games are set on the basis of the collective wisdom of the whole population of bettors. The odds in fact are set in an active attempt to induce an equal amount of money to be wagered on both sides. This is why the betting line often shifts as a game approaches—the teams have not changed in strength, but the amount wagered on one side has become excessive, so the line is moved to induce more betting on the other team. Consequently, the odds or point spread on a game reflects not the opinion of any one bookmaker whom you can outsmart, but the amounts bet and the overall beliefs of everyone betting, and generally tends to reduce the choice between sides to a matter of guesswork. However, when there is a deeper need to prove one's power through the ability to bet correctly, people can lose track of such realities in the situation.

One man, whom I will call Earl, underscored this point when he told me of his surprising lack of interest in winning at the racetrack the day before. "I took home a couple of thousand dollars," he said, "and I don't know why, but it just doesn't seem like a big deal this time." He and I wondered for a while about this mystery until he casually mentioned that he had not picked the winning ticket. His friend, who had accompanied him to the track, had gone to the ticket window when Earl was in the bathroom, and as a lark had bought Earl a couple of tickets on a long shot. "Oh, when the horse came in, it was exciting all right," Earl said, "but, you know, it was like eating cotton candy. Nice for a minute, but then it sort of disappeared." This was unusual for Earl, who could talk at length about the fine details of handicapping horses, his notable wins in the past based on his extensive knowledge of the horses, the jockeys, the effect of the conditions of the track, past performances in big races, and so on. In this case, though, Earl could not attribute the win to his knowledge. All that he gained from this race was money, and, despite his focus on this, it was not what his addiction was about.

Another man had a system for betting on football games. It was very important to Garry to be able to outthink the betting line. This was so important, in fact, that in his view he never lost. Whenever his team failed to cover the point spread (win the bet for him), it was the fault of a much-cursed player or coach. If only he had not fumbled, or called the wrong play, then the system would have worked. Garry had made the right bet.

Garry's need to be right, as showed by winning via his use of his personal system, had originated in a history of feeling that he was the loser in a lifelong competition with his fraternal twin brother. *Thinking* had been highly prized in their family, but his brother had been universally judged to be the smarter twin. In light of this, it was not hard for either Garry or myself to understand the importance to him of reversing his helpless sense of being the "dumb" one, and his rage at the unknown bookmakers who were trying to outsmart him, which made his gambling into an addiction.

———

Garry's story also points up the way other people may become important as part of a gambling addiction. You may recall that with other addictions sometimes the addictive object, such as a drink, may itself stand in for a lost person. For example, you might remember the man sitting on a curb holding his bottle of wine and declaring that it was his friend (chapter 11). In these instances, a feeling of helpless isolation is counteracted through an attachment to the addictive object. In gambling addiction, a relationship to an important person may appear, as it did for Garry, as the competition. Or, another person may be the source of nurturance or supplies. For example, some people suffering with compulsive gambling have described a feeling of satisfaction from obtaining a bank loan that is similar to winning money on a bet. In both cases, there may be a feeling that one's needs are being cared about. This thinking can apply to a bookie who extends credit, and even to imaginary figures, such as Lady Luck, who may smile upon you, acknowledging your value. The importance of this is to think through the way you may place others in roles that are mostly symbolic, generally with a consequent loss of some ability to think clearly in the situation.

———

One attribute that is unique to compulsive gambling among addictions is the peculiar role of reality in this addiction. Like other addictive acts, the purpose and drive behind compulsive gambling arise internally, and the act's accomplishment of repudiating helplessness is also an internal, emotional achievement. It would be difficult for most addictive behaviors, like taking a drug, to actually achieve a reversal of powerlessness in the real world beyond the mind.

But gambling can do this. It provides a realistic, though tiny, chance of reversing its central harmful effect (loss of money) if one continues to perform the same behavior. If you suffer with compulsive gambling, you know that this reasoning can become a destructive rationalization for "chasing" your losses, betting ever larger amounts, and losing more and more. The grain of truth in thinking that the next bet will solve at least your financial problems has added to the difficulty of stopping for many people suffering with compulsive gambling. A slightly different form of this was illustrated by a woman with compulsive gambling whom I saw, who was in a near panic at the thought of no longer playing "her" number in the lottery. After a great many years of playing this number without any success, she was terrified that as soon as she stopped, the number would come up. There was indeed no way to deny that this was a possibility, however remote. At last, she could only stand to stop playing when she truly understood that what she was trying to achieve by winning had nothing to do with financial riches. She could stop playing, in other words, when she saw that even if her number did come up, it would not be the answer to the needs within her.

If you suffer with compulsive gambling and have been tortured by the tiny bit of truth in the idea that the next bet might be the big win, it will be helpful to remember this woman's story. Like her, even if you win it will not matter in the long run—since compulsive gambling is not about money. Like every addiction, it is about much more important things.

———

Another characteristic of compulsive gambling that seems to set it apart is that gambling inherently results in intermittent reinforcement—sometimes you win, sometimes you don't. As you may know, this kind of variable reinforcement is known to create habits that are especially difficult to break. This is because a negative result (not winning) in the course of this sort of variable pattern does not discourage further attempts, since negative results are routinely followed by positive ones—and this effect may be strong even if the positives are outweighed in number by the negatives.

However, though intermittent reinforcement can play a role in excessive gambling in general, the effect of this pattern in *compulsive* gambling is limited—because it bears only on the "habit" part of gambling, not the addiction. As I described earlier in discussing the difference between abuse and addiction (chapter 9), habits are only subsidiary factors when it comes to the deeper issues at stake in a true addiction. If you suffer with gambling addiction, then, the message is that although the peculiar habit-prolonging quality of intermittent reinforcement can make it harder to stop gambling, if you recognize this pattern, it need not stand in the way of mastering your addiction.

A final point about intermittent reinforcement is that it is not unique to compulsive gambling. Many other addictive acts have variable success rates. Each drink, drug, plate of food, Internet game, or trip to shop at the mall is not as satisfying of the addictive drive behind it as every other instance of the addiction. As with compulsive gambling, the reason the addiction persists is not because of its intermittent reinforcement, but because of the persistence of its underlying purpose and drive.

———

Another idea frequently raised about compulsive gambling is the notion that it is driven by the "thrill of the action." You may recall that this was what Mark (chapter 4) thought about his own betting. When we investigated this, though, we discovered that it was not the action that was thrilling, but the prospect of winning. There was no thrill for him in the action if he expected to lose. However, he had never noticed the difference between the thrill of the action and the expectation of winning, because whenever he bet, he expected to win. In turn, this expectation was based on his emotional need to win. If you suffer with compulsive gambling you may find the expectation of winning to be familiar. Being aware that you tend to think along these lines, you have reason to pause and reflect before making this the rationale for a bet.

Another reason for the popularity of the "thrill" idea as the drive behind compulsive gambling is the false idea I mentioned in chapter 8 ("Myths of Addiction"): the notion that people perform addictive acts in order to get a "high." As I said before, this is basically just a restatement of the ancient mistaken moralizing about addictions as pleasure-seeking behaviors. No addiction is fundamentally motivated by a search for pleasure. On the contrary, addictions are compulsively driven whether they lead to pleasure or not, and are determined by deeper factors than pleasure-seeking, as I have endeavored to show throughout this book.

A last variation on the "thrill" idea is expressed in the feeling that, win or lose, it is a thrill just to be "in action" (gambling). Here, the excitement is still ultimately dependent on the expectation of winning—there would be no thrill if you were certain you would lose—but it is more indirect; being "in action" itself is a solution to helplessness. When you think about it, this is not hard to understand. If you were trapped underground, it would be exhilarating just to crawl into a tunnel that offered the chance of getting out, whether it eventually led to freedom or not. Being "in action" is like this—the very act of playing is already a reversal of hopelessness and helplessness because it inherently offers the chance of a solution. This is basically the same idea as the satisfaction that people with alcoholism often feel just by ordering the drink. It should be clear that this is very different from the notion that what is being sought is the thrill itself. This is a helpful point to keep in mind, if you are a person who finds it thrilling just to be in action.

———

There are many forms of gambling. Sometimes, it does not matter which form is used or is available any more than it matters whether you are drinking beer or vodka if you suffer with alcoholism. But sometimes there is meaning in the choice. If gambling serves as a proof of mastery, skill, or intelligence, as was the case for some of the people I described above, it is necessary to gamble in a way that can supposedly demonstrate this, such as betting on sports. But the opposite may be true. One woman told me that she preferred the lottery over all other forms of gambling precisely because it was random. Her whole life she had resented the unfairness of favoritism bestowed on others. She was determined not only to win but to force others to have to compete with her on equal terms.

———

You may wonder what makes one person focus on compulsive gambling, while another person with an addiction drinks alcohol. The answers are best understood by getting to know people individually to find out their specific life stories. Among the factors that may play a role in compulsive gambling are an unusual focus on money in a family of origin or actual gambling in parents, with whom chil-

dren identify. But it cannot be denied that money is highly important to nearly everybody in our culture, often carrying meanings of
power and value. So it is not surprising that some people with no
particular family history will find in money a suitable focus for an
addictive drive. Given, too, the large overlap of compulsive gambling with other addictions (about 40 percent of people with compulsive gambling also suffer with alcoholism), there is no need to
hypothesize an entirely separate group of people prone to this
addiction over others.

———

Lastly, I must make a point about criminality and compulsive gambling. Many people suffering with this addiction have become
involved in illegal activities such as embezzling money in order to
have more funds with which to gamble—almost always to chase
losses. Illegal acts are so common that they are actually part of the
official diagnostic criteria for "Pathological Gambling" in the
DSM-IV. (Remember, though, that the DSM-IV is merely a
descriptive document without reference to understanding the condition. As I have mentioned before, it incorrectly characterizes
"Pathological Gambling" as an "Impulse-Control Disorder"—
which, as a compulsion, it is not.) However, if you suffer with
addictive gambling or care about someone who does, you should
know that the criminal activities associated with compulsive gambling are not the same as criminality, or sociopathy, in general. This
is not to say that illegal actions taken in the pursuit of this goal are
any less illegal. But when people with compulsive gambling steal
money, it is nearly always after they have run out of other sources
and is essentially another compulsive activity driven by the same
forces that lie behind the gambling addiction itself. The intent of
people with compulsive gambling who steal is generally not to
enrich themselves by taking from others, but through continued
gambling to recoup their losses. In fact, there is commonly a
thought that one will win enough to pay back people who are
owed. This is consistent with the fact that many compulsive gamblers work very hard, sometimes at two or more jobs, in order to

obtain more money to gamble. As a group compulsive gamblers are not trying to take advantage of others so much as they are driven by any means to satisfy the compulsion to gamble. The importance of the distinction about motives is in how to deal with the crimes. Because illegal acts committed as part of compulsive gambling are not a symptom of underlying sociopathy, it is better for courts to include treatment as a key part of any sentencing, rather than simply to lock people away.

SEVENTEEN

# *Sexual Addiction*

Of all addictions, sexual addiction may be the most private and experienced as the most shameful. Therefore, I will begin by addressing what may be the preeminent issue for you, if you suffer with this problem. Sexual addiction is like every other addiction—it is not more strange, more shameful, more perverse, or psychologically different from addictions focused on alcohol, gambling, or shopping. As an example, you may recall Robert's story (chapter 12), in which his phone sex addiction was just one of his two addictions. As mechanisms of the mind, there was no fundamental difference between the two addictions when you looked beneath the surface.

The underlying sameness of sexual addiction and other addictions is another example of the unity of all addictions. Of course, it is also true that the "choice" of displacement of the addictive drive to sex may have meaning, just as the choice of focus of an addictive drive may be important in other addictions. However, as with the relationship of money to compulsive gambling, or specific biological effects to drug addictions, it can be expected that in sexual addiction, although the focus is on sex, it is the *meaning* of sex that is important. Steven's story—whose beginning was on page 2 of this book—is an example.

————

A hard rain made it difficult for Steven to see out the windows of his car. His search was already hindered by the fact that in this weather the prostitutes would be huddling in doorways, instead of strutting openly as on most nights. But he had to find one. Almost every night, he had to find one. He had been cruising for prostitutes for years and knew many by name, and even a little about them as people. He favored some over others, because of how they looked, or because they did what he wished, but he had only a general sense about what made them so appealing. "So necessary," he corrected himself scornfully, as he drove. Steven took little pleasure from his search. It was true that he often achieved orgasm as a result of his liaisons, but he was clear in his own mind that if he could, he would rather take a few nights off and watch TV. Cruising was time-consuming and potentially danger-ous. Because he was almost exclusively interested in having fellatio performed on him, he was not as worried about contracting the HIV virus as he otherwise would have been. But there were other dangers—of being caught by the police, becoming exposed and los-ing his job, or being mugged or blackmailed. Prostitutes were also expensive, and Steven did not have any extra money from his civil service job. He once figured out that if he had never spent time with a prostitute he could have bought the beautiful boat he had always wanted.

The rain came down harder, and the temperature continued to drop. The forecast had said chance of snow flurries, but if this kept up it would be a full-blown snowstorm. Visibility was getting worse by the minute, and Steven decided to turn home. It was when he was halfway to the city condominium where he lived by himself that he came to a decision to see somebody about his problem. He was frustrated that he could not find a prostitute that evening, but he knew it was more than that; he had been coming to this decision for a long time. "This is just fucking ridiculous," he muttered to himself as he finally gained the entrance to his building's parking garage.

———

Steven was a thirty-five-year-old, tall, heavily built man with a thick beard. If he had been wearing a red checkered shirt and jeans instead of a coat and tie he might have been a model sent from central casting to play the stereotypical lumberjack. He greeted me with a strong handshake and fit himself carefully into the chair in my office, which suddenly seemed a bit small. After some brief pleasantries, Steven turned right to his reason for coming.

"As I said on the phone," he began, "I have a problem with going to prostitutes. It's been going on for years and I'm sick of it."

"What do you do with them?" I asked.

"It's basically fellatio. That's what I'm interested in. I tell them what I want, they do it, I pay them. That's it."

Steven did not say more and there was a pause.

"You make it sound pretty cut and dried," I said. "There must be some feeling about it, too."

He shrugged. "Maybe. Sometimes. I just want to get rid of it."

"Sure. It would be helpful to know more about the details, though, to understand it better."

Steven looked uncomfortable. "I guess. Maybe we can talk about something else first," he said. "I think that would be easier for me."

I nodded. "Okay. Why don't you tell me about yourself?"

———

Steven told me he grew up in a small city with both his parents, and two sisters, three and five years older. The family had no major problems, at least that could be seen from the outside, and lived in a middle-class neighborhood where Steven had many friends. His father was a pharmacist and his mother was a homemaker. Steven said the only tension in the family was between him and his older sisters, whom he viewed as favorites of both parents. When he was young the children often fought, and he remembered many instances of losing fights with them, of being physically held down and taunted, and of being forced to run errands for them.

"I wanted my sisters to include me in their games, so I guess I put up with a lot of stuff because of that," he said one day. "Besides, there wasn't much I could do. They were bigger than me, and if I ran to my mother, she pooh-poohed everything. To tell you the truth, I think she was fucked up. I think it was part of some problem that she had. She was always telling me I shouldn't be rough on them, without noticing what they were doing to me. It really felt like she had some kind of secret pact with them. And nobody really gave a shit about me." He took a deep breath. "Anyway," he went on in a softer voice, "I couldn't be running to my mommy all the time. I wasn't going to be a sissy."

I thought about what Steven had said. I asked him, "Where was your father in all this?"

He gave a bitter laugh. "He was the biggest sissy of all. *I* was tougher than he was. I don't think I ever saw him stand up to my mother." He shook his head. "Forget him. He was no help."

———

It was not long after we began meeting that Steven began to speak more freely about what he did with the prostitutes.

"I saw one two nights ago," he said one day, "a woman named Stacy. I've been with her before. She's pretty good."

"Tell me what's good."

He paused a moment. "Well, first off, she's my type. I'm a big guy, and I like big women. I don't mean fat, I mean tall, strong—a woman who can handle herself. And," he said with a shrug, "she goes along with me."

"Go on."

He took a breath. "Well, as I told you, she performs fellatio on me. And . . ." He paused, then seemed to make up his mind. "And she says the stuff I want her to say." Steven paused again. I waited for him to continue. "I tell them that I want them to ask me to suck my dick," he said, not looking at me. "Sometimes I want them to ask me a couple of times." He stopped talking and there was a silence.

"That's part of what makes it exciting?"

He cleared his throat. "Well, if you want to know the truth . . ." He took out a handkerchief and wiped his nose, then took a few moments to stuff the handkerchief back in his pocket. "If you want the truth . . . that's pretty much the thing that's exciting about the whole deal."

There was another pause. I said, "Her asking, that's what's important?"

He nodded.

"Can you say some more about it?"

He shrugged, then sat a second. "I don't know what else there is to say. That's always turned me on. I think it's in my bones or something."

A few seconds went by, then I said, "What does it feel like you're doing to them?"

Steven coughed. He removed his handkerchief and swiped at his nose again, before replacing it in his pocket. "Well . . ." He cleared his throat. "I think, I'm putting them down. You know, compared to me."

There was another silence. I said, "So, when you go cruising, are you specifically thinking about that interchange between you and the woman?"

Steven looked surprised. "Yes, of course."

"What I mean is, does it seem to you that you're driven by a buildup of sexual tension, or is it the idea of their asking you that seems to drive you on—if you can distinguish between them?"

Steven thought for a minute. "Well, it's not sexual tension, I'm sure of that. The fact is that I have trouble sometimes getting it up when I'm with them, you know? I mean, I'm not seventeen anymore, and I'm out almost every night."

I nodded, and said, "Do you always request that the women do exactly the same thing? Does it ever vary?"

Steven thought again. "No, not really. Sometimes, the women don't want to do it—saying what I want—so I try to do without it."

"How does that work?"

He shook his head and frowned. "It doesn't."

"How do you mean?"

"Well, first, I've got to say it makes me so damned mad." He shook his head. "I'm not real proud of this, but sometimes I throw stuff around. I don't think I know what I'm doing. I don't hurt the women or anything, it's just that I lose it, sometimes." He took a breath. "Anyway, what do I mean it doesn't work? It's no good, that's all. Half the time I can't get off. And even when I do, it's not worth the trouble. I could stay home and masturbate and save the money."

There was a silence. I said, "Well, I guess we know where to look for the source of this addiction, then." Steven looked at me with his eyebrows raised. "I think you're saying it's not really about sex," I said, "it's about the asking."

———

As Steven and I continued to meet, we gradually clarified what you have probably already figured out. Knowing his life story, it was not hard for us to see that he was driven to repeat the asking scene with prostitutes because it enacted an enraged reversal of the powerlessness that he had suffered at the hands of his older sisters when he was small. Now, the prostitutes stood in for his sisters, and he could "put them down" as he had felt—and at times literally was—put down by his sisters. Furthermore, the rage he felt when the prostitutes refused to comply with his wishes is readily understandable as the rage at his powerlessness that drove his addiction to begin with. When he could not express this long-standing feeling in his addictive act, it emerged as a blind fury.

We also came to understand that Steven selected tall and strong women among the prostitutes not for the reason he initially thought—that he was a big guy, so he liked big women—but in fact it was the opposite. Since the prostitutes were standing in for his sisters, who, when this all began, really were bigger and stronger, it was valuable for the meaning of the act that they looked the part. Put another way, Steven choose these particular women not because he was a big guy, but because once he had been a little guy.

_____

Eventually, then, we worked out the purpose and drive behind Steven's sexual addiction, and they fit the general pattern of the psychology of addiction. And the meaning of his addictive behavior turned out to be quite different from the simple expression of a sexual drive—just as other addictions are driven by meanings that are not evident from their superficial focus. With this awareness, Steven, like others with addictions, could begin to take control of his addictive behavior.

However, you may still question why Steven's addiction was specifically sexual. He might, after all, have developed another way of expressing the feelings behind his addiction, without it involving sex. Why was this a *sexual* addiction?

First, an indirect answer. As you know, it is common for addictions to shift focus. When this happens, it appears that one addiction replaces another. This can be true when sex is the object of the addiction, as well. So, from this point of view, there does not have to be a specific reason for the sexual focus—it may be one among many possible ways to express the underlying purpose and drive. This is admittedly not a satisfying answer to the question I raised, but I mention it because it would be wrong to think of sexual addictions as having such a separate identity that they cannot be interchanged with other addictive focuses.

More significantly, there is something special about sex—needless to say. It is a central part of everybody's identity and emotional life. Because of that, conflicts involving sexuality are extremely common, and they regularly involve matters far beyond physical sex alone. Problems with worthiness, potency, attractiveness, lovability, capacity to be an equal with other adults, capacity to relate in an emotionally intimate way, questions about the right to have pleasure for oneself, and more, are frequent accompaniments of difficulties that have a focus on sex. Since sex is such a meeting ground for feelings, it is to be expected that sometimes the emotions that give rise to addictions have a significant sexual component, or may be expressed through a sexual means.

How would this apply to Steven? It would be simple if Steven had been involved in some specifically sexual interaction with his sisters, but he was not. However, that did not mean he had no awareness of sexual roles and stereotypes. In fact, Steven remembered very clearly from an early age that part of what was humiliating for him was his idea that "they were girls, and girls are supposed to be weaker than boys." His view of his mother as favoring his sisters contributed to his feelings—*all* the females in the family seemed to be against him. And, his father's passivity contributed to his considerable anger and anxiety about the power of women.

Although Steven had not reached puberty at the time the trouble occurred with his sisters, when he did, he brought with him into adolescence all the rage and the special determination to establish himself as a dominant man that he had built up over the years. Not surprisingly, these feelings became closely linked with his emerging sexuality. As a teenager, he frequently masturbated with thoughts very much like the ones he later enacted with prostitutes. His subsequent addiction, then, reflected feelings that had acquired a sexual character years before. Putting this another way, Steven's addiction was sexual because of its roots in experiences that came to have a sexual meaning for him.

———

For other people suffering with sexual addiction, of course, the issues behind the addictive act may be quite different. You may recall that Robert (chapter 12) addictively called 900 numbers for phone sex because he felt trapped in his marriage, and when he made the calls he felt free. As one more illustration, here is a brief look at another person's struggle with a sexual addiction.

———

Ron did not come to see me because of his sexual addiction, but because he was lonely and depressed. At twenty-eight years old, he had never had a steady girlfriend, and had few men friends. His job in a large corporation kept him in his cubicle, or at least he kept himself there, from the time he walked in each morning until he left. He ate lunch at his desk and did not share in water cooler talk with other employees because, he said, he had no interest in sports or gossip or the latest sensational news.

Ron wanted to have more relationships, but he said that he did not know how to go about it. When he went on a few dates, he had felt awkward, and had said little. He never felt the women he dated had a good time, so he hardly ever called them again. The one or two times he did call, he was politely turned down.

It was only after we met a few times that Ron told me that he spent a good deal of his time when he was not working watching pornographic videotapes and, rarely, having sex with prostitutes. He had been viewing the tapes since he was about eighteen years old, and had been seeing prostitutes for the past four years. He explained that he had repeatedly tried to give up these sexual activities, because he felt it was "abnormal" to spend so much time on them, and because he knew that his involvement with them increased his isolation and added to his reluctance to allow anyone to get to know him.

Ron had grown up with both his parents and a brother four years younger until he was seven years old, when his mother died in an automobile accident. When he first told me about this, he said that he remembered little either about his mother or about her death. He also had no clear memories of his or his father's reaction to their loss, and said he could not recall any time, then or later, that he and his father talked about his mother. Ron's father did not remarry, and Ron described the three of them in the family living a quiet life, with little he could recall to document the passing of the years. He said he could not think of any problems from his childhood, but he also could not remember times that were especially happy, or any occasions when the family did special things together.

Hearing this story, I wondered if Ron, and perhaps his father and even his brother, had been depressed for many years. It was impossible to know what the family had been like before his mother died. But it was clear that the pattern of isolation that Ron exhibited as an adult had been almost lifelong.

I also wondered, of course, about the connection of his early loss with his sexual addiction. However, Ron did not speak about his mother after telling me of her death, so if there was a connection it was not evident on the basis of what Ron was saying. Indeed, Ron had little to say about his addiction altogether. When I asked about what he liked to watch in the videotapes, for example, he had almost no thoughts about it. "I like to watch them have sex," he said. Asking him to elaborate, he could only think of the fact that he was not interested in anything he described as "kinky," and that he did not care for scenes involving any kind of group sex. Other than that, he said, "It's pretty simple," and it was clear that this was just how he felt about it.

We had been working together for a little while when Ron told me one day that he was thinking of finding a prostitute again. He had continued to rent pornographic videos, but had not been with a prostitute since we started meeting.

"What brought this to mind?" I asked him.

"This always happens. I think I told you that I would go with prostitutes more, if I could afford it. When it's been a long time, I feel like I've got to go find someone."

"You've been watching the videotapes, though."

"Yes."

"They're not enough?"

"No. Not after a while."

"What happens after a while to make them not enough?"

"They're just not the same. It's not the real thing."

What Ron was saying seemed obvious. But he had said so little about his sexual feelings that I asked him if he could say more about this.

"I'm just thinking about the real thing when I'm watching them anyway," he replied.

"Thinking about having sex with a woman."

"Yes."

"And when you're watching the scene, you're in it."

"Yes. I'm the guy in the scene."

I thought a minute. Ron had said this before, but today was the first time he had drawn a distinction between watching the pornographic tapes and being with a real woman. "What's the difference between the tapes and the real thing?" I asked him.

Ron looked at me blankly. I waited a moment, but he seemed at a loss to find something to say.

I said, "My question doesn't make sense to you?"

Ron looked troubled. After another few seconds, he said, "I don't know how to answer."

"Well, what comes to mind?"

For the first time since we had met, I thought I saw some feeling in Ron's face. His cheeks reddened, and it looked like he almost had tears in his eyes. There was a silence, then he said with a slight quaver in his voice, "It's warmer with a real woman." A tear rolled down his cheek, and we were both quiet for a minute.

I said softly, "After a while, the tapes aren't enough. You need the warmth."

His head bent, and he began to weep silently.

———

When Ron said that what drew him to the pornographic videotapes was pretty simple, he was telling me something that was deeply true, although neither of us understood it at the time. After the session in which he cried, he began to talk about the fantasy he had watching the tapes—actually, he realized for the first time that he had a fantasy. It was indeed simple—that he was very close with a woman, close enough to feel her warmth, and close enough to be warmed by her. This is what he had to seek, and what compelled him to watch tape after tape, year after year. His powerful yearning for closeness was also what made him so awkward and uncomfortable when he was with a woman, except with prostitutes whom he knew would allow him to be close.

When Ron began to understand this, he started for the first time to feel some control over his urges to watch pornographic tapes. At the same time, in our sessions, he began to talk more about his loneliness, in the present and the past, which led to his yearnings for closeness. He still did not have any clear memories of his mother, but in small ways he began to bring her into the room—in references to his uncle, her brother, about whom he did have fond memories, and to the garden she had tended behind their house.

Ron's sexual addiction was an effort to reverse the helplessness of his loss, the loneliness and emptiness into which he had been thrust when his mother died, and which had continued in the years afterward with his depressed father. It seems clear that it was during these years that Ron himself began to withdraw. The intensity of the drive behind his addiction reflected the kind of basically healthy insistence on not being helpless—for Ron, not being left alone—that I have tried throughout this book to show is present behind all addictions.

––––––

If you suffer with a sexual addiction, you may find that, like the people I have described, you can trace the meaning of your addiction to issues of helplessness that have little to do with adult sexuality itself. Certainly, if you are aware of specifically sexual experiences that have been important for you, those could bear on your addiction. But even if that is the case, keep in mind that it is always the meaning of the events that matters, not just that they occurred. Working this out is an area where you might want to find professional help (I discuss this in the next chapter).

––––––

Before closing this chapter, a word needs to be said about the relationship of sexual addiction to so-called sexual perversions (better called "paraphilias"). The latter are conditions in which some special requirement must be met for a person to reach orgasm during sex. Steven, for example, was excited by his enacting a form of dominance over the prostitutes he sought. He had trouble reaching climax if they did not agree to participate in the scene he was driven to create. Traditionally, the term "sexual perversion" has been reserved for circumstances in which the special condition is obligatory—when it is impossible to reach orgasm without the performance or presence of the required action or prop. In Steven's case, this was not entirely true; he preferred the scene to be as he asked, but he could reach orgasm without it.

More important, as Steven's story makes evident, a sexual "perversion" is no more and no less than a manifestation of underlying feelings and conflicts—no different from any other manifestation of emotional distress. Unfortunately, as you know, the word "perversion" itself has come to mean deviant in a particularly degrading way—an important reason to replace it with the word "paraphilia." Part of the bad reputation of paraphilias, of course, comes from awful stories of other people being forced to participate in these acts against their will. But apart from coercing others into situations in which they are not freely participating, the need for special requirements to achieve orgasm ought not to have any quality of degradation, or any special moralizing about it.

But is there any connection of paraphilias with sexual addiction? The answer is seen just by comparing their descriptions. Paraphilias are variations from usual ways of having sex, while sexual addictions are intense drives to have some form of sexual activity. It follows that some of the time, the underlying themes that lead to paraphilias may also lead to addiction. As an example, consider a man who suffered with the paraphilia of exhibitionism. His need to exhibit himself arose from a need to be seen and admired, to be acknowledged as a man, via the reactions of others to his self-exhibition. These same factors lay behind the addictive repetition of this behavior. When the meaning of his paraphilia became clear, so did the meaning of his addiction. Hence, sexual addictions may, or may not, involve paraphilias in the particular *form* that they take. Likewise, paraphilias may or may not be addictions—they may simply be requirements for the individual while having sex.

This is important to keep in mind if you suffer with a sexual addiction, or care about someone who does. More than once, I have heard someone angrily refer to a person with an addictive sexual activity as "a pervert," not grasping the meaning of either perversion or addiction, or the lack of basis for moralizing about either.

EIGHTEEN

# *Treatment*

Throughout this book, I have tried to show how you can take control over an addiction by understanding its psychology—using that knowledge to turn the tables on the urge to repeat an addictive behavior by using the urge itself as a signal. I have tried to show that, using this signal, you can find an alternative solution that more directly addresses the underlying purpose behind your addictive act. In a sense, I have hoped to provide the awareness about how addictions work that you might have been able to discover if you were in a therapy yourself with someone familiar with the ideas which I have published in the scientific literature, and that I have presented in this book.

I certainly hope that if you do have an addiction, the understanding I have described here will by itself—with some practice—be sufficient to gain control of your addictive behavior. However, there will likely be many of you who will want to use this knowledge as a springboard to pursue treatment in a professional setting. In this chapter I will discuss some of the major issues in the treatment of addictions. Before turning to professional treatment, I will consider self-help groups.

## TWELVE-STEP PROGRAMS

As you know, these programs have helped some people, but they also have significant limitations, many of which I have already discussed. I will first briefly review some of the limitations and problems of twelve-step programs, then discuss how and why they can be helpful for those who make use of them.

To begin with, as a one-size-fits-all approach, these programs tend to be uninterested and unhelpful in understanding the individual emotional factors that determine addictive behavior. Just as serious, they tend to shame those who do not benefit from their approach. People who do not improve are regularly told that they have not "gotten it" or have not "worked the program" hard enough.

Making people feel foolish or bad if they do not benefit is consistent with AA's uncritical attitude toward itself. Unlike professional approaches, there is no effort within twelve-step programs to advance their understanding of the treatment of addiction, alter their program based on its results, or suggest other treatment if theirs is not working well. Such an approach would obviously be unacceptable in any medical, psychological, or other professional treatment. It reflects the self-reinforcing nature of having a group of people all of whom believe in the same program. Without attempting to investigate or understand their successes and failures, AA and the other twelve-step programs are insular by nature. Put another way, these programs do not seem to recognize the nature of their "sampling bias." By attending only to their own success stories, they create an impression that everyone outside their group, if they only believed or worked hard enough, would do as well with their approach.

A corollary of this is that a number of people who have done well in AA have written or talked about it, while, needless to say, one does not see many articles from people who have not been able to benefit from AA. This is another kind of sampling bias, unscientifically tilting public impression toward the correctness and usefulness of AA. One particularly unfortunate result of this has been its influence on people in positions of authority to make health care decisions. Too many people in governmental or court positions buy the idea that twelve-step programs or counseling based on them are the only, or the best, way to approach the problem of addiction.

Some of the traditions and advice of twelve-step programs are also harmful, as I have discussed (particularly in chapter 8, "Myths of Addiction"). For example, advice such as to try to avoid being angry is, as you know, particularly unwise counsel to give to somebody struggling to understand and master an addiction. Likewise, myths of needing to surrender your willpower, or that you should count your days of sobriety—both tenets of AA—are also frequently unhelpful or even harmful. Surrendering your willpower suggests that because you have an addiction you should give up on your ability to manage it, and is the opposite of what is needed if you are to use your understanding to actively take control over it. Counting sober days contains the moralistic and often destructive idea of returning to zero after a slip, which inappropriately gives the messages that you have failed and that you deserve this harsh punishment. As I said earlier, many people have told me of how injured they have felt by this, with its punitive character sometimes even precipitating further addictive behavior.

Indeed, there is quite a bit of unfortunate moralizing in twelve-step programs. For example, in Step Four, you are directed to take a "fearless moral inventory" of yourself. From a positive standpoint, this may be helpful to some people who have difficulty examining themselves. But this also carries the unmistakable message that having an addiction means that you had better spend time looking at your moral failings, as if either addiction or the emotional factors that contribute to it were at heart moral issues.

————

The many limitations of AA and other twelve-step groups have made them unpalatable to the majority of people who have tried this approach, but without a doubt there is a group who have found that they were helped to achieve sobriety through their devotion to this program. How does it work? Besides its quality as a mutual support, when it works best it relies on substituting an external omnipotent power for an addictive action—for instance, drinking. Members are encouraged to acknowledge that they have failed to be able to control their own lives, and to turn over their will to a "higher power." AA asserts that this will be helpful in controlling what they call their members' "misuse of willpower,"[1] to which AA attributes the problem of addiction. But from the perspective of the understanding of addictions I have been describing in this book, it is not hard to see another way that this could be helpful.

AA is encouraging people to make a shift in their source of power and strength. When people can make use of this idea, they give up their addictive behavior which had produced a needed sense of mastery and control, and replace it with the AA concept of the "higher power," or an idealized view of AA itself.[2] That is, the restoration of power against helplessness that was sought through an addictive act is supplied instead through a *relationship* to an omnipotent figure—one that can provide a sense of strength and security. With such a connection in one's mind, there is less sense of helplessness. And when this works, it is clearly an improvement over the addiction.

The main limitations of this approach follow from its not helping to understand the basis for addictive behavior. Because of this, it does not aid in finding actions that would more directly address what is driving your own individual addictive act, or in understanding yourself so that you can take control of the addiction without relying on the twelve-step organization or its "higher power" concept. This becomes important for people who do achieve sobriety in AA but then lose it. Often, they find that their previous devotion to AA or the higher power idea has waned, leaving them with nothing within themselves to manage their addiction. It is at just this point that they are often told that they need to devote themselves harder to the organization's ideas—rather than understand what has caused the slip. For some people, this can result in a brittleness in the sobriety they achieved through twelve-step programs. When they cannot reinvest themselves in the organization or its ideas at the point of resumption of drinking, they often leave it, sometimes feeling worse about themselves than when they began.

―――

Although it is not the principal goal of twelve-step programs, it has been noted by some that they may be helpful for people who have had a problem with acknowledging limitations in themselves.[3] Although AA's emphasis on humility and admitting defeat is excessive, it is true that some people may gain from this in their capacity to question themselves in a healthy way. For them, this can be a valuable benefit. However, I do not agree with AA's overall view that people with addictions have an insufficient amount of humility. That idea is an aspect of the moralistic view of addictions that is so much a part of twelve-step programs. For those people who have gained in the area of humility, then, I believe it is a benefit that aided an aspect of them that is separate from the problem of their addiction.

Another useful aspect of twelve-step programs can be their focus on a shared commitment to take good care of yourself. This is valuable especially for those who have some problem with "self-care" as I described in Chapter 11. Again, this problem, while sometimes present along with an addiction, is a separate matter from it. However, this pleasant, supportive quality of twelve-step programs does explain why there are some people who like to attend AA meetings even though they do not have an addiction themselves. Group support is valuable for almost everyone.

―――

To summarize, twelve-step programs can be useful under certain circumstances. For those of you who can make use of the "higher power" idea, these programs may help you to abstain from addictive behavior. If you do decide to try one of them, you may find it helpful to take from the program what you can use, while leaving aside some of their less helpful, or actually hurtful, ideas. You should be aware, however, that you may experience some pressure to accept everything in the program. Do not let yourself, in any event, feel ashamed or as though you are to blame if this one-size-fits-all approach is not for you.

———

Twelve-step programs can also be a supportive adjunct to a professional therapy, so long as your investment in the twelve-step program does not prevent you from being thoughtful about the meanings behind your addiction. There are many people, in fact, who have been able to combine twelve-step programs with an individual or group professional therapy. If you do this, you may find that the need for the twelve-step program lessens over time as you come to understand your addiction better and have other more specific ways to master it. Should you find that your investment in a twelve-step program decreases with greater understanding of your addiction, you will also have the possibility of eventually being able to end treatment. AA and its analogues have, of course, no provision for termination—the program is intended to be a permanent lifestyle.[4] In my experience, some people are able to internalize enough of a sense of empowerment that they are eventually able to stop their attendance at AA meetings. However, there are many others who, while they can benefit from the program, cannot fully internalize the key element of empowerment—so they must attend forever in order to remain sober. Indeed, the anxiety that some people suffer about leaving AA can contribute to their fervor in insisting that *everyone* must stay forever, and to hostility toward those who feel less need to continue in the program. The lack of an end point in twelve-step programs is one of the unfortunate consequences of their not addressing the individual factors that lead people to have an addiction. Since the treatment relies on the attachment to the organization and its ideals, rather than making use of your mind to understand your addiction, it often does not leave you in a strong position to master your addiction yourself.

## PROFESSIONAL THERAPY

Since addictions are psychological problems, it makes sense that people who are trained and knowledgeable about human psychology are in an especially strong position to help you with them. Indeed, a well-known study that looked at prediction of treatment outcome in people with addictions found that the most important prognostic indicator in these people was the level of their emotional strengths, not the level of severity of their addiction itself.[5] There is, in fact, a big difference between people who are trained to think about your problem psychologically and others who mainly know the twelve steps of AA. Of course, it is valuable for otherwise well-trained therapists to be familiar with the psychology of addiction, and not every therapist has been trained or experienced in this field. I will return to how to find a good therapist at the end of this chapter.

———

To begin, as I hope has been clear, old concerns about psychotherapy not being helpful for people with addictions are simply wrong. They were based on mistaken notions that therapists could not both pay attention to the addiction itself, and at the same time, help people with the emotional factors behind them.[6] As I hope you can see from the cases I have described in this book, it is quite possible to pay very close attention to an addiction while understanding the psychology behind it. Indeed, this is the best way to approach the problem. Even when crises arise, such as a need for hospitalization for detoxification, they may be taken in stride both in practical terms of dealing with whatever needs to be done immediately, and in working to find out the factors that have led to the crisis.

The other reason concerns had been raised about psychotherapy for addictions was based on the mistaken idea that if you have an addiction, you are incapable of thinking about it or dealing with the emotions that lie behind it. Besides being insulting to people with addictions, this idea was harmful in discouraging therapists from working in this area. Fortunately, more and more therapists have learned to discard this inappropriate advice.

This brings up a related issue—whether people should, somehow, stop their addictive behavior first before even beginning a psychotherapy! As strange as it sounds, this has been advised in the past—again mainly because people did not understand addiction or did not believe that people could address their addictions in therapy. A consequence of this notion was an old model in which people were actually turned away from therapy and told to go to AA, or another twelve-step program, then come back when they were sober (or otherwise abstinent). Of course, this left people with no choice, and the many who could not make use of twelve-step programs were out of luck. A related matter was an idea that even in therapy, therapists should first only talk about narrow practical details of an addiction, such as reminding people to avoid walking down the street where a bar is located, before considering any other aspects of a person's emotional life. As you can tell from the many stories I have described, this is not necessary and in fact it delays the work of the treatment.

With regard to continued addictive behavior during therapy, as I have said before, while "slips" are not desirable, they can be turned to advantage in helping to learn about the factors that precipitated them. In fact, there are basically only two kinds of reasons why continued addictive behavior should lead to an interruption in therapy. The first is when addictive behavior leads to a crisis or an emergency that must be attended to before all else. The second reason is more general—it is essentially a judgment about whether continued addictive behavior interferes with the therapy itself to such an extent that it cannot usefully proceed. An example of this would be addictive behavior, such as drinking, causing a person to miss so many sessions that the treatment cannot advance. However, it should be clear from all the cases I have described in which some degree of addictive behavior continued during treatment, that interrupting therapy ought to be a very unusual event. It is, after all, more common than not for people to have slips during treatment, just as people usually do not suddenly cease other behaviors they are concerned about at the moment they enter a treatment for them. Indeed, except for the obvious concern about immediate dangers from an addictive behavior—which of course need to be addressed—the notion that anyone should be cast out from treatment just because he or she still suffers from the problem that led to beginning treatment is plainly illogical.[7]

A final word about therapy in general. I said that twelve-step programs do not consider whether people are appropriate for their approach, nor do they refer people elsewhere because they think something else would be better. Professional therapists, however, routinely make just this sort of evaluation and adjust accordingly. A therapist may, for example, suggest that you try a twelve-step program along with individual therapy to see if you can benefit from the combination. Or, you may be referred to a professional group therapy or couples therapy instead of, or along with, individual treatment. Therapists may also make suggestions about the frequency of meeting according to your individual situation. Each of these plans has merit in specific circumstances. Naturally, you should expect that the therapist will discuss his or her thinking about these ideas with you, but the point is that treatment should be the result of a careful assessment of you, individually. You cannot wear the same size as everyone else, nor should you.

## SUCCESS AND FAILURE

In describing the stories of people in this book, I have tried to convey that success is hard-won. Like the people I have described, most folks who are struggling with addictions do not become well overnight, and their course of treatment is not a straight line.

On the whole, what allows people to succeed in treatment is a capacity to be thoughtful about themselves, even if they sometimes are not aware that they have this capacity when they begin. People who truly cannot think about their own thoughts and feelings, or cannot attend to the therapy in any significant way, may be better off in another form of treatment that does not look at individual factors.

Sometimes people begin a therapy and appear to have the ability to pursue it, but then bog down. What goes wrong when therapy does not succeed? To begin with, it is critical to distinguish treatment failure from what is merely a delay in moving forward. Here is a brief example of the latter.

————

Hank was a forty-two-year-old man who had come for treatment because of his addictive use of marijuana and alcohol, and after some initial gains, it appeared that he was making no progress in treatment. He had spent most of his childhood in foster homes. We had come to understand that when he used drugs, he experienced a sense of empowerment against the helplessness he had felt ever since he had to endure the frequent moves and losses of his youth. Hank called the feeling he had about using drugs "getting away," and his intense urge to use them arose whenever he felt he was ignored or rejected. Through using drugs, or just the thought of using them, he felt he "got away" from the awfulness of his rejection to a place where he was not subject to the whims of those in charge, who did not care about him.

Despite this understanding, there had been only very modest progress in relinquishing his use of both of his drugs. When he felt an addictive urge, occasionally he could catch himself and figure out what had precipitated it, and there were times when he could find a more specific solution to his feeling. On some of these occasions, he was able to put his feelings of rejection into perspective on the basis of what he understood about them, so he was not emotionally caught up again in his old sense of helplessness. At some other times, he found he could either speak up for himself or take an action that directly dealt with his feelings of being slighted. For example, after he received a poor review at his work, an occasion that always would have precipitated drug use in the past, he arranged to see his supervisor's supervisor to talk about the way he had felt overlooked and ignored.

But these successes were infrequent. No matter how hard we worked together, and no matter how clear his understanding of his

addiction seemed to be, after a point his addiction appeared relatively unaffected. Since such apparent plateaus are not unusual in
any psychotherapeutic treatment, for addictions or anything else,
we both persisted with the general idea that there must be more
that we did not yet understand.

The light began to dawn for us when Hank again used drugs just
before I went on a vacation. He had experienced this as another
rejection. But what was new was that he began to speak of his ideas
that I had left because he was not doing well. He knew that this was
not true—he knew that I left because it was a planned vacation—
but the idea of my leaving him brought something else to his mind.
He had the thought, "If I do stop using drugs, then he will be
gone forever"—because Hank would no longer need to be in treatment. For this man who had suffered so much abandonment, this
was intolerable. Hence, we found out that he had continued to use
drugs for the very same reason we already knew about—to reverse
his feelings of helpless abandonment—but we had not appreciated
how this fear of abandonment had silently arisen in his feelings
about the treatment itself. His long plateau in therapy was now
comprehensible. As we worked with this new awareness, Hank was
able to let himself use the tools he already had to take control over
his addiction. Once his fear of what would happen if he got better
was in the open, it became safe for him to give up drugs, as we continued to work on the matters that underlay his addiction.

———

Hank's story is only one example. Other people hit a plateau specifically because of the progress they are making. For example, when
people begin to see the anger and hurt that may lie behind an
addictive behavior, they often have to accept this part of themselves
slowly. One woman told me that she hated angry people and was
certain that she was never going to be one of them. Since there was
a lot of anger behind her addiction, this meant that we had to tread
slowly through the complexity of her feelings. In general, it is a fact
of life that treatment has its overtly slow parts. But most of the
time, these periods are no more quiescent than the apparent life-

lessness of a tree in winter—a lot is going on that cannot be seen from the outside.

Sometimes people question whether there is "time" for this process, in the treatment of something as potentially dangerous as addictions. I have already said that there must always be an ongoing evaluation of whether a therapy should be interrupted because of a crisis or emergency. However, the fact is that there is no time to *not* investigate the feelings and conflicts underlying addictions. It is just the failure to do this that wastes people's time in repetitive treatments that do not ever get to the heart of the matter and do not help in controlling the addiction—as when people came for their two-hundredth admission to the detoxification program in which I used to work.

In terms of whether an addiction can be at least controlled before the deeper issues are resolved, this happens regularly. For some, this means total abstinence, for others it means some degree of addictive behavior while they are resolving underlying issues—though abstinence is still the final goal. But as long as the addiction is not dangerous or there is not a steady downhill course, the therapy can and must continue.

———

What about real treatment failures? Assuming that the therapist is knowledgeable and competent, there are just a few basic ways that therapies fail, and they are related to each other. One is if a person is not truthful with the therapist about his or her addiction. I am not referring here to hesitancy to say things, which is perfectly normal. Nor am I speaking of minimization of a problem, which is also quite common, especially at the beginning of treatment. However, a pervasive failure to let the therapist know whether you are repeating your addictive behavior can effectively undermine the process.

The second way treatments fail is when there is an ongoing powerful negative reaction to a therapist, not because the therapist is inappropriate, but as a repetition of old angry feelings toward important early figures in a person's life. When this persists it can make it impossible for the two of you to work together. Again, I must immediately qualify this by saying that both negative and positive feelings toward a therapist are perfectly normal and expectable. In fact, talking about these feelings that regularly arise in the relationship between you and your therapist is, as you may know, an especially good way to explore and understand them. Often, these feelings that occur "in the room" are experienced as much more meaningful than if the same feelings were talked about in a more abstract way. So, I am not referring to *having* negative feelings about a therapist.

The problem arises only when these feelings are not talked about, but instead are enacted in a pervasive way. For example, one man with a gambling addiction had been beaten often by his father as a child for not living up to his father's standards. Over time, he transferred many of the same feelings of bitterness and rage toward his therapist. In itself, this might have been a fruitful source of investigation. Indeed, knowing his past, this transfer of negative feelings to the therapist was to be expected. Unfortunately, though, the form that these feelings took was in an absolute determination to prove that his therapist could not be helpful to him, to frustrate the therapist in the way that he himself had suffered as a youngster. He did this mainly via a kind of pseudocompliance, virtually "yes-ing" the therapy into destruction. The problem here was that his father had tried to beat him into submitting to the father's superior knowledge and wisdom. Now, this man was never going to "submit" to anyone's taking a "superior" role with him, which included any therapist who would presume to have something to offer him.

Again, in itself, this problem is not insoluble. Whether it leads to treatment failure depends entirely on whether the individual with these powerful feelings can find some way to work with the therapist, even while he still harbors this intense reaction. Under many circumstances, this kind of problem can be successfully resolved. But not always. Sometimes the problem wins. So, if you find yourself in a therapy in which you can recognize that your negative feelings toward the therapist are a repetition of elements of your own life, you should be watchful for whether this is under-mining the treatment. And if matters reach a complete blockade, you and your therapist may want to obtain a consultation with another experienced therapist who can often be helpful in sorting this out.

The third major way that therapies fail is when people drop out of them in the middle. Sometimes this happens as the result of the kind of negative feelings I just described. At other times, people leave prematurely because the feelings brought up seem too much to face. If you are engaged in a therapy and are contemplating quitting, you should give yourself the chance to talk this over carefully with the therapist. This is all the more true if you are thinking of leaving because you have negative feelings toward the therapist. Remember, if you have selected a therapist who is trained in psychotherapy, he or she will listen to your criticisms or concerns with the aim of both considering their realistic basis (therapists must always consider their own role in their interaction with people they treat) and trying to understand any underlying basis for them within you. You do not want to be one of the people simply in a plateau phase of treatment who quits before the therapy can move on.

## HOW TO SELECT A THERAPIST

In this chapter, I have been talking about psychotherapy, the kind of work I have described in all the cases in this book. This kind of treatment differs from addiction "counseling" in both its focus and purpose, and in the training of the therapist. Addiction "counseling" is mainly directed at motivating you via underlining the costs to you of addictive behavior, informing you about the tenets of AA, and supporting you in sticking with that program indefinitely. Psychotherapy for addictions is, on the other hand, interested in uncovering the emotional factors within you as an individual that create the meaning and drive behind your addiction, enabling you to master addictive behavior by working out its causes. A result of this is that you are able to manage your addiction yourself; it is not necessary to permanently attend treatment.

The training of many counselors, compared with psychotherapists, also differs. As I mentioned concerning the myth that you should be treated by someone who also has an addiction (chapter 8), an unfortunately large number of people who are addiction counselors feel they are qualified just because they are familiar with the AA program. Often this group of counselors have little or even no training in human psychology. Consequently, while they may be supportive, they are not prepared to help you with the meaning of your addictive behavior or to add to your own self-understanding about it.

How do you find a good therapist, then? What you want is someone who has a sound background in treating and understanding emotional issues, and who also has an interest and experience in treating addictions. Admittedly, this can be a hard combination to find.

In searching for such a person, start with someone who is well-trained in treating emotional problems. It is better to have someone with this expertise who is somewhat less versed in addictions than to begin with someone who is familiar with the usual way to look at addictions but who has little expertise in human psychology. Someone with solid psychotherapy credentials can learn about the psychology of addiction, but it is not realistic to expect counselors who have not had years of training and experience in human psychology to be able to serve as psychotherapists.

Not all approaches that are identified as therapy, however, are oriented toward the sort of in-depth work that I have been describing. There are various descriptors for the kind of work I have been illustrating throughout the book, such as "insight-oriented," "psychodynamic," or "psychoanalytic" psychotherapy. These all usually describe therapy of the type I am suggesting. In contrast, there are other forms of therapy that are generally described as "behavioral" or "cognitive," which typically focus on labeling and behaviorally modifying behaviors or thoughts that are known—that are on the surface of the mind—but do not investigate underlying issues that lead to these patterns of acting or thinking. As a consequence, these approaches are unlikely to get to the heart of the problem, or to help you make full use of the understandings of your behavior that you have developed through this book. Finally, you should be aware that some psychiatrists, while excellent clinicians for certain conditions, are principally interested in medication treatment and have little interest or expertise in psychotherapy.

Overall, in speaking with potential therapists, you should not hesitate to ask about their interest and orientation toward psychological issues, and in particular how they would describe the kind of psychotherapy in which they feel they are expert.

———

Depending on where you live, it is not always easy to find people with a psychodynamic orientation. Two organizations that may be helpful with this are the American Psychoanalytic Association and Division 39 of the American Psychological Association (this is the division of the American Psychological Association that is involved with in-depth psychological work). Ask them about phone numbers for local affiliate groups in your area. Once you call the local affiliate, ask if there are members with a known interest in addictions. Even if the people at the affiliate society office do not know specific therapists with this interest, they should be able to offer names of members who can help you locate a therapist.

Through this route, you may find someone who is a good, psychodynamic therapist but who says that he or she does not have a lot of experience in dealing with people with addictions—though he or she has no misgivings about seeing people with these problems, either. In this case, treatment may be satisfactory, so long as the therapist appreciates that your addiction is a big part of what you want to understand—not something to be left out of the treatment to be dealt with elsewhere. Unfortunately, even well-trained therapists may have the misguided idea that if you suffer with an addiction, you are not a candidate for a more sophisticated treatment and send you off to a standard addiction program. Don't let this happen to you. On the other hand, as I have said before, there is nothing wrong with *combining* a traditional addiction counseling or a twelve-step program with psychotherapy. In this case, you want to be sure that the therapy includes trying to understand the addiction, and the nonpsychotherapy component is pitched toward being supportive without interfering with your efforts to understand yourself in your therapy.

Another route to locate a therapist is to contact an addiction treatment clinic. Here, you likely will not have a choice of whom you see, and the clinic itself may have a particular approach that influences all its therapists. If the entire clinic follows a traditional counseling model and has little or no interest in viewing addictions as psychological problems that can be investigated and understood, you may have to try elsewhere. However, some clinics provide a range of therapists, some of whom have greater training and interest in psychological matters. Before enrolling in a clinic ask about this, and if there are more psychologically attuned therapists then ask to be assigned to one of them.

Clinics also almost always provide professionally run groups, which may be combined with an individual therapy at or outside the clinic. The usefulness of these groups will hinge on both the way the group is designed to work and the training and outlook of the people leading them. If you are interested in being in a group, try to join one that genuinely tries to explore the issues arising in an addiction. One way to identify these groups is that they are not restricted to continuing for a fixed length of time, such as eight or ten weeks, and they do not have an educational agenda (some groups are designed as a kind of mini-course). Groups that are open-ended in time, by contrast, allow members to deepen their work in how they relate to each other and in how they help one another understand the feelings that go into addictive behavior. The opportunity to explore and experiment with feelings about relating to others, besides the therapist, who are actually present with you in the room, is a unique value of group therapy. And although groups cannot delve into the individual factors that make you who you are, there is no reason not to combine group and individual therapies to have the advantages of both.

———

This brings me finally to the question of how to know when therapy is done. You are generally going to want to have two areas finished. The first is to have a confident control of your addictive behavior, so that when an addictive drive arises, you understand what it is about and have good means of dealing with it other than repeating it. And the other goal is to understand more fully the feelings and conflicts that you have discovered lie behind the addiction so that they lose some of their power over you. When you have accomplished both of these goals, you are done.

———

Although this chapter has been about obtaining outside help, of course you can also make use on your own of the understanding of addiction that I have described throughout this book. Putting this way of thinking about addiction to work for you will call upon your abilities to think about yourself, your thoughts and your emotions. But as you know, having an addiction does not make you any less able to do this than anyone else.

Addictions *are* in the mainstream of the human condition, so their emotional basis can be understood as well as any other aspect of human suffering. Once you understand those powerful feelings that drive you to repeat an addictive behavior, you can use that understanding to achieve a genuine and lasting mastery over your addiction.

# NOTES

## Chapter Five: I Have to Do *Something*

1. *Diagnostic and Statistical Manual of Mental Disorders (DSM-IV)* 4th edition. Washington, D.C.: The American Psychiatric Association, 1994.

## Chapter Six: Hooked by the Mind: Physical and Psychological Addiction

1. Robins, L., Helzer, J., and Davis, D. Narcotic use in southeast Asia and afterward. *Archives of General Psychiatry* 1975, 32: 955–61.

## Chapter Seven: The Genetics of Alcoholism

1. Pickens, R., et al. Heterogeneity in the inheritance of alcoholism. *Archives of General Psychiatry* 1991, 48:19–28; p. 23.
2. Heath, A., et al. Genetic and environmental contributions to alcohol dependence risk in a national twin sample: consistency of findings in women and men. *Psychological Medicine* 1997, 27: 1381–96; p. 1393.
3. Isselbacher, K., et al. (eds.). *Harrison's Principles of Internal Medicine*, 13th edition. New York: McGraw Hill, 1994, p. 339.
4. Sapolsky, R. It's not "all in the genes." *Newsweek*, April 10, 2000, p. 68.
5. *Newsweek*, May 25, 1998, p. 72.
6. Merikangas, K. The genetic epidemiology of alcoholism. *Psychological Medicine* 1990, 20: 11–22.

7. Ibid.
8. Cadoret, R., et al. Development of alcoholism in adoptees raised apart from alcoholic biologic relatives. *Archives of General Psychiatry* 1980, 37: 561–63.
9. Merikangas, K. The genetic epidemiology of alcoholism. *Psychological Medicine* 1990, 20: 11–22.
10. Ibid., p. 14.
11. The nine studies are cited in Merikangas. Forty percent is about the average of these studies, with proportional representation of the studies based on the number of people in them.
12. See note 1, chapter 7.
13. Kendler, K., et al. Temperance board registration for alcohol abuse in a national sample of Swedish male twins, born 1902 to 1949. *Archives of General Psychiatry* 1997, 54: 178–84.
14. Heath, A., et al. Genetic and environmental contributions to alcohol dependence risk in a national twin sampler: consistency of findings in women and men. *Psychological Medicine* 1997, 27: 1381–96.
15. Pickens, R., et al. Heterogeneity in the inheritance of alcoholism. *Archives of General Psychiatry* 1991, 48: 19–28; p. 27.
16. Ibid., p. 19.
17. Roe, A., et al. Adult adjustment of foster children of alcoholic and psychotic parentage and the influence of the foster home. Memoirs of the section on alcohol studies, Yale University. *Quarterly Journal of Studies on Alcoholism*, no. 3, 1945 [cited in Goodwin 1973].
18. Goodwin, D., et al. Alcohol problems in adoptees raised apart from alcoholic biological parents. *Archives of General Psychiatry* 1973, 28: 238–43. In this study, combining his two most severe categories of drinking showed no significant difference between children of alcoholic and nonalcoholic biological parents.
19. Cloninger, C., et al. Inheritance of alcohol abuse. *Archives of General Psychiatry* 1981, 38: 861–68.
20. Goodwin, D. *Alcoholism, The Facts, 2nd edition.* Oxford, England: Oxford University Press, 1994.
21. Cloninger, C., et al. Inheritance of alcohol abuse. *Archives of General Psychiatry* 1981, 38: 861–68.
22. Foroud, T., et al. Genetics of alcoholism: a review of recent studies in human and animal models. *American Journal on Addictions* 1999, 8: 261–78.
23. Ibid.

CHAPTER EIGHT: MYTHS OF ADDICTION

1. *Twelve Steps and Twelve Traditions,* Alcoholics Anonymous World Services, 1952, p. 42.
2. Sapolsky, R. It's not "all in the genes." *Newsweek,* April 10, 2000, p. 68.

3. Waldrop, M. *Complexity: the Emerging Science at the Edge of Order and Chaos.* New York: Touchstone Books, 1992.

4. Ibid., pp. 81–82.

CHAPTER NINE: WHEN IS ABUSE NOT ADDICTION?

1. Dr. Norman Zinberg was the first to emphasize this. (For instance, in his paper "Alcohol addiction: toward a more comprehensive definition. In *Dynamic Approaches to the Understanding and Treatment of Alcoholism* [eds. M. Bean and N. Zinberg]. New York: Free Press, 1981.)

CHAPTER TEN: THE INTERNET, SHOPPING, EXERCISE: HOW CAN YOU TELL IF IT IS AN ADDICTION?

1. This example is taken from Dodes, L. Compulsion and addiction. *Journal of the American Psychoanalytic Association* 1996, 44: 815–35.

CHAPTER ELEVEN: EFFORTS TO UNDERSTAND

1. Wieder, H., and Kaplan, E. Drug use in adolescents. *Psychoanalytic Study of the Child* 1969, 24: 399–431; Milkman, H., and Frosch, W. On the preferential abuse of heroin and amphetamine. *Journal of Nervous and Mental Disease* 1973, 156: 242–48; Wurmser, L. Psychoanalytic considerations of the etiology of compulsive drug use. *Journal of the American Psychoanalytic Association* 1974, 22:820–43; Khantzian, E. The ego, the self and opiate addiction: theoretical and treatment considerations. *International Review of Psychoanalysis* 1978, 5: 189–98; Khantzian, E. The self-medication hypothesis of addictive disorders: focus on heroin and cocaine dependence. *American Journal of Psychiatry* 1985, 142: 1259–64.

2. Dodes, L., and Khantzian, E. Individual psychodynamic psychotherapy. In *Clinical Textbook of Addictive Disorders, 2nd edition* (eds. R. J. Frances and S. I. Miller). New York: Guilford Press, 1998.

3. Wurmser, L. Psychoanalytic considerations of the etiology of compulsive drug use. *Journal of the American Psychoanalytic Association* 1974, 22: 820–43.

4. Dodes, L. Addiction, helplessness, and narcissistic rage. *Psychoanalytic Quarterly* 1990, 59: 398–419.

5. Khantzian, E. The ego, the self and opiate addiction: theoretical and treatment considerations. *International Review of Psychoanalysis* 1978, 5: 189–98; Khantzian, E. Self-regulation vulnerabilities in substance abusers: treatment implications. In *The Psychology and Treatment of Addictive Behavior* (ed. S. Dowling). New York: International Universities Press, 1995; Khantzian, E., and Mack, J. Self-preservation and the care of the self. *Psychoanalytic Study of the Child* 1983; 38: 209–32.

6. Khantzian, E., and Mack, J. Self-preservation and the care of the self. *Psychoanalytic Study of the Child* 1983, 38:209–32.
7. Wurmser, L. The role of superego conflicts in substance abuse and their treatment. *International Journal of Psychoanalytic Psychotherapy* 1984, 10:227–58.
8. See note 3, chapter 11; Kohut, H. The analysis of the self. New York: International Universities Press, 1971.
9. Krystal, H. Alexithymia and the effectiveness of psychoanalytic treatment. *International Journal of Psychoanalytic Psychotherapy* 1982, 9:353–78.

CHAPTER THIRTEEN: TEENS

1. NIDA Notes, 2000; vol. 15, no. 1. Bethesda, Md.: National Institute on Drug Abuse.
2. NIDA Notes, 2000; vol. 14, no. 6. Bethesda, Md.: National Institute on Drug Abuse.
3. Gambling disorders in Louisiana. *The Wager*: publication of Harvard Medical School Division on Addictions, 1996, vol. 1, no. 50; Alberta adolescent substance use increases with gambling involvement. *The Wager*: publication of Harvard Medical School Division on Addictions, 1996, vol. 1, no. 43.
4. Blos, P. *On Adolescence.* New York: Free Press, 1962, pp. 12, 14.

CHAPTER FIFTEEN: WHEN AN COMPULSIONS ADDICTIONS?

1. Dodes, L. Compulsion and Addiction. *Journal of the American Psychoanalytic Association* 1996, 44: 815–35.
2. Fenichel, O. *The Psychoanalytic Theory of Neurosis.* New York: W.W. Norton, 1945.

CHAPTER SIXTEEN: THE VICTORS AND THE VANQUISHED: COMPULSIVE GAMBLING

1. Sources of access for underage gamblers. *The Wager*, publication of Harvard Medical School Division on Addictions, 1996, vol. 1, no. 20.
2. *Boston Globe*, series on gambling, February 1997.

CHAPTER EIGHTEEN: TREATMENT

1. *Twelve Steps and Twelve Traditions*, Alcoholics Anonymous World Services, 1952, p. 42.
2. Dodes, L. The psychology of combining dynamic psychotherapy and Alcoholics Anonymous. *Bulletin of the Menninger Clinic.* 1988, 52: 283–93.

3. Mack, J. Alcoholism, AA, and the governance of the self. In *Dynamic Approaches to the Understanding and Treatment of Alcoholism* (eds. M. Bean, N. Zinberg). New York: Free Press, 1981.

4. Rosen, A. Psychotherapy and Alcoholics Anonymous: can they be coordinated? *Bulletin of the Menninger Clinic.* 1981, 45: 229–46.

5. McLellan, T. Psychiatric severity as a predictor of outcome from substance abuse treatments. In R. Meyer (ed.). *Psychopathology and addictive disorders.* New York: Guilford Press, 1986, pp. 97–139.

6. Dodes, L. Psychotherapy is useful, often essential, for alcoholics. *The Psychodynamic Letter.* 1991, 1: 4–7.

7. Dodes, L. Abstinence from alcohol in long-term individual psychotherapy with alcoholics. *American Journal of Psychotherapy* 1984, 38: 248–56.

# INDEX

counting days of sobriety, 96–97,
226
denial, 102
gene for alcoholism, 8, 80–90
hitting bottom, 93–94
importance of physical addiction,
69–79
need for surrender, 95–96, 226
self-destructiveness, 94–95

narcotics:
pain and, 75, 92
in self-medication hypothesis, 131
*see also* heroin
needs, and putting others first, 37–38
neurotransmitters, 69
changes in levels of, 77
"high" and, 98
*see also* dopamine
New Hampshire, 195
nicotine, 74–75, 103
intentionally elevated levels of, 104
nucleus accumbens, 77–78

Obsessive-Compulsive Disorder
(OCD), 181, 193–94
overuse, addiction vs., 78*n*, 103–15

pain, narcotics and, 75, 92
paraphilias, 221–23
parapraxis, 128
parents:
addictive behavior as substitute
for, 134–36
death of, 66–68
enabling by, 178–80
relationship with, 63–65, 66–67
of teenagers, guidelines for, 164
teenagers' desire to be different
from, 161–62
teenagers sent to therapy by,
154–59
peer pressure, *see* interpersonal
pressure

peptic ulcer disease, 81, 84
personality, addictive, 100–101, 126
personality disorder, 126
perversions, sexual, 221–23
phenylketonuria (PKU), 81
genetics of, 83–84
phone sex, addiction to, 142–43,
144–45, 146, 147, 210, 217
physical addiction, 69–79
binges and, 71–72
brain chemistry myth in, 98–100
effects on brain, 77–78
incidental nature of, 75–76
neurotransmitters in, 77
psychological addiction vs.,
69–79, 104
in relapses, 76
smoking and, 74–75
switching addictions and, 70–71
and unity of addiction, 70–71
withdrawal in, 91–92
physics, human behavior and,
99–100
pornographic videotapes, 218, 219,
220–21
powerlessness, *see* helplessness,
feeling of
prediction of urges, 6, 22–25
projection, 176–77
prostitutes, in sexual addiction, 2,
211–17, 218, 219
protein, 81–82
Prozac, 194
psychoanalytic therapy, 238
psychodynamic therapy, 238
psychology, recent rise of, 79

questionnaires, for alcoholism,
120–23

rage:
addict's relationships affected by,
170–71, 172
in alcoholism, 171, 172